Perfect Day

An Intimate Portrait Of
Life With Lou Reed

Bettye Kronstad

JAW
BONE

PERFECT DAY
An Intimate Portrait Of Life With Lou Reed
Bettye Kronstad

A Jawbone book
First edition 2016
Published in the UK and the USA by Jawbone Press
3.1D Union Court
20–22 Union Road
London SW4 6JP
England
www.jawbonepress.com

ISBN 978-1-911036-06-7

All of the photographs used in this book are from the author's
collection, except: *jacket front* Hulton Archive/Getty Images;
page 141 Michael Putland/Getty Images; *page 144 Cafe Royal*
Bettmann/Getty Images; *Amsterdam* Gijsbert Hanekroot/Redferns.

JACKET DESIGN Mark Case

Printed in China by Everbest Printing Investment Ltd.

1 2 3 4 5 21 20 19 18 17

contents

the elevator........... CHAPTER ONE

New York City, winter 1968.

Just as I pushed the down button there was a *ding* and the elevator to my left opened, pouring a crowd of people out into the hospital hallway. After the last person stepped out, I took a step toward the empty elevator, when suddenly a voice behind me cried, 'Hey, you! Beautiful!'

The voice was compelling, an order. So I turned around.

'Yeah, you,' he said.

I didn't say anything, but my eyes took in a skinny guy in a blue denim shirt with white mother-of-pearl snaps half undone, exposing an abundant growth of chest hair. A wide, worn leather belt was slung low on his narrow hips, holding up his stylishly weathered bell-bottoms. The hems were appropriately frayed and shredded from being dragged on slick city streets and flared out around him in a perfectly composed puddle. His hair was in an Afro, but a soft, curly light brown one, carefully coiffed. He had his thumb hooked over his belt buckle, and the rest of his hand hung down, carefully pointing to his crotch. He was looking straight at me, a bemused but commanding expression on his face.

'What are you doing in here?' he asked. 'You look normal.'

I took the punk in, paused a minute, then looked him straight in the eye.

'I am,' I said.

By now he was standing directly in front of me. My first impression was that he had a serious ego, but I knew this often implied quite the opposite. He was disarming, the kind of guy who let you know how he felt about you; he didn't play any games.

I turned on my heel and walked into the open and waiting elevator.

Ouch!

I felt a sting on my bottom. As I turned around to face the front of the elevator, I took a look once again at this wannabe rock star with a pretty face. He was smiling. Had this guy just slapped me on my bottom?

I calmly stared forward, blatantly avoiding his gaze, ignoring him. I arranged a slight smile on my face that I hoped had just the right amount of a hint of a sneer. It gave me the look of an ice queen, and with my long-legged, fashionably thin Scandinavian blondeness, if I kept my mouth shut long enough, people thought that's what I was.

As the doors began to close, he shouted out, 'I'm here to visit Lincoln. Do you know him?'

I still didn't say anything, but yes, I knew Lincoln. He was a smart man who'd had an unfortunate accident when he made a suicide jump in front of a train at 59th Street and Lexington. Regrettably—for him—his attempt failed, and he'd sliced off an arm and a leg instead.

'Well, if you do know Lincoln,' said the skinny guy as he stuck out his hand to hold the elevator doors open, 'ask him about me. My name is Lou Reed.'

He paused so I had time to let the name sink in, like it should mean something to me, and continued to stand there staring at me. I had no idea who Lou Reed was. Later on, Lincoln told me he was the principal writer and lead singer of The Velvet Underground. Like everyone else in the city who was seriously interested in rock'n'roll, I'd heard of them and I liked their music, but I hadn't gone out and bought any of their albums.

For me, this certainly wasn't a love-at-first sight experience; nor could I foresee the intensity that lay ahead of us. Our relationship would last five years; we were engaged for several of those years, although we were officially married for less than one.

While Lou projected a rock star persona—and there remained little doubt that his visceral, larger-than-life personality could pull off this act flawlessly—from where I was looking, he seemed dissipated, almost defenseless. It was like he was reaching out to me from some unknown place, and was compelled to seek me out, perhaps without even knowing why. As we stared at each other a myriad of unspoken messages traveled back and forth between us, and it was unmistakably transparent that whatever our communication set, it was not dependent upon language.

The elevator door began to close, but he kept his hand over it, denying it permission. He saw in my face that his name had fallen on deaf ears.

'I'm his best friend,' he said. 'Ask him!'

Again the elevator wanted to close, and again he pushed it back. But it punched back at him, again and again, banging and shuddering.

Soon the alarm will go off and all hell will break loose, I thought—*especially in this place.*

But all I did was look at him as he looked at me.

All at once his hand fell slack at his side and, as the doors finally began to close, he continued to stand there, unmoving, staring at me with this confident, but kind of silly, dazed expression on his face that didn't at all compliment the arrogant hipster who looked like he'd just stepped out of Central Casting.

Then, quietly, he said, 'So will you ask him about me?'

That's when the doors closed, and I thought, with probably a faint sigh of relief escaping into the empty chamber.

Oh, that's all I need: another nut job.

I'd only been in New York about a year and a half. I'd started out in Greenwich Village in a fifth-floor walkup, but now I was living in university housing near my soon-to-be ex-fiancé while I worked my way through a comparative literature English course for my bachelor's degree at Columbia, typing up the law professors' cases and conducting some of their research.

But it wasn't until after the elevator doors completely closed, shifted gears, and began to drop that I pulled my jacket closer to me, inserted the razor sharp teeth of my zipper into its box, and pulled it up to my neck. And immediately forgot about the dude with the—all right, I noticed—pouty, Betty Boop lips and girlish, upturned nose who, nevertheless, gave me my first and only butt slap.

* * *

Spring 1968.

I hadn't spoken to Lou in a couple of months, although I'd seen him visiting Lincoln in the hospital. I cared about Lincoln, and Lou meant a great deal to him. It was about the only time I'd see Lincoln laugh, and after Lou's visits, Lincoln looked supported and greatly encouraged. Lou seemed to give him hope that he could survive his recent tragedy, despite the devastating injuries to which he now needed to adapt.

Lincoln always told me when he was expecting Lou, and invited me to join them, but I never did. Although we'd established an implicit understanding when we met near the elevator, what Lou and I actually said to one another hadn't been much. But after I saw what a good friend he was to Lincoln, the idea of getting to know Lou a little better seemed more attractive. If I happened to be there when Lou was visiting, he'd wave me over to talk with them, but I'd just smile, wave, and walk on by. I didn't want to be a distraction during his visits, because he seemed to have such a positive impact upon Lincoln.

Besides, I had a great deal on my mind. I'd applied for a New York State scholarship, and had just received its acceptance. Not only was I planning how best to break off my engagement, I needed to finalize the details of the trip to Europe I was planning to take with my college friends. I had finally finished the application for my passport, but I still needed to secure the student package deal I was purchasing for my trip.

I was also busy preparing for my studies at Columbia in the fall as a full-time student, which was very time consuming—filling out papers and getting them signed, finding new housing, selecting the courses that I'd take in the fall. I was thrilled about winning a full scholarship to an Ivy League school—I no longer needed to work at the law school full-time and attend evening classes to get my degree!

The year 1968 was one of the most tumultuous years in the history of this country. In modern times, if ever the country was close to a revolution, this was the year. I was one of those college kids who protested against the Vietnam War. On October 21, 1967, I was tear-gassed while attending the demonstration against that war in Washington D.C., along with thousands of others. While walking through campus to work on April 23, 1968, I watched as students began lining up at the foot of Lowe Library's steps for the student riot there. I was swept up in it, tear-gassed again, and felt the hard edge of a New York City cop's billy club.

With burning tears streaming down my face, I managed to extricate myself from the riot and blindly stumbled down the hill at 116th Street and Broadway to my new student room, into which I'd recently moved. Unlike many protestors, I somehow avoided arrest.

In 1968, along with the continuing escalation of that senseless and vicious war, hundreds of thousands of American boys—including friends from school I grew up with—were getting maimed and killed. Then Martin Luther King, Jr. was assassinated and, only two months later, on the 1968 election campaign trail for the Democratic Party's presidential nomination, Robert F. Kennedy, Jr. was shot and killed. I adored Kennedy and thought he was the leader this country needed, and I loved King, a great shining light in the nation's fight for racial equality. Along with hundreds of thousands of other college students and American citizens, my heart was broken. What was happening to this country?

All of these events led me to anticipate my trip to Europe with extraordinary relief and great expectation. The truth was, I couldn't wait to leave this country, no matter how much I loved it. My father and his family were European immigrants. I was raised with a European sensibility, which included an unspoken, gentle cynicism about America that one never shared, of course, with anyone outside the family.

And the country *was* a mess! As well as the student protests taking place all over the country, race riots were breaking out in the streets. It was a depressing political atmosphere to live through, and it hurt to the core. I was deeply disappointed in this country, and couldn't wait to leave for saner shores.

Indeed, social unrest continued after I returned from Europe, when I literally stumbled upon a demonstration that would have a profound impact upon me and how I viewed the world, and would become a major factor in informing my belief in and dedication to the music of Lincoln's friend, Lou.

I remember that early, humid morning in June 1969. Since January 1967, when I first moved to New York City, I had made my home in Greenwich Village, near Sheridan Square. Even though I moved uptown to Morningside Heights, I continued to spend a great deal of time in the Village, and I still saw many of my friends who lived in my old neighborhood. After all, it was only a twenty-minute subway ride uptown.

It's three in the morning and I am walking back to the subway station after attending a party at a friend's house in my old apartment building, about to enter the enclosed triangular park that forms at the apex of three streets that merge downtown on Sixth Avenue and Sheridan known as Sheridan Square. Park benches are enclosed within the fenced-in park; old maple and beech trees, bent, delicate, and elongated, are outlined against the night-lights where nary a star can be seen between the roofs of the buildings looming skyward. This is the oldest part of Manhattan, construction having begun in the 1600s.

It is a terribly, terribly civilized place surrounded by cobblestoned streets amid brownstones at least a couple of hundred years old. The old fence that surrounds Sheridan Square is iron-spiked, at least six and a half feet tall. During the early fall or spring and summer months, people sit quietly reading, sipping coffee or tea. In the winter, they soak up the sun and watch the quiet snowfall.

A ghostly quiet has settled over the empty square. Copper lantern streetlamps softly glow in the mist. I am just crossing the street when suddenly a deafening roar of outraged human cries is heard, and before my astonished eyes, the doors of the old Stonewall Inn burst open and belch forth hundreds of furious, marginalized men and a few women in black and barely there out onto picturesque, sedate Sheridan Square.

The crowd empties out onto Sheridan and starts swinging west toward Sixth Avenue. I reach out and grab onto the old iron fence nearby. As the mob surges by me, heading uptown, I am pushed, shoved down, and trampled upon. After a couple of minutes on the pavement, I shake my head to clear my thoughts and watch as residents, roused by the ruckus, stumble out of their row-house apartment buildings or privately owned townhouse doors. Scratching their bed heads and scowling, they look around to see what all the fuss is about at this god-awful time in the morning.

I struggle to rise to my feet, determined to gain a foothold on the solid bricks of the old cobblestoned streets. Despite my dazed condition, I'm slowly beginning to realize what is happening. This is a storming of the Stonewall Inn, and everybody knows what kind of bar *it* is!

These men and a few women are, for the first time in the history of this country, storming the streets to let the world know they are no longer going to accept any more of the humiliating treatment, discrimination, disrespect, or comprehensive marginalization forced upon them by the 'straight' world—indeed, the very society that many who live in the Village shun by never setting foot above 14th Street, unless they're in a speeding cab. Because above Union Square, they are judged as creatures of a dark and distant alien planet, merely because of the way they talk, the manner in which they dress, the music they make or listen to, the books they write or read, and the people to whom they choose to make love.

All around Sheridan Square, little pockets of people have gathered in an informal assembly. Amid hushed whispering and a yawn or two, a decision appears to have been made. Further up Sixth, I can see people streaming into the streets and up the avenue. Nodding, assenting, and mumbling, their bathrobes flapping and slippers slapping the moist stones of early morning, the citizens of Sheridan Square and the surrounding neighborhood join the growing throng.

The gays are mad as hell, and they aren't gonna take it anymore!

Well, this is our neighborhood, and neither are we!

Straightening my second-hand black leather jacket, I pick myself up, dust myself off, and join the fray.

* * *

Lincoln and I spoke on the phone at least once a week, and I visited him every week or so. Then Lou asked Lincoln to telephone me to find out if he could call me. It had been a month since we'd seen each other, and I wasn't sure how I felt about seeing him.

Lincoln assured me that Lou wasn't really the arrogant hipster I'd met in the elevator. It was all an act. He was a very serious writer, and a good one. I respected Lincoln and had seen how Lou was a loyal friend to him—and *that* I liked. Although I rejected his advances toward me in the elevator, when Lincoln told me that Lou was a serious writer and I'd heard his music, I felt somewhat intrigued by him.

I hadn't thought much of him that day in the elevator, but I was interested in writing, and it slowly began to dawn on me how great it would be to know a writer whose work was breaking new ground and getting noticed.

I suppose I hadn't taken him so seriously at the beginning. It was only later that summer, while I was sitting in a square in Montparnasse, Paris, that the reality of his originality and brilliance shocked me. I was having my usual bowl of freshly brewed morning coffee and a roll of French bread, baked only hours earlier in a shop behind the cafe, reading the *International Herald Tribune*, when I suddenly came across an article about The Velvet Underground, how they were contributing to the intellectual and artistic progression of rock'n'roll—not only with their music, but because Lou Reed was writing under the influence of classic literature and using innovative, sophisticated writing techniques in the lyrics of their music.

My immediate reaction after reading it was—*that guy?* From personal experience I knew how easy it was to see Lou in the role he'd cast for himself: the loud, larger-than-life personality who got drunk and boisterous past all reason. But the article struck home with me because he had talked to me at length about his writing when we first got to know each other: how important it was for him to get a line *just right*, or tell a complete story—with characters, plot, and a point of view. He wanted his songs to have *a beginning*, *a middle*, and *an end*. Although it had been difficult to follow his ramblings—he was drunk at the time—I was still able to understand what he wanted to accomplish in his writing.

Secretly smiling to myself, I tore the article from the newspaper and tucked it into my bag to read again, later. I hadn't seen him for several months, but I now realized that Lou was finally being taken seriously as a writer—which was what he seemed to want and need most of all.

* * *

Before I left for Europe, I told Lincoln that he could give Lou my number, and that he could call me. The next day I got a message from him on my answering machine; however, I was still hesitant to call him back. But Lou called again and left another message. It took a few days before I finally called him back.

I agreed to meet him at the West End bar, several blocks from where I lived on Morningside Heights. It was a very popular Columbia University watering hole made famous by Beat writers like Jack Kerouac, Allen Ginsberg, and William Burroughs, who had hung out there. Bob Dylan and many other up and coming musicians of the time played at the West End. It was a famous place, but it had great food and an artsy, intellectual, neighborhood feel to it. Everyone went there.

Lou was sitting in a booth across from the bar, directly opposite the front door, so he could see me as soon as I arrived. He immediately got up and walked over, took my hand, kissed it, and then bowed like a courtly gentleman. I was a little surprised because he seemed very subdued—shy, even—so different from when I first met him!

Lou escorted me back to his booth and asked if I wanted something to drink. He already had a scotch on the rocks. I wasn't a drinker but said I'd have a glass of Chablis. He went to the bar and brought it back to me. A waiter came with a menu, and I quickly ordered a burger and fries. So did Lou.

At first he asked about me. I told him about my new scholarship, and how excited I was to begin attending school full-time in the fall, when I returned from my trip through Europe. I was hitchhiking with a married couple who I'd met in class. Surprisingly, I found myself liking him.

But Lou had been steadily drinking one scotch after another through dinner. Toward the end of the evening, as he started talking about the things that were happening in his life, he got plastered. He talked about how important his writing was to him, which was very interesting to me. But then he started going on about the conflict he was having with John Cale, with whom he'd formed The Velvet Underground, and with whom he wrote their music. He was extremely upset about it. If the band took the direction John wanted, Lou said, they'd never be a success.

I realized that the band was going to split up and Lou didn't know what he was going to do afterward. The more he talked about it, the more upset he became—and the more he drank. By the end of the evening, he had become loud and started yelling.

As Lou became more and more drunk and obnoxious, I suggested we leave. Reluctantly, he called for the check and paid, but he insisted on walking me home, several blocks from where we were. I told him there was a subway stop only two blocks away on 110th, but he insisted on escorting me to my door.

Staggering home with Lou hanging onto me for five blocks wasn't my ideal way to end the evening. But although he could be obnoxious, he was also very funny and smart, and I appreciated his sense of humor. Despite some insufferable behavior, he made me laugh.

He wanted to come up, but it was really late, and I wasn't comfortable having boys in my room. I rented my room from a widowed professor's wife and her adolescent son. I told Lou we should say our goodbyes at my front door.

'Good,' he said, then kissed me on the forehead, turned away, and walked off, stumbling.

I hadn't the slightest idea how he was going to make it up our steep hill on his own. I watched his lone figure staggering off into the night, lit only by the amber light of the street lamps. With his black T-shirt and leather pants, he virtually disappeared. All I heard were his black boots scraping and scuffing on the harsh pavement, staggering and stumbling up Morningside Heights.

As he disappeared from view, the image of a mortally injured black panther slinking back to its cave and licking its wounds sprang into mind. Panicking, I ran after him and cried, 'Hey! I forgot to buy a pack of cigarettes at the corner store. Wait up!'

Because he was slurring so heavily, I couldn't understand most of what he was saying, but as we staggered to the top of the hill, we laughed while he talked, until we got to the stairs of the subway stop on Broadway. I helped him down the first step, and when I saw his hand clasped safely onto the stair railing, I gave him a quick kiss on the cheek, turned, and ran in the direction of the store. Almost immediately thereafter, I returned to make sure he'd made it safely down the stairs without falling and breaking his neck.

The last I saw of him, he was taking one step at a time and holding dearly onto the railing, before disappearing into the bowels of the underground station. As I walked back down the hill, my thoughts were filled with him. I liked him, and I felt badly for what he was going through. He was very interesting and charming, but his drinking scared me. I realized I was frightened for him, but it also turned me off. My instinct said to stay away from him.

During the next week I ran around town getting my passport and vaccination shots and shopped. I didn't pack my room because I was coming back in the fall and it was being held for me. Lou called the next day and left a message on my machine to call him back, raving about the wonderful time we had.

Most of the time we did, I thought, *but toward the end? Maybe not so much.*

The next thing I knew it was the middle of the week, only a couple of days before I left for Europe. I was leaving the apartment for a doctor's appointment when the phone rang. I lived on the top floor of an old brick building on 116th Street, around the corner from Riverside Drive. The cavernous combination living/dining room, which the professor had created by knocking down the dining-room wall separating the two rooms, was flanked by a huge flagstone fireplace; three Romeo & Juliet cast iron balconies of double lead glass louvered floor-to-ceiling doors opened onto a panoramic view of the Hudson River. Only the very tops of the Hudson River Park trees lining the banks of the river could be seen as the river traffic floated by.

During the day, the white sail of an occasional yacht broke the monotony of commerce rallying up and down the river. At night, the deep oily underbelly of the glistening Hudson snaked past our wall of windows. A hawk would occasionally drift by on an air current, then dive into the river to pluck its lunch from the rich riverbed below, punctuating the trace of living and dead marine life emanating in the air. It was invigorating, but dank and a little seedy. Seeing the view from this high up in the sky, all one's senses were challenged, yet all your dreams felt real and very possible.

Although the telephone was ringing insistently, I decided to ignore it, as the answering machine was set to pick it up after seven or eight times. I had just closed the door and was turning the key in the outside lock when I heard Lou's voice on the machine. I couldn't hear what he was saying, but recognized hurt and anger in his voice, which was loud, and why I heard it through the heavy front door.

Instinctively, I opened the door and ran to pick up the phone. I didn't want to cause Lou any more misery. I knew he was going through a difficult period and I didn't want to hurt him. A part of me could see through his extreme behavior—a man who was hurt and vulnerable.

I picked up the phone as he was speaking, and quickly said, 'Hello?'

Lou was in the middle of expressing his disappointment at not hearing from me before I left for Europe when suddenly, mid-sentence, he stopped speaking. A prolonged silence followed, neither of us speaking. Finally, after saying 'Hello?' again, and not getting a response, I thought he'd hung up.

I was just about to put the receiver back into its cradle, when suddenly he said, 'Hello?'

'Oh, you're still there! I thought you'd hung up!' I said.

'Yeah,' Lou said. 'I'm still here.'

There was a slight pause, and then his voice got a little louder. He was whining. 'I've been calling you all week and leaving messages! Have you been getting them? Don't you return phone calls? I don't understand why I haven't heard from you!'

Really? Did he remember I was leaving the country for almost half a year? Had it not occurred to him that I might have something, other than immediately returning his calls, to do? Yes, he was a talented and semi-famous musician in town, but don't push it, buster.

I was irritated, but I was determined to remain polite. My family was Scandinavian, and they were not especially known for their innate ability or desire to participate in polite chatter. They told you simply and easily how they felt. Like me.

'I've been really busy. I'm leaving for months in a couple of days, and this week has been crazy! I meant to call you, but I really didn't have the time, between running around and getting all the last-minute things that needed to get done. I still have to pack! I've had a lot to do.'

He didn't say anything.

After some time passed, I said, 'Lou?'

I honestly wasn't sure if he was still there, although I hadn't heard the receiver click or be slammed. From his tone, it could have happened.

Finally, he answered, 'Yeah.'

There was another pause.

'So, you are still there,' I said brightly, hoping to pick up the pace and sweeten things up a bit.

'I'm still here.'

'Oh, okay, I didn't hear you say anything, so I didn't know …'

He was hurt. I could hear it in his silence.

'I didn't say anything,' he answered.

'Oh, okay,' I said awkwardly.

'I just thought you'd call back after I left so many messages,' he said.

'I only got a couple,' I said, wincing a little.

He raised his voice slightly. 'I left three—*or four!*'

Rather than quarrel, I quickly said, 'I'm sorry, Lou. I was just so busy.' There was another pause, and I filled it.

'I have been meaning to call, and have been thinking of you. I had a nice time, too.'

I was not being entirely truthful, but it seemed the right thing to say at the time.

'Well, I'm glad to hear *that*,' he replied.

'Oh, yes,' I said. 'I loved to hear about your music. You seem to really care about it, and I respect that. '

I had, I admit, listened more carefully if a Velvet Underground song came on the radio. Lou's lyrics created stunning images, which clashed just uncomfortably enough to illuminate the struggling everyman in today's world. Lou Reed cast art in song, I had to give him that.

'Oh, I'm glad to hear that!' he said. 'Can I see you tonight?'

I laughed. I wish I hadn't, but it just came out of me. The idea of seeing someone I'd just met at the last minute on the night before I was going overseas for nearly half a year was ridiculous!

'You think that's funny?' he asked. I'd offended him.

'Oh, I'm not laughing at you or your suggestion, I'm sorry. Please, don't take my laughing the wrong way. I wasn't laughing at you, but the idea that I would have time to see anyone!'

'Well, can't you take off a couple of hours?' he asked. 'Surely you have dinner. Don't you eat?' he demanded.

'Not really,' I said. 'I mean, I eat, of course, but I just grab something. I haven't sat down to dinner in I don't know how long,' I hastily continued. 'I haven't even packed yet, and I'm leaving the day after tomorrow!'

'Aren't you going backpacking?' he asked. 'How much do you need to pack, if you're only taking enough to carry around on your back,' he asked, sarcasm sliding into his tone.

I knew he thought the whole back-packing-across-Europe a hippie thing, which, if anything, amused him. But I wasn't a hippie! Everything that I wore matched or was coordinated! Nor did I appreciate the sarcasm in his voice he'd barely deigned to disguise.

'I don't really have the time to see anyone, I'm sorry,' I repeated, firmly.

'Okay, okay!' he said. 'How about tomorrow night, then?' he asked.

He obviously hadn't heard a word I'd said.

'If I can't see you tonight, how would I be able to see you then?' I asked. 'That'll be my last night before I get up at 5am to make my flight the next morning.'

'Oh, come on, don't you have a minute to say goodbye to me before you leave?'

I couldn't believe what I was hearing. Was he dense? Or just arrogant?

'You're leaving!' he cried. *'For months*!?'

Why was he was pressuring me? I began to lose it.

'Look, Lou, if I was going out the night before—which I'm not— do you honestly think there would be no one else I'd rather see than you on the last night before I leave the country?' Then I added, *'For months*?'

'*No!*' He almost yelled it. 'Come on!' he urged. 'One drink!'

Why was he pleading? Didn't he realize he'd offended me?

'Lewis, I can't!'

This was the first time I used his real name, but only for emphasis. I liked it. The man I knew when he let his guard down was more a Lewis than a Lou, anyway.

'Look, just meet me for a drink,' he said quietly. 'We can meet at the West End, like before.'

I didn't say anything.

'It won't take too long … one little drinky-poo?'

'No!' Now I was raising my voice. Look what this guy was doing to me!

'You sure?' he asked meekly. He sighed, but it also sounded like he was steaming a bit, too.

Honestly!

'Well, okay, I just wanted to say goodbye. In person.'

'I appreciate that, and thank you for thinking of me,' I said evenly.

I gave him time to acknowledge my overly polite tone. Surely he knew I meant it by now.

'Well, all right.'

Nevertheless, I continued to employ the full-frontal silent treatment.

'I'll be thinking of you.'

You do that, I thought.

But, instead, I said, 'I'll be thinking of you, too, Lou.'

Now, where did that come from, I wondered. *I had no idea!*

'Really?' he quickly said.

Suddenly it occurred to me: this guy is really interested in me! Before that moment, the thought hadn't entered my mind. Surely, girls—and guys—threw themselves at him? He was a lead singer in a rock'n'roll band! Didn't everybody fall all over them? Then I thought of the perfect exit line for Lou Reed.

'Yes, of course! When I get to Scotland, I'll have a scotch for you!'

'You're going to Scotland?' he asked quickly. 'When?'

Oh, no.

'Yeah, we're hitching up to Edinburgh from London. There's an arts festival up there my friends want to see, and so would I. I'll be sure to—'

'—that sounds fabulous!' Lou said, cutting in. 'Won't you be scared, hitchhiking?'

'No,' I replied. 'Everyone does it. It's a rite of passage around here.'

'Oh, okay.'

'I gotta—'

'—as long as you stay safe!' he said.

'I will,' I answered.

Then, as an afterthought, thinking this would surely end it, I said, 'For you.'

'Aw,' Lou said, 'that's sweet!'

'Okay. Gotta go! Goodbye!'

'Hey!'

Now what?

'Thanks for seeing me back to the subway.'

For a moment I froze. So he knew I hadn't run out of cigarettes. But quickly I said, 'Absolutely! I'll call you when I get back.'

'Will you?'

'Yes! *Goodbye!*'

'Goodbye, princess,' he said. 'I'll miss you.'

And then he was gone.

reading
poetry......... CHAPTER TWO

Through Lincoln, Lewis learned I'd just returned from my European travels, and once again he asked Lincoln to ask me if he could call. I said it was okay, so he began calling me. Just before Lewis was to move out on the Island he called and asked if I would come to Max's and see him perform his last show with The Velvet Underground, a gig that had been extended throughout the summer of 1970. I promised I would.

In the late evening of August 23, 1970, it was almost as hot and humid as it had been earlier that day, although a more lightly tempered breeze coming off the Hudson River cooled my back, buffeting me a bit, as I trudged from Riverside Drive and 116th Street up our steep Morningside Heights hill to the Broadway subway station. I boarded one on the downtown side after a not unduly long wait, and the train, because of the hour, was slightly less stifling than it normally was in the dog days of August on the island of Manhattan.

Arriving at 23rd, the short walk to Max's Kansas City on 18th Street was all downhill on Park Avenue South and effortless. It was always cooler downtown, but even on a relatively peaceful Sunday evening, one could feel a prickle of excitement and anticipation entering the lower body of Manhattan, which historically contained its arts districts, and I was reminded of my first days when I first moved here, marveling at all the changes in my life that had happened in three short years. I had just come back from traveling around on another continent, and now it seemed I'd be entering yet another 'worldly' enclave.

Although I had never been to Max's, I'd heard of it, as it was one of the more popular and notoriously hip haunts of the downtown music and arts scene. I wasn't sure what to expect, so I slowed down before entering. Once inside, I looked around, and saw a tall, shaggy-haired man lounging against the wall near the front door. Lou had given my name to Mickey, the owner, who had a kind of proprietary air about him. I walked over and told him I was here to see The Velvet Underground.

The man looked me up and down, then asked if I was a friend of Lou Reed's. I answered yes. He said Lou was expecting me and told me to follow him upstairs. Once we climbed the stairs and arrived at the relatively small performance space, Mickey turned around and smiled, wordlessly gliding off and disappearing into the crowd. The place was packed solid with the usual crowd of characters I would get to know when Lou and I began steadily dating, but on that night, I knew no one there but him.

I was instantly aware of how hot the room was, the temperature at least 20 degrees higher than it was downstairs, although the air conditioning was blasting away. I looked around at my new surroundings. Packed with people shoulder-to-shoulder, the crowd seemed to be waiting restlessly with what felt like a heady but fierce anticipation for the band to begin playing. Further back I saw the band were already on the small, slightly elevated stage, setting up their equipment, and getting ready to perform.

Perhaps it was because of the heightened tension in the room, but suddenly time seemed strangely suspended. The lights were already low, and it was dark. It was so crowded that one could hardly make out the shapes of individuals in the room. As I found a space to stand somewhere in the middle of the crowd and not that far from the front, I felt like I'd entered a giant, exotic cocoon fused with sights and smells of a primitive but unified animal-like spirit.

Suddenly I heard Lou's voice over the speakers. I could barely make him out on the dimly lit stage. At first, I stood and listened, but then everyone started screaming and shouting, jumping around and hugging each other. Lewis started some onstage patter, but through the din it was virtually impossible to see him or hear what he was saying.

Then the opening chords began to play, and just as I was beginning to acclimate myself to the live sounds of a band I'd only thus far heard on the radio, maybe about halfway through their first number, 'I'm Waiting For The Man,' a space opened up between me and the stage, and Lewis saw me in the crowd.

For that instant, we made eye contact. He seemed to pause for a bit, then resumed singing. Although he didn't acknowledge me from the stage, as the set progressed he appeared to direct his performance to where I was, which was really surprising and took me back a bit. I danced almost the entire time I was there, as I didn't know if I was imagining he was singing to me, or if he really was; in either case, I was somewhat overwhelmed, and I decided to let myself go and just dance to the music.

No one danced with one partner, but with each other all at once. Although the crowd moved like one huge, rhythmically gyrating animal, everyone also seemed to be alone in their own world, wrapped up in the sound of The Velvet Underground. Occasionally one could spot in the crowd drinks held high overhead, sloshing around all over everyone below, but no one seemed to care. The room was permeated with the sights and smells of pot, booze, and probably some seriously illicit drugs. The band played notoriously loud, and Cale's droning climbed over, around, and through us, yet you could also hear Lou singing—screaming, really—over the instruments. Lewis sang his heart out—sometimes, I could have sworn, right at me. It was a bit intimidating.

I had an extraordinary time that night, and in truth, it is one of the best experiences I've ever had at a rock'n'roll show. The audience was alive, one giant whip of electrical current let loose. There wasn't one person who wasn't rockin' to the music and thrilled by Lou's unusually energetic stage antics in what would go down as one of his best live performances.

Lou knew it was The Velvet Underground's last show, and I knew it, too; but the rest of the audience didn't, although I was unaware of that fact at the time. This was actually the first time I'd ever seen him perform, and I thought he was incredible! He possessed an enormous amount of power and stage presence, and he looked to me like had reached down inside of himself to give all he possessed for his last show. I learned later that some members of the band didn't even know this was their last night, because they were scheduled to play for another week.

After their final song, Lou suddenly jumped down off the stage and strode into the middle of the crowd, grabbing me. He was wringing wet, sweat pouring down his face, but he pulled me to him anyway and kissed me brusquely on the cheek, yelling something in my ear.

I couldn't hear what he was saying over the bedlam of the closely packed, screaming audience. He pulled back to catch my eye, and we experienced a moment where we looked at each other face to face, eye to eye. His look was urgent, almost pleading, but then the moment was gone, and he was surrounded by people crowding in on us to get closer to him. As we were separated by the ongoing crush, I remember the wild, almost haunted look he cast in my direction. Then, over everyone's heads, as we were pulled further apart, he yelled something out to me, cupping a hand around his mouth.

I couldn't really hear him, only see him mouthing words. As he stabbed himself in the chest with his index finger, pointing first to himself, and then me, he mimed, '*I. Will. Call. You!*'

But then he was swallowed up by the crowd, disappearing out of sight. I didn't know where he went, but I wasn't interested in being part of the crowd, so I managed to get through the room, which was still filled to overflowing. Pockets of spent, disheveled people soaked with sweat, their clothes sticking to or limply hanging off them, slumped against one another. Sweat was pouring down *their* faces, too, and many in the crowd had a queer but sublimely satisfied, almost otherworldly look. I was as hot, flushed, and sweaty as everyone else, probably the mirror image of those I pushed past as I tried to make my escape from the heat and intensity of the place. I noticed the heavily applied eye makeup on many of the drag queens sprinkled throughout the room streamed down their faces in rivers of black, eidolic tears, and I thought with not a little irony that they could have been falling for the demise of a seminal rock'n'roll band's final performance. The aftermath was overpowering, and after the band left the room, it felt like something living had just died.

Finally I managed to get to the stairs and climb down them and out onto the street, relieved to get away from the mayhem and feeling of oppression that had fallen upon me. I sprang through the crowd that had migrated out onto the sidewalk in front of the bar, where luckily I was almost immediately able to flag down a passing cab to take me uptown and home. Beat and sprawling on the back seat as the cab picked up momentum and streaked through the traffic lights on Park Avenue, timed for speed on a late Sunday night, I was suddenly struck by what I had just witnessed onstage that night. All the pieces of Lou I'd seen and talked to suddenly fell into place, and I was overwhelmed by a feeling I cannot describe. It was overpowering, and somewhat frightening. Quietly, I noticed time was moving in a regular, more ordered fashion once again. I watched gratefully as the familiar landscape outside my window streaked past quickly, in real time.

Yes, the band had been fabulous! Yes, Lewis had been in top form. I'd spent the night dancing my heart out to The Velvet Underground's final performance, and had experienced a wonderful time. But I'd never quite be able to entirely shake the realization that this had been the last time Lewis would be singing his songs with the band he started, and put his heart and soul into for nearly a decade. However amazing the evening had been for me, it had mostly been about the music and Lou's performance, and getting lost in the moment. But the thought that this was also a final moment in time had never quite left me.

Suddenly, my exhaustion fell over me, and I remember inadvertently shivering, then curling up and lying down on the back seat for the long ride back home. Tomorrow was Monday, and I had to be at work at 8:30 in the morning. I wondered how Lou was feeling, and where he'd gone. I knew he planned to move out to his parents' house, but I didn't know then that he had moved there directly after the show.

* * *

Lou kept his word and called me that week. After he left The Velvet Underground and moved to his parents' house on Long Island, we began dating. Before long, we were seeing each other regularly.

When Lou moved out to the Island, he was different, more like the man I'd only had glimpses of when I'd seen him in the city, before he had so many Johnny Walker Reds under his belt that he became drunk and obnoxious. I had good reason to want to take it slow and get to know him better, and I was glad I had the opportunity to do so. After hours of long telephone conversations, where we discussed everything from our favorite books to the best bagel in town—and, naturally, had the first and most important discussion for couples in this town, about where to find the best pizza—Lou asked if he could come into the city and take me out again. I agreed.

Within a couple of months, he was coming in every weekend to see me. When he wasn't drinking or feeling the pressure to perform—which he was often want to do, mostly when he was out in public and around his crowd—I came to learn that Lewis was a remarkably quiet and thoughtful man, gentle and sweet.

Then he invited me out to his house for a weekend on Long Island to meet his family: his parents; his sister, Bunny; and his grandmother, who was also living with them. We developed a routine where every other weekend he would come into the city and stay with me, and the next weekend I would go out to the island and stay at his house.

Out on the Island, we spent time in his room, talking about writing, music, or what poems or songs he was working on. We'd go out to dinner with his parents or borrow the family car and have a quiet dinner at the Reeds' favorite Chinese restaurant. Then maybe go to a movie, or to the bar he hung out at afterward for a couple of drinks, where we just talked.

Our early dating was easy, going out, spending time with his family, seeing movies—the usual stuff—and it was then, as we got to know each other over these months, that we fell in love. It was a surprisingly old-fashioned courtship, but the kind that appealed to me. Because even though it wasn't hip or cool—and I would never admit it—in my heart, it's the kind of girl I was. Lou knew that, and frankly that could have very well been one of the things about me that he valued most. I was happy that he didn't pressure me but seemed to enjoy us taking our time to get to know one another, as much as me.

Surprisingly, despite the very different worlds we had been brought up in, we had a great deal in common: our love for the written word, poetry, and rock'n'roll, and a kind of instant, very easy, unspoken simpatico. We fell into a very natural kind of rhythm, spending our weekends together away from our jobs, and my studies, without a care in the world, really.

* * *

Although I always looked forward to my weekends with Lewis and his family at their home on Long Island, the weekend coming up was different. I needed to mentally prepare myself.

Having left my family back home in Pennsylvania, I was alone in New York City. When Lou's parents unhesitatingly welcomed me into their family, they filled the emptiness in my heart created by the loss of mine with warmth and affection.

The Reed family home was a modest ranch house built, like thousands of others, during the prosperous years following World War II to accommodate the suburban sprawl that exploded the middle class onto the Long Island landscape. It was decorated simply but tastefully, and I bunked overnight on the very comfortable couch in their den, with the sheets, blankets, and feather pillows Lou's mother always provided for me.

Sometimes, late at night, Lou crept in, and we snuggled together, talking long into the night—sharing and planning our dreams together, before falling asleep in each other's arms. In the morning, as the family sat around a breakfast table heavy with smoked salmon, whitefish, lox and bagels; hot, steaming coffee; and a panoply of local pastries and delicacies, nothing was ever said about our nights together, and they were innocent enough, too. I seemed to blend seamlessly into the family weekend plans and routine.

But given what had occurred the previous weekend, when Lou spent the weekend at my apartment in the city, I wanted to make our time together especially lovely—to bring some hope, confidence, and happiness back into his life.

Because the week before, on a Friday evening in February 1971, another drunken night at Max's Kansas City had ended with me practically carrying Lewis out the front doors of the club to the curb of Park Avenue South and 18th Street.

I successfully captured the only cab cruising the avenue at this hour. Once it pulled up, I managed to get Lou, dead out, safely inside. Quickly closing the door so he wouldn't fall onto the pavement below, I walked around to the street side and got in.

At the sound of the door shutting behind me, Lewis shot straight up in his seat and, in a state of considerable confusion and dismay, looked around. But as soon as he saw me next to him, he aimed his head directly onto my lap and fell into it again. I gave the cabbie our address and we sped off north into the early morning mist, which was rising in a manner not unlike the mist that I imagine escapes from behind the curtains obscuring the Great and Mighty Oz.

For the city that never sleeps, it was unusually quiet. As the cab sped off, I was finally able to lie back on the headrest to ease my splitting headache and catch my breath. Perhaps the whooshing sound of the cab speeding over the early morning moisture of the smooth asphalt on Park lulled me to sleep, because I was suddenly jolted awake from a disturbing dream by a cacophony of baffling rushing sounds above.

I opened my eyes just as the cab swerved through the 42nd Street Tunnel and emerged back onto Park. I saw a pair of falcons burst from between one of the towering office buildings on the west side of the avenue, flying toward us and then low overhead, furiously beating their wings. Although I was inside a moving vehicle, they frightened me, and I ducked instinctively to avoid being hit by them, which made absolutely no sense at all. I must have fallen asleep, but it was also clear to me how much Lou's drinking upset me.

Lou's snoring returned me to the present and tore through my fears. I looked down, and Lou was still asleep on my lap, his nose between my thighs. There was a painful familiarity to this scene, so once again, I lay my head back, but this time warily, without closing my eyes. I didn't want to fall asleep again; I needed to keep my head straight so I could think. Because I didn't know what I was going to do. After his poetry reading at the St. Mark's Church Poetry Project the night before, I knew I had to try to help restore his confidence, what was also shattered all over my lap. But it wasn't too long before we pulled up to my corner at Broadway and 116th. On the other side of the transparent plastic barrier between us, the driver turned around and asked how I was doing.

'Can you make it?' he asked.

An unmistakable Queens accent filled the enclosed space. I sighed with relief to hear it, and it brought me back to earth and my actual geographical location: Gotham, New York. I began trying to wake Lou, gently shaking his shoulder and running my hand over his forehead. His head was damp, and his hair was soaked, plastered flat to his skull.

'Huh?' Lewis exclaimed, sitting upright.

Somewhat shaken, I pulled myself together enough to ask the driver how much I owed him. But then Lou unexpectedly put his hand out to stop me from reaching for my bag and shoved his other one into his pants pocket, pulling out a wad of bills.

'I got this,' he said.

Suddenly we were thrown forward. Another cab had plowed into us from behind. Lou hit his head on the plastic barrier, and I hit my forehead on the window beside me. Lou flopped over onto the seat, and I thought he'd passed out. I immediately started cursing—a habit I'd picked up with relief and surprising agility, living in town.

The cabbie pulled up short and said, 'All right, all right, let me see what the fuck just happened. Sit tight and shuddup, will ya?'

Getting out, he added, 'Check your boyfriend, see if he's alive. He's drunk out of his mind, so he's probably fine. Let me know if you can't find a pulse.'

Then the door slammed shut and the cab shook. Queens was pissed.

I shook Lou and called out his name.

'Lou! Lou! Wake up!'

'What, did we just get rear-ended?' he asked, looking up at me. 'What the fuck, at this hour in the morning?' He threw the wad of bills in his hand on the back seat and said, 'Well, there goes his tip.'

With that, we both doubled over laughing, stumbling out of the car. We were fine—maybe a couple of bumps on the head, but that was all. The yelling between the two cabbies was probably entertaining, but we resisted rubbernecking, and Lou dragged me across the street to get me out of there.

By the time we got to the other side of the street, the shouting was over. A police siren started up on Broadway; a tugboat hauling a garbage dump on the river below bellowed out a warning for another vessel to get the hell out of the way.

When we got to the sidewalk on the other side of Broadway, Lewis slipped behind me and pulled me to him. He moved his body into mine and wrapped his arms around me. Oh, that felt nice! I leaned into him a little, and he placed his knees into the backs of mine, where they fit perfectly.

We had been together for several months, and things were good. Pressing himself up against me, he shoved his nose into my hair and plunged it down into the neck of my sweater.

'You all right?' he asked.

'Yeah.'

'You smell so good,' he said, taking a deep breath and laying his head on my shoulder.

For a second we stood there in the early morning—a fairly typical hip, young New York City couple dazed by the light of the morning as it broke around us. Like statues, we watched our cab pull away from us on Broadway. Shimmering in a kind of golden, otherworldly light, Morningside Heights looked like an Edward Hopper painting. I noticed everything was moving very, very slowly, like we were inhabiting an underwater world. The magnolia on the lawn of the entrance to Barnard Hall was in its last throes of fall color. With only a few leaves left, they clung stiff and lonely to their soon-to-be abandoned residence, like tenants thrown out on the street for non-payment of rent. One fell and hit the cement sidewalk below. It sounded like a truck crashing into a brick building. God, my head hurt!

This must be how dogs hear. No wonder they're a nervous wreck in this town.

'Come on, baby,' Lou said, 'let's go home.'

I was so relieved that a sigh escaped from my lungs before I could suppress it. I must have shuddered a little, too, because Lou stopped and turned me to him. After looking at me and saying nothing, he lifted my head between his hands and pulled me to him. Without a word, he pressed his lips to my forehead. They tingled, like a shot of ginger. He kept them there for quite some time, and I heard the words he didn't have to say out loud to me. I let my guard down and moved closer, if only to hear his latest fairytale. I was suddenly very, very tired.

Aware of the stillness around us, he asked me something quietly. They were words I loved hearing. We were entirely alone, and not another living being or speeding vehicle was in sight.

'Is there *any* orange juice in the fridge?' he asked.

I smiled, and the anxiety and fear I'd felt all evening lifted, like a swallow flying out of a hayloft at dawn, or how my spirit rises hearing Beethoven's Seventh. The sound of his voice stopped the shaking I was unaware of until then, and I was glad that now I could lean into him and relax. My watch on this night was over.

As we took the final steps back to the safety of the three-bedroom apartment I was now sharing with two other students, I began ruminating about the evening we'd just had.

* * *

Lou and I had followed at a slight distance behind the East Village crowd who, in their usual navigational pattern, shuffled off to Max's after spilling out onto the street from St. Mark's church, where the poetry reading had been held. They broke into little groups, casually chattering as they walked along or hailed cabs, several piling into one after another.

We walked quietly, saying little, because Lewis had just experienced a historically significant but disastrous evening. This was the first time he'd participated in a poetry reading. Beforehand, we'd only been members of this audience, listening to, among others, Allen Ginsberg, Gerard Malanga, Jim Carroll, Patti Smith. Then, Lou read several of the poems taken from his latest batch, which he'd also sent out for publication consideration earlier in the week. It was the first time Lou had read any of the poems he'd written since his self-imposed exile at his parents' house after leaving The Velvet Underground in the summer of 1970.

We'd started that weekend snuggled together in my single bed, enjoying a blissfully lazy, late Saturday morning. Afterward, we made it to Tom's Restaurant around noon for our usual breakfast of eggs on English muffins and a double order of extra-crispy bacon. Lou gulped down orange juice and I sipped a V8 with a slice of lemon. We downed several cups of their delicious coffee, then headed off to an afternoon cruising the second-hand bookstores on Broadway. Lou picked up a worn collection of twentieth-century American poetry, and I bought a paperback biography of Stanislavsky and the Russian Theatre.

We began the evening with an early dinner at the West End. Lou wanted to keep his head clear for the reading later on that evening, so he drank only a couple of Johnny Walker Reds. Over dinner, he read out loud the poems he had lined up for the evening. At first he was shy and hesitant in his delivery, but his confidence grew with encouragement. He sat up taller, and his delivery got stronger each time he read them. He added two more poems, which he said were risky, because they were so personal. One of them was about me. I was surprised at his choice, because in it he confessed that he was in love with me. Its title was simply my first name.

Although I was afraid this might embarrass me, I didn't let on; I kept my head down, quietly smiling, as he practiced reading the poem out loud. He'd read it for me after he'd written it, a couple of weeks ago, when we were in his bedroom out on the Island. I'd been touched, but I was at a loss for words to express how I felt. I had simply kissed him afterward—which is what I usually did when he read poems or songs he'd written about me or said I inspired.

We went over the poems he read about three times, then decided that should do it. Better not to over-prepare, so that he could appear like he was reading them for the first time. I knew from my acting training that this would encourage a fresh delivery and allow more insight into his performance.

Entering the church, we ran into Gerard Malanga, the poet and photographer who had worked with Andy Warhol for years. He and Lou talked about what they would be reading that night, and Gerard was delighted to hear Lewis was participating. Before he left to chat with a couple of other poets who were just arriving, Malanga—who didn't seem to be able to keep his hands to himself—gave my bottom a squeeze. I never told Lou about Malanga's roving hands because I thought he was harmless and, in those days, girls routinely tolerated this kind of machismo nonsense.

Danny Fields came over to Lewis and immediately engaged him in conversation, ignoring me. Lou knew Danny had been nursing a crush on him for years, ever since he worked with The Velvet Underground, writing a book about the band's early years. Patti Smith came up, and, putting her arms around Lou's neck, laid her head on his shoulder. It was pretty clear to both of us that she hoped everyone was looking, because Lou was a cool friend to have. But I smiled at her, and eventually, she disengaged from him so we could begin looking for a seat, hopefully, in the back. As soon as people saw Lou was in the house, they came up to him, hugging him or shaking his hand, exclaiming how happy they were to see him. Soon, Lou relaxed and began flirting—sometimes subtly, sometimes not so much—with everyone within a mile's radius of him. That was his *modus operandi*. It meant he was feeling like his old self, and I was happy.

It has been said that there was a year or two when everyone in Warhol's Factory, including Andy, made a play for Lou. At the very least, he was richly received with open arms into the cult of characters populating Warhol's industrial space, which had recently moved to Union Square. Lou was extremely practical and very ambitious. He used his sexuality whenever it could further his career, but he wasn't emotionally invested in anyone but me. I wasn't sure other people knew this, but I did, and he'd already grudgingly acknowledged it to me.

'Bettye, I'm just being practical,' he'd say.

I wasn't the jealous type—it's not my style; never has been. If your guy wants to be with someone else, let them, and move on. If they really want to, they will; it's only a matter of time. If they don't, and they're just playing you, they'll get the message that you'll be happy to see them go if they continue treating you disrespectfully.

Eventually the moment came and Lou got up to read his poems. I held my breath. The church grew as quiet as a graveyard.

After the reading was over, Lou said nothing for a very long time. It hadn't gone well at all, and he knew it. As we followed the dispersing crowd, Lou's hands were in his pocket. His head was down, and he kicked whatever he found in his path on the sidewalk. I didn't say much, hoping he'd feel better if we just kept walking. We had over twenty blocks for him to get his thoughts together before we met up with everyone at Max's. I hoped that, during that time, he could articulate his feelings, thinking he would feel better if he expressed himself, rather than bottle them up, as he usually did.

Aside from Danny, who clapped loudly when Lou read a poem about homosexuality, nobody said much to Lou after he completed his reading, or after he went back to his seat. Allen Ginsberg congratulated

Lou on his work before he left. Jim Carroll did, too. But whatever else was said to him was nothing more than lip service. I felt very uncomfortable for him and noticed that, unlike when we arrived, people avoided him as they left.

The mistake Lou made in front of that audience was obvious. Rather than being the cool Lou Reed everyone expected to entertain them, he'd been straightforward and sincere, revealing the man behind the myth. After his reading, and the audience's mild reception to his work, he announced that he was giving up music to concentrate on writing poetry. Everyone in the audience was shocked. Some seemed embarrassed for him. I was as surprised as everyone else, but I didn't let on.

Lou knew the rules of this crowd. *Never* be sincere—it was so very uncool. And Lewis had always been the epitome of cool. But for him to stand up in front of the crowd to proclaim a new love, and then announce he was giving up music, was a recipe for disaster. It was clear that many of those in attendance were wondering, *what happened to our Lou?* You could hear them thinking, and some of them whispering. *The rumors must be true! Lou really did have a breakdown!* Lou Reed and John Cale had led one of the most influential and revered bands in rock'n'roll, and now he wanted to give up music and become what? *A po-et?*

Everyone knew Lou was an excellent writer. 'Heroin' contained groundbreaking lyrics and subject matter, along with 'Venus In Furs,' 'White Light/White Heat,' and 'Pale Blue Eyes.' There were so many! His latest, 'Rock And Roll' and 'Sweet Jane,' from the Velvets' final album, *Loaded*, were destined to become rock'n'roll classics.

Even if most of Lou's crowd hadn't read his poetry, they had heard it was getting published in several influential music magazines after he left the Velvets. But to give it up and work as a typist in his father's accounting firm, and try to become a serious poet? And, at almost thirty years old, to move in with his parents in the middle-class suburb of Baldwin, Long Island? The New York City Son discovered by Andy Warhol? A member of the Factory, and the venerable Velvet Underground? He *was* crazy!

At the beginning of the evening, people had crowded around Lou when we first got to St. Mark's Church, telling him how much they'd missed him, how glad they were to be there for his reading that night. But I sat in the audience as he read his poetry, I heard and felt their reaction—the stillness that fell over the audience. This didn't seem to be the oh-so-cool Lou, who everybody loved, everybody wanted—and some got a piece of. *Where was he?*

I remember feeling hurt, angry, and confused. I didn't know many of these people then—and some, not at all—so I didn't fully understand what was going on. Only that Lou was very angry and incredibly hurt. But he wasn't gonna let 'em see it! Instead, he donned his Lou Reed persona. That was the reason for his surprise announcement. Not because he was really dropping his entire musical career to write poetry, but in defiance of them.

For months, Lou had talked about how these people hadn't heard him. They didn't know or care about the person under the persona, which was one of the reasons why he created one in the first place. Because then nobody could hurt him. Underneath it all, however determined he might be, Lou Reed was a very sensitive man, and he was tired of playing games. He was sick of sucking up to people he could care less about who might help his musical career.

Because *what if* he wanted to be just a writer? *What if* he wanted to concentrate on writing poetry? What business was it of theirs? Whose life was it, anyway? Why couldn't he do what he wanted?

'*Fuck that*,' he was saying. 'I can do whatever I want—fuck you all! If I want to stand up here and read my poetry—whomever and whatever it's about—and you withhold your approval or judge me because I no longer want to serve you in our mutually bullshit, symbiotic relationship? Well, then, *fuck you.*'

He was rejecting them because they were rejecting his work, and that was very personal to him, because his writing *was* him.

'Guess what, assholes,' he flung back at them. 'Not only am I going to write about whatever and whomever I want, I will throw away my entire musical career just because I can, and do nothing *but* write poetry. And I'll be as successful with that, as I am with my music—far more than most of you. I'll do whatever I want, you pretentious pile of posers!'

He was, in fact, furious.

We had discussed Lou giving up his career in music and pursuing a career as a writer—a poet—quite a bit, and I had encouraged his writing. But I knew he hadn't made that decision yet, because he loved rock'n'roll. It was a difficult decision for him to make, so I was a little surprised at his announcement, but I knew him well enough to understand how he felt—and why he did it.

Afterward, we went to Max's, but to be honest I don't remember all the details of that night. I got pretty plowed myself. I remember Lou with his head in his arms on a table in the back room at some point in the evening, incredibly sad. He felt totally rejected by the very people he counted on for support, while he tried to make some sense of his career and his life, during a major turning point within it.

I have always remembered this night as one of the most painful nights I ever saw Lewis experience in public. He reacted by drinking like a fish, snorting whatever he could get his hands on, becoming inconsolably sad, and then falling down drunk. But he was acting out his hurt and anger—a pattern I would see repeated so many times over the next several years that it became heartbreaking. Ultimately, it became unbearable.

new york, new york........ CHAPTER THREE

I woke up and Lewis was staring at me, lying on his stomach, head propped up on his elbows, in my face. Startled, I looked at him without moving, unintentionally staring back at him. Then I blinked. I didn't know if this was a dream or another typical morning waking up next to Lou Reed. In the two years we'd been together, the one thing I could always rely on was that life with Lou was never predictable.

A smile spread slowly across his face. He was beaming, like a kid who's been waiting for his parents to take him out for ice cream. He kept staring at me, smiling, but I saw that he was totally genuine—tender, even. So I lay there for a while, neither of us moving, staring at each other. I remember thinking how lucky it was that you couldn't fall into someone's eyes, no matter how much you loved them, because, at this moment, I was afraid I'd never come back.

'Lewis,' I said, shifting my body in discomfort, my eyes never leaving his. I brought my arms around my head, locked my hands into place, and, to add a sense of normalcy, yawned.

'Hmmmmmm …?'

'What are you doing?' I asked.

He stared at me a moment longer and then ran his forefinger down the outline of my cheek, moving a strand of hair away from my forehead.

'I love watching you sleep,' he said.

'Oh?' I asked. 'Why?'

'Your face is so beautiful when you're sleeping.'

He said it so quickly that it almost sounded rehearsed. It was a compliment, but his concern about looks—even when sleeping—was challenging to me.

I'd moved to New York City three years earlier and quickly learned that the way people looked and dressed was almost more important than anything else. In New York, if you were considered good looking, all you had to do was keep your mouth shut, smile, pout, or snarl. It seemed to me that if you were lucky enough to be born good looking, automatically, people were nice to you.

I'd become adept at concealing my thoughts and nearly all of my true feelings, mostly when Lou and I were out in public. When we were alone together, relaxed, and could be ourselves, we were very comfortable together, and agreed on most things.

Lou followed astrology; in fact, although he may not have asked directly, he would always find out what signs the planets were in the horoscopes of those whom he worked or allowed to be close to him. Lewis was a Pisces, the sign that rules my moon; I'm a Scorpio. Both Pisces and Scorpio are water signs, water being the element that represents our emotions, as does the Moon in our horoscope. This made us compatible—we both felt things deeply but were outwardly emotionally reserved. Lou wasn't one for small talk; neither was I. There wasn't much said between us, because there really didn't need to be; we instinctively knew what the other was thinking or feeling. Ours was an easy pairing.

But we weren't alone much anymore, not like we used to be, on weekends—out at his parent's house on Long Island or at my apartment in the city. Now that we were launching Lou's solo career, we had to network on the party scene, which often made me feel on edge, because I was unfamiliar with making deals and trading favors; it simply wasn't part of my background. But I'd learned that's how the world worked, especially in this city.

Lewis loved all the parties and social gatherings around town. He was a famous flirt, sometimes outrageously so, and with everyone. Woman or man, it didn't matter—all were fair game. I didn't mind, because I knew it didn't mean anything to him; it was all just an exercise. Lewis was determined to make it this time around on a world-class scale, because he absolutely believed The Velvet Underground should have. He wasn't going to let that kind of failure happen to him again.

I missed our weekends together out on the Island at his parents' house, especially those times we sat on the floor of his childhood bedroom with all his recording equipment spread out around us. After he finished working on his poetry or a song, he'd record it and ask for my reaction. Often Lou asked me to sing his songs, as he recorded them, because he loved my 'boy's choir' voice—a quality I acquired after years singing in my high school and church choirs. With the exception of the songs on the *Berlin* album, Lou had me do this throughout our relationship—and it was actually when we experienced some of our more intimate moments.

My believing in Lewis gave him confidence and renewed his self-respect. It is what he needed, especially after leaving the Velvets. This was a great deal of what bound us together and cemented Lou's trust in me, but at the time I was only doing what came naturally to me. I loved him and believed in his work, and that's how I was brought up—to support my man.

In the beginning, it was obvious to us that people wondered where Lou found me. You could almost hear some of the hip, famous musicians, models, artists, journalists, and writers traveling in the same circles as us thinking, *Now where was it that Lou picked her up? Where did this girl come from, again?* But few asked. In truth, it didn't really bother me, and Lou even less. Anyone who knew Lou will tell you that he trusted very few people. But he trusted me. I had been embraced by his family, and he knew I wasn't in it for the money. We were in this together and, ultimately, we were going to make him a star.

When we spent the first year and a half of our relationship hanging out with his parents on Long Island, I never imagined how my life would change as Lou's star rose. The years after he left The Velvet Underground and retreated to Long Island have been called his 'lost' years, but this was hardly the case. Lou came from a marvelous, supportive family, and going home gave him the support and security to regain his confidence and find himself. We met John Cale for dinner after Lou moved back into the city with me, and I heard him tell Lou that he thought it had done him some good. But that meeting was cut short when Lou suddenly got up and looked at me to let me know we were leaving. I said a hurried goodbye to John, and then we left. Lou didn't even say goodbye to him, and John seemed a little startled that the meeting had ended so abruptly. But they had a famously contentious relationship, so it wasn't all that surprising to me. I hadn't caught what set Lou off, but he never talked about it, and it was clear he didn't want to, so I never asked.

Lou was writing, and while he was employed as a typist at his father's firm he spent much of his time working on his poems, consistently sending them out for publication consideration. He was the boss's son, so nobody said anything about the work he produced there. He published several poems in the *Harvard Advocate*, the university's literary magazine, along with a few other magazines.

Lou and his family got to know me very well. They were incredibly warm and welcomed me with open arms. My family was back home in Pennsylvania, where I mostly grew up on my family's two farms. After World War II, Dad found peace working the smaller, seventy-acre one. Now, without family, I was alone in the city, and Lou's family became my surrogate one. I loved and respected his family, and they were very fond of me. They thought I was good for him, and approved of our relationship.

I would be a bridesmaid for his sister, Bunny (whose wedding was the first time I saw Lou wearing his yarmulke). By then, about three years into our relationship, we had become officially engaged; Lou first asked me to marry him a year after we began dating, but I didn't want to make it official until he had kick-started his solo career.

I directed my thoughts back to Lewis, who was still smiling at me—and staring! At times, he could be incredibly sweet, almost like a love-struck high-school kid. It looked like this was one of those moments. Okay, that was nice, but I wasn't sure I liked anyone watching me sleeping. It felt like an invasion. I also thought it was a bit weird. But Lou looked harmless enough, so I let it go.

My mind wandered off to later that night and whether we would end up at Max's again. It was here that I saw my high-school hero, John Lennon, quietly having dinner with Yoko. If there was anyone I would have liked to have been introduced to, it was John Lennon, but Lou always scoffed at The Beatles' music. He walked right past John, not even acknowledging his presence. I thought Lou was jealous of John, but I never mentioned it. Lou was very competitive, though, and I'd seen this behavior with him before. That's why I never asked to meet anyone he didn't automatically introduce me to.

All the visiting rock stars congregated at Max's. David Bowie, Mick Jagger, Ray Davies, Rod Stewart—to name a few—usually ended their nights and early mornings here, along with their bands and entourages. During that time, Max's was the rock star playground of New York. People danced upstairs or on the tables in the back room—it didn't matter—you could virtually do just about anything. Everyone passed around cocaine or casually placed it on tables in the back room for all to share, like you might leave out snacks for houseguests. Almost everyone got roaring drunk. I suppose all kinds of things were happening in the bathrooms, but I avoided them like the plague.

As everyone let loose of all the pressures and tensions that built up from touring the world, they screamed and shouted, laughed, slapped each other's backs, and hugged in drug-induced and alcohol-fueled endearments. Almost everyone got in on the act. Glasses were thrown against walls, insults were hurled; then people hugged and kissed, made up, and apologized.

David, Lou, and Iggy—especially these last two, wired on cocaine and booze sometimes beyond all comprehension—egged each other on with one exhibitionist escapade after another. They were amusing, like elementary school kids roughhousing during recess, and we found it entertaining. But at the core, their shenanigans were really rather innocent; they were kids at heart who just wanted to have fun. Sometimes, serious conversation about art, writing, and of course music transpired, and those were great; but they were also fueled by drugs and alcohol, and sometimes things got heated and lost in the moment.

When Andy Warhol and his entourage showed up, the place lit up like Christmas. Usually, Andy just took one photo after another, enamored, as he was, with his newest playmate, the Polaroid Instamatic, which had just come out on the market. Whirring and spitting out one instantly developed photograph after another, he freely handed them out to anyone who asked—and even if you didn't. This allowed him not to say much or anything at all, which made Andy happy.

Andy was, essentially, an observer, his Polaroid the perfect foil. He and the artist Brigid Polk, a central member of his entourage, would huddle, whispering, with all the Factory members strung out and piled up around them as they held court. One could practically see steam rising from some of those conversations, they were so heated. Occasionally, one of the Factory reprobates, harried out on heroin, would nod or mumble and whimper and then lay back down, sometimes on top of each other—arms, legs, torsos tangled up or wound around one another—on floors, tables, or whatever closest horizontal surface was present—out to the world.

Everyone loved and respected Andy, and so did I. He was a gentle soul—a genuine artist. He'd learned during his early advertising career what was necessary to make a buck in a country that didn't support the arts. After Lou left the Velvets, however, he often treated Andy badly, intentionally snubbing him. It hurt Andy and it embarrassed me. This was because, to a large extent, he blamed Andy for the Velvets' failure to achieve success on the level Lou thought they deserved. After Andy's initial, rather modest investment in the band, he didn't financially support, manage, or guide them in any meaningful way, if at all. Andy thought lending his name to the band was enough, but Lou didn't agree. As a result, when we saw Andy at functions, Lou tried to avoid him as much as possible; when he couldn't, and it looked like Lou's fangs were about to come out, I'd do my best to distract him.

* * *

Looking into Lou's hopeful eyes on this morning, as he smiled and continued staring at me, I thought that maybe Lou was too dependent, and sometimes a little crazy; perhaps we worked too hard and he played even harder, but I loved him and our work together. A girl could do worse in the world, right? The man was crazy about me. So I went with it.

'How long have you been there, watching me sleeping?' I asked him.

'Oh, I don't know,' he said, coyly, reaching up and smoothing another wisp of my hair away.

It already seemed like too long a time for me. What I needed was a dose of the ordinary; a cup of coffee and some V8 with fresh lemon. Then a walk around the block to the newsstand to get the *Times*, order a bagel with a dollop of cream cheese at the corner diner, and read what was going on in the world. Because it was very different from the one in which I now inhabited. Sometimes I wanted to get far, far away—if only for a little while.

Little did I know that Lou would use this scene of us lying in bed that morning in a song. 'Make Up' on *Transformer* starts with the lines '*Your face when sleeping is sublime / And then you open up your eyes.*' But then Lewis turns it into something quite different—a gay anthem. This is one of the many examples of Lou's brilliance: taking the real moments in his and others' lives and creating something totally unexpected and unprecedented. He liked watching me put on makeup, too: '*Then comes pancake factor number one ...*'

Lou learned writing techniques in the classes he took as an English major with Delmore Schwartz, a largely unsung but gifted American poet who was his professor and mentor at Syracuse University. One of the strategies Schwartz taught Lou about writing was to give the reader something unforeseen: seize the predictable outcome, do a 180-degree turn, and use that. If your original meaning changed, go with it. This could be very helpful in the writing process and, if the end result became really interesting and challenging, people would think it—or you—brilliant. A writer had little to lose with this tack, because you could always throw it out, if it didn't work.

Lewis wrote about the strong and the weak; juxtaposed unkindness with affection; and contrasted the most undesirable segments of society with the innocent and vulnerable living in it. He was relentless in exposing the underworld of the city, while extolling the virtues of the society he routinely chronicled and damned. Before him, no one had written about the disenfranchised in this country.

Lewis applied the techniques and tricks of great writing and literature to rock'n'roll. Few, if any, pushed the genre into this arena. The potent mixture of Lou's characters from the streets of New York City, along with the experimental sound of The Velvet Underground, gave a curious intensity to Lou's music.

There was little doubt in anyone's mind—especially mine—that Lou possessed a kind of genius. Lewis went straight to the core of truth—and, more often than not, it was the stuff that nobody wanted to talk about.

He excavated the raw and menacing truths that populated all the dark, unacknowledged places of this majestic city, and mined it for gold.

And it worked. He reaped significant return in his writing, despite the fact that at times, for Lou, the material he was drawing from was excruciatingly painful. He found his own pain reflected in the lives of the outsiders he wrote about; but as he dug into the painful parts he unearthed in their hearts, he was successful in revealing a hazardous but exquisite dignity about them.

Burrowing into all these forbidden and untapped regions of the human condition carried some treacherous risks to Lou's state of mind and body. Mounting pressure from management and record companies, touring conditions on the road, and late-night partying or coming down off a performance high all took their toll. Lou got too absorbed in alcohol and drugs trying to escape it. The stress of all these elements came with a price on his head, for which, in the end, he paid in spades. But because of these demands put upon him, I, like most everyone around him, gave Lou considerable latitude. I felt intense pressure, too, but there was little consideration for me, especially from 'upper management' as his solo career grew more successful. Our relationship would become like his writing: cruel, then tender; loving, then we'd battle, make up, and move on.

It hadn't started out like that. In the beginning, I loved him without reservation, and was devoted to making him happy. I was determined to help get the stories and messages contained in his lyrics out to the world, because I fervently believed in them—and him. I still did. But I became embroiled in the business of making him a star. This is very different than the wish for a man to become one.

* * *

One weekend we promised Lou's parents we'd spend some time out on the Island with them. Lou had spent several weekends in a row with me in the city and we felt bad about not seeing them. The weather was perfect. Spending a couple of days soaking up the sun at the family's private beach club seemed like the least we could do!

I took the train out to the Island after work, and Lou picked me up at the station. We ordered in pizza and had it delivered, enjoying a casual dinner in their comfortably cool, air-conditioned home. Lou had a couple of drinks and we all watched television, chatting and catching up. Then everyone turned in early, for which I was grateful, as I was exhausted from the work week, school, and the travel out on the Long Island Rail Road.

We all rose refreshed the following morning and enjoyed Saturday brunch, which Lou's mother put together for us. Our plans included Lou's parents dropping us off at the club while they went out shopping. Later, the four of us would meet there for dinner. Lou and I had on our summer whites and brought our swimsuits with us as we took off in the family Mercedes. We were looking forward to spending the afternoon stretched out on the club's lounge chairs sipping piña colada's while blissfully staring out over the Atlantic Ocean.

As the tide rushed toward the beach, tennis balls lobbed furiously back and forth over the net in the tennis courts next to us. Sometimes Lou and I retrieved the balls that were hit over the fence and threw them back to the players. Fully uniformed attendants in blazing white came by like clockwork to ask what we wanted to drink, or Lewis waved his hand and minutes later they arrived. He smoked calmly, looking pensively out at the ocean, like he did when he was dreaming up new lines for songs.

But this time he didn't have his notebook, which he normally used to jot things down for his next album. Because today he was giving me my first tennis lesson. It had been a subject of conversation during our brunch earlier, when everyone found out I didn't play the game.

I liked badminton, though, and I spent my summers playing it with my stepsister at home or at friends' houses. Neither of the high schools

I attended had a tennis team, so it was the only net game we knew. But everyone in New York played tennis. The game was practically a prerequisite for the people in Lou's social circles, so he was determined to get me up to speed with his family and friends.

I grew up riding horses, ice-skating on our pond, playing croquet and badminton in our back yard and at social events. I played second base in softball—baseball was considered too tough for girls back then—and center in basketball in high school, although there wasn't an official girl's basketball team, either. I was a high hurdler and long-distance runner for the high-school track team, participating in virtually all the athletics offered to girls in the rural community I grew up in. Tennis wasn't one of them, but Lou knew I'd been a jock, so he didn't think it would be difficult for me to learn another competitive game.

After several rounds of drinks, and just before the dinner hour, when the courts cleared for everyone to go inside and change, Lou took out the rackets and tennis balls we had brought with us. I'd had only one cocktail that afternoon, because I wanted to be alert for the game.

The ocean waves were crashing against the cement wall just on the other side of the fence of the tennis court Lou chose. He had brought one of his sister's rackets for me, and unzipped his from its protective jacket. He explained the rules and how the game was played, and I took my place on the side of the court facing the water. Lewis told me to serve underhand; he'd work on teaching me to serve properly in the next lesson. For now he said to lob the ball over the net and get used to placing it according to the rules.

Lewis then whacked his first serve at me, which I hit back with all my might. The ball immediately flew over the fence and landed in the ocean. Patiently, he pulled out another ball from his pocket, and served a second one. It was as ferocious, if not more so, but I hit it with less force this time, and he ran and got it, lobbing it back. I ran into the net and hit it too hard, and it landed over the fence and into the ocean, again. This time he looked at me pointedly before pulling out another ball from his pocket and serving. I ran to it but missed.

'Damn!' I cursed.

'Don't worry about missing it so much,' Lou said. 'But try hitting the ball on *this* side of the fence! I I don't have that many balls.'

I smiled—and said I'd try.

I served this time, but the ball went sailing high up into the air like a high fly ball. Lou looked at me like I was unhinged.

'This isn't softball, you know,' he said, keeping his eye on the ball, as it dropped to earth.

He served again. This time the ball slammed into my stomach. I doubled over, the air knocked out of me. I turned my back to him, because I didn't want him to see my pain, furious I'd missed it. Instantly, he was at my side, putting his arms around me.

'Are you all right?' he asked.

'I'm fine,' I said, straightening up, although I still felt it.

'You sure?'

'Yep.'

'Okay, as long as you're all right.'

Maybe if you eased up a bit, I would be, I thought.

'Hey, why don't we change sides? You take mine and I'll stay here.'

'Right,' I said, walking to the other side of the net, my back to the ocean.

When I got in position, he gently lobbed the ball over to me.

'Why don't you serve, this time? I'll try to hit it back more gently.'

Now there's a concept, I thought.

Lightly, I asked, 'Anybody play badminton around here?'

'*No.*'

I lobbed the ball over to Lewis, and he went for it, slamming it back at me. Somehow, I managed to get to it in time, and walloped it back at him—straight over the fence.

'Sorry,' I yelled out to him.

Wearily, Lou pulled out another ball and bounced it on the asphalt next to him.

'Need more practice!' I yelled.

'*Yes*!' he replied, serving the ball, and whacking it as hard as he could. I ran and got to it in time to lob it back, but the ball sailed up and over the fence, again.

'Oh, this is ridiculous,' Lou shouted in frustration. 'I've run out of balls!'

'Hold on, I'll go get you one,' I shouted, running off the court to retrieve it.

'No, don't,' Lou cried. 'You're going to have to learn to keep the ball on this side of the fence and in play on the court. *Just forgedaboudit.*'

By now I was already on the other side of the fence, and I kept on walking. When Lou saw me ignoring his orders, he started pacing back and forth on his side of the court. I tossed the ball over to Lou by hand so he could serve. I didn't trust what would come out of my mouth next.

'Now, why didn't you serve the ball back to me, instead of throwing it? This isn't *softball*, Bettye,' he reminded me, tossing it back.

As I stuck my hand out and caught the ball with one hand, I looked at him like perhaps he should take his own advice.

'Well, you know, you said you were going to serve nicer balls, but you keep walloping them at me,' I said. 'I don't think that's helping!'

'You need to learn how to handle the opposition!' he shouted back. 'No one's going to do you any favors in this game.'

I knew the last thing in the world I should do was open my mouth, because now I was really pissed. I threw the ball up in the air and hit it overhand. Miraculously, it was a perfect serve, but Lou missed it.

'All right, that's it!' Lou said with disgust, and started walking off the court.

'Aw, come on, Lewis,' I cried. 'Just serve the ball! Looked pretty good to me, that time. I got it where it was supposed to go, didn't I? You missed the ball!'

'Nah, I'm done,' Lou said, and kept on walking.

'Lewis,' I shouted. 'Come on, don't give up on me yet.'

My competitive nature got the best of me, and before I could stop it, I said what I'd been thinking.

'Have I ever given up on *you*? In a matter of minutes?'

I was used to being a good athlete, and the point in competition is to win. But he'd been whacking balls at me, and playing with a lot of misplaced anger. I was tired of being the brunt of it.

His response was to pick up the ball, ram it into his pocket, and walk off the court. Then, from the other side of the fence, he turned to me.

'You've got some nerve saying that to me,' he said, lowering himself onto the lounge chair. 'Here I am, trying to get you to fit in with everybody, and what do you do? Accuse me of being—'

'*Spoiled, and childish?*' I shot back.

He didn't say anything but picked up his glass, drained it of all its melted ice, and slammed it on his side table.

'Why don't you just trot on back to the country where you came from? I don't need you, you're just a pain in the ass!'

By now, he was gesturing angrily at an unresponsive ocean.

I stood watching him as the burning sun dropped closer on the horizon behind him. It would, in an hour or so, disappear into the depths of the ocean. In its lengthening shadow, malice spread out around us.

Now, how are we going to come out of this one, I wondered.

I held on to my pride and walked off the court, saying nothing. I was disappointed in myself and troubled by what I'd heard.

Lewis was waving both arms for the attendant like he was flagging down an emergency vehicle. I got back to my chair and stretched out. My glass had only leftover warm water in it, but I drank it all. Even though I was equally furious and crushed, I knew that a) he didn't mean what he said, and b) he'd gone too far, playing hardball to teach me a lesson, which had little to do with the game of tennis. So I had nothing more to say.

An attendant came rushing over and asked Lou what he wanted.

'The same, and could you make them doubles?' he answered through clenched teeth.

'Not in mine, thank you,' I said, looking up at the kid.

Ignoring my instructions to the boy, Lou looked out onto the water. The kid returned with our drinks in a New York minute. Lou took his immediately, emptying it in one gulp.

'Another,' he said imperiously.

I hadn't touched mine, although I would have liked to. But he'd gotten my dear mother's 'Irish' up.

'Could you bring me a coke, please,' I asked.

'Certainly,' the boy replied, taking Lou's empty glass from his outstretched hand that he'd raised with a drop-kick wrist. Casting his eyes upward, as he caught mine, the attendant rolled them in Lou's direction. Turning, he beat it out of there as fast as he could.

Watching the kid rush off, I thought of an Oscar Wilde quote:

Some cause happiness wherever they go; others, whenever they go.

'Look, princess,' Lou said, after a while. 'I'm sorry. I didn't mean that.'

I said nothing.

'Did you hear me?' he asked, reaching over, and touching my arm.

Our chairs were placed side by side, facing the dying sun.

I continued staring out at the water. A fleet of seagulls flying overhead began screeching their haunting call, either because they'd spied their evening meal or were enthusiastically applauding the tension in the air between Lou and me. Grudgingly, I conceded it was probably the first reason. The gulls didn't care about the human condition—and Lewis, I thought, didn't seem to give a damn about me sometimes. With his last remark, he'd confirmed my greatest fear: that he was using me as sole support for his new career, not because he loved me.

'Come on, princess,' he whined.

You bet I'll ignore you now, buddy.

Finally, he practically yelled, '*Bettye?*'

'What?' I answered, not turning to him.

Lewis got up and came over to my chair. He kissed my forehead and knelt down beside me.

'I'm sorry, princess. You know I love you. I can be a real schmuck sometimes.'

I didn't say anything for a long time. Instead, I listened to the seagulls as they left, screaming, off to a place where water met darkening sky.

'The lesson I learned is that you play some serious hardball, Lewis. Not a damn thing about tennis.'

'I have to beg to differ,' he replied.

I half-heartedly laughed and lifted my face in the dying light. He moved in, as I knew he would, to kiss me.

'I am sorry,' he whispered.

The wind was rising.

Slowly standing up, Lou said, 'I couldn't do anything without you.'

Yeah, that's what I'm worried about.

But thankfully I kept my raging paranoia to myself.

I'd told him the truth and let him know I'd punch back if he played hardball with me. That was Lou's lesson. I learned little about the game of tennis from him, and I've only played it a couple of times since. But I gained some valuable insight into how he played the game.

* * *

As Lou continued to stare at me that morning, I had time to consider our relationship. I saw he was ambitious, single-minded, and, in his pursuit, often thoughtless of me and my needs. But I was raised as many girls at that time were—to accept it, as women throughout history had. Women who wanted a successful man in their lives were taught to acknowledge and accept that men like this were selfish and driven—often beyond reason. For these men, it was part and parcel of achieving their destiny, which we, as women, were expected to nurture.

So far, when Lewis screwed up, he apologized, regardless of his motivation—selfish or not. I would have driven myself crazy analyzing Lou's motivations, and with the speed our lives began to take off, I didn't have the energy or time.

For now, I needed to trust in his love for me. My gaze traveled back over the fine features contained in his beautiful face as he lay, stretched out on the bed, gazing into my eyes.

Me—I just looked like where I came from. But Lewis? He had looks that produced stars in our firmament.

'Baby, I said,' let's go get some coffee.

'Okay, princess,' he said, laying his head down on my abdomen and falling, almost instantly, asleep.

four in a bed............**CHAPTER FOUR**

Lou and I lurched into our first apartment together, a small studio on East 73rd Street, off First, with the *Rolling Stone* writer Ed McCormack and his wife, Jeannie. It was after four o'clock in the morning, which was when the bars closed in Manhattan back then. We were laughing, drunk and coked out of our minds.

Well, I probably wasn't as bad as the others, and certainly not like Lou and Ed, because I didn't drink or snort coke as much as them. Usually, I pretended to act very high so I didn't have to take any more substances, because I didn't like to feel out of control when I was out with Lou. By now I was a full-time acting student at the Neighborhood Playhouse, studying with Sanford Meisner. Escorting Lou around town was where I honed the performance skills Meisner taught us.

I could also keep an eye on everything going on around me—an eye that was straight so that I didn't end up in bed with any Tom, Dick, or Harry. There was enormous pressure to sleep with everybody during the 'free love' era. If you didn't, there was definitely something wrong with you: you were frustrated or frigid. Or—the worst possible thing on the face of the earth—straight. In the days of free love it was uncool and old-fashioned to want to keep your body to yourself and only share it with someone you loved. This was certainly the case with the Lou Reed crowd, which always had some vestiges of the people who hung around at the Factory. Then there were the hip, coked-out rock musician/writer, agent/manager, actor/director, producer/show-business crowd—the one into which I had somehow gotten myself.

One of the advantages of being Lou Reed's girlfriend was that when I was with him, no one came on to me anymore. I never felt safer than when I was with him, because I was left alone. Nobody tried to jump my bones. They just looked, which is all I wanted. I could feel the same freedom when I went out with Lou that I did with my fellow acting students from the Playhouse when we went out to dance in gay bars. Dancing made me happy because I could forget about any responsibilities I had for school or Lou, and I could let myself go a bit.

At the start of our relationship, after a day of acting school, hitting the auditions and getting rejected—as was usually the case for working actors—I could let off a lot of steam by going out with Lou. Oh, I'd get callbacks, but then it was standard practice for a director or producer to pressure an actress either directly or by implication to sleep with them if you wanted to land the role. My feeling was that this was my body, and nobody was getting it unless I loved or cared about them a great deal.

All the snorting and drinking going on around me was, in truth, a little scary, but I would never admit it. As a twenty-year-old renegade from Pennsylvania country, I joined in, mostly to conform. I also wanted to keep things charming and fun to avoid being judged or harshly evaluated. Was I smart or pretty enough; talented, rich, or educated enough for Lou's crowd to have serious conversations with me? I was much younger than everyone around me. There was a seven-year age difference between Lewis and me, and at twenty that's very noticeable. I was easily influenced by him and what he wanted. I thought it better to not talk and to laugh a lot, dance, and be happy.

Most of Lou's friends had already graduated from college or had their master's degrees, but I had only a couple of comparative literature and English courses from Columbia University, where I had been working toward my bachelor's degree before transferring to the Playhouse. Nobody in Lou's world knew how difficult the Playhouse was; most had probably never heard of Sanford Meisner, although he was already considered one of America's greatest acting teachers. For me, the superficiality that came with all the posing that occurred at parties Lou and I attended was almost a welcome relief from the strict routine at school. Lou told me he knew a great deal of the parties or functions we attended were mostly nonsense, but he said it was necessary to be seen in the right places, so along I went.

I'm a Viking, and I have one hell of a constitution. At four or five in the morning, I was usually the one still in a vertical position when no one else was, because all I really wanted to do was dance.

When I first began dating Lewis, I was just a kid having a good time on a break from college. Except Lou's world wasn't college. It was the real world. As Lou was beginning his new solo career without The Velvet Underground, there was an enormous amount of pressure on him to succeed where they had failed before—especially since he was largely considered responsible for breaking up the band.

I agreed to help Lou launch his solo career while pursuing my own in the theater, but I was probably too young to comprehend how much pressure I was actually putting on myself. I just kept everything light and breezy. This was probably why Lewis found me so attractive. I was fun to be around, upbeat. I was mad for Lou and I looked up to him. I was relatively smart, somewhat sensitive, rather idealistic, and I understood what he had to say. I had been a bookworm all my life and had written poetry since I was a kid. But I also always kept him safe; I reassured him when he felt insecure about his new solo career and got him home safely when he was too drunk or stoned. He knew when he was with me that I genuinely loved him, and that gave him a sense of security in a world full of back-scratchers.

Sometimes I called on a small core of my trusted friends from acting school to help me get Lou safely out of the gay bars we went to. Things could get rough in the early hours of the morning—we could have easily got beaten up or robbed. Or I had to get us out of strange scenes Lou somehow got us into in weird people's houses in the East Village after all the bars closed and my friends had gone home for the night. Like this night.

Back home, Ed, his wife, and I flung ourselves onto the burnt-orange, crushed-velvet, tuxedo-style couch Lou gave me $200 to buy at the local furniture store. It truly was the best-looking one of the bunch, and the only place he agreed I could buy furniture for our new place. Lou staggered over to the easy chair he insisted on buying—a black leather reclining one like the sort old men ease themselves into at the end of their work day to watch the news. It was the one piece of furniture Lou seemed to care about and insisted upon getting.

Despite our paltry budget for home furnishings, no expense was spared on Lou's chair. It cost twice as much as the couch. But we weren't living in suburbia, nor was I cooking and serving him nightly dinners in front of the television. I'd had quite enough of working in the kitchen while growing up in my parents' home, and Lou had no idea I was even capable of cooking, because we usually ate out or had Chinese or pizza delivered.

Lou made a grand gesture of placing the chair prominently in the corner of the living room of our studio apartment and said that was where he was going to write. But what Lou mostly did was sit in it and drink cheap scotch. This was a bit disappointing to me, but then that's what writers do, right? They drink. And that's what Lewis did this night, too, as he stumbled back from pouring himself yet another scotch in our tiny kitchen.

The light in the bank of windows on the far wall was beginning to turn an early morning grey. Ed was talking about the interview with Lou that they'd recently done, and how he had gotten some real insight into him. I was getting bored again, which of course I could never admit. As his girlfriend, it would have been sacrilegious. The crash of ice cubes I heard as he fumbled around in the freezer made me feel guilty for not performing like the perfect hostess, but I knew he enjoyed fixing everyone's drinks.

I listened to Ed expound upon what he thought were especially profound insights into how Lou thought and worked. I nodded and laughed when it sounded like it was the right moment, which is what I usually did when people began talking about Lewis, because the person I knew had little resemblance to the one they were talking about. Lewis and I had our own private world, and I was glad most of these jive-asses didn't inhabit it. We were going to make Lou the biggest star on the planet, although this wasn't all that clear to me in the beginning of our relationship.

So, when Lewis came staggering out from our tiny kitchen into the living room with our guests' drinks, who cared if he looked like a common drunk? They thought he was hysterical. I was a little embarrassed at his condition, but I could always hide my feelings by laughing, along with everyone else.

He had another drink for me, too. As he handed me an incredibly stiff scotch, which I took with a splash of soda—a very large splash when I was making it—I could see there was no soda in this baby. It was a serious drink, and Lewis meant business.

'Love you,' he said.

'Love you, too, Lou,' I said.

I brushed my lips up against his cheek and softly shoved my nose down his collar to catch the scent of his faintly astringent, masculine smell. I felt the rough, fine growth of beard on the lower portion of his face. It softened the sharp lines of his jaw, but it also somewhat reassured me that the man of the house was present and—despite his condition—accounted for.

After running his hands through my hair, which he loved, he straightened up to the five-eleven height his high-heeled rock-star boots topped him out at and toddled over to the corner in front of his chair. Suddenly he whirled around and looked at us. Ed, Jeannie, and I were sitting all lined up, however askew, on the couch opposite him. He almost looked like he was onstage, and he immediately took control of the room. With a kind of theatrical flourish—which I appreciated, being an acting student—he put his drink down on the occasional table to the right of the chair.

Commanding our attention by looking at us like we were three eager young college students in a classroom, Lou began to instruct us upon some finer, more obtuse points, comparing elements of Edgar Allan Poe's horror stories to Raymond Chandler's 1940s LA detective novels. But this was, unbeknownst to Ed and his wife, about the 200th time I'd heard this lecture—at least that's what it felt like—in somewhat similar early morning settings, although I'd never before heard it in my own home; nevertheless, I struggled up into a more upright position, plastered a quasi-interested look on my face, and smiled.

Somewhat tipsily, Lou launched into the lesson.

'*Now*,' he began, and I remember thinking he should continue with *children*, although of course I didn't say it. I, like everyone else, had learned early on that one never, ever interjected anything into a Lou Reed lecture. If anyone else wished to contribute to one of Lou's teaching moments, the consequences could be brutal. His putdowns were legendary and lethal. But instead of carrying on with his lecture he suddenly lit up like a child who was anticipating the huge splash a brightly colored ball he'd just thrown into the pool was about to make, and excitedly clapped his hands together.

'Why don't we open up the pull out couch so we can all jump into bed together?' he exclaimed.

Everyone froze in place. What followed afterward seemed to move in slow motion. Nobody said anything, nor looked at anyone else, except Lou, of course, who was looking at the three of us like he was about to dive in after the brightly colored ball and make a much bigger splash. He smiled impishly and stuck his right forefinger into his cheek and began screwing it forward then backward into his face, which I guessed was a suggestive gesture. He puckered his lips into that *Betty Boop* way of his, stuck his tongue into the other side of his mouth, and popped out his cheek into another suggestive, almost garish gesture, opening his eyes up very, very wide, coyly batting his eyelashes. I actually wasn't sure of the overall desired effect he was going for. Then, with his other hand splayed out on the opposite side of his head, he began to wag it back and forth like an old time actor from one of those 1930s black-and-white ragtime films that are often on late-night TV.

'Whaddya all say?' he asked.

I assumed this was meant as a feeble gesture to fill up the gaping space of silence that had spilled all over the place. Our Upper East Side studio apartment had suddenly begun to feel even smaller, if that was possible, and more crowded. Still nobody said anything. Lou's suggestion fell flat as a lead ball into our modestly furnished apartment, and created a huge belly flop, rather than the intended splash.

'Huh?' he added.

Then he began wiggling his bottom like an Al Jolson dancer.

I got up like something had just pricked me on *my* bottom and said, 'I've got to visit the little girl's room'—a term I'd never used before. 'Be back in just a minute.'

I began making my way, glass tinkling, toward the bathroom on the other side of the living room, across from the kitchen by the front door. Walking fifteen feet into our living room, you reached a wall of windows on the exterior wall of the apartment—the only feature that was remotely pleasing to the eye. It looked out onto someone else's back yard, where there were trees that provided shade in summer.

I'd recently planted a variety of potted plants on the windowsill to add a bit of life and color to the apartment. I grew up on both of my family's farms in Pennsylvania, and I was a gardener, although no one actually knew that about me, either; in fact, most people didn't know much about me at all, which was fine with me, because I've always been a very private person. Like my body, I didn't share my life with anyone except Lou.

As I made my escape to the bathroom, Ed's wife said something so softly to her husband that neither Lou nor I could hear what she'd said. He began laughing—a little too loudly, I thought—and she followed suit a bit too quickly, but I began to laugh, too. When I got to the bathroom door, I turned around and, for some reason, began shimmying as I backed up into it, smiling and waving, closing the door behind me.

What the … ?

I truly didn't know what to do next. I could hear them laughing and talking, and it actually sounded like they were getting a little excited about Lou's proposal. I could hear Lou and Ed's voices rising, then falling; an ascent here then there. I began to feel very uncomfortable.

I sat my drink down next to me on the sink to my left and automatically turned the faucet on—something I often did when I periodically went into bathrooms to sit for a while and think about what to do. The confined space allowed me a moment to think about the sometimes-strange goings-on that happened at parties or functions that we were attending, and I could be alone and hear my thoughts. If anybody came to the door, at least it sounded like I was using the bathroom if I turned the faucet on.

Considering how popular the bathrooms were at many of the scenes Lou and I frequented, I wasn't being paranoid, because there was usually a line of people waiting to get into the bathroom. Often it was to shoot up or have sex. But in this rather unusual set of circumstances, I was desperately searching for something to at least sound normal, even if it was only more acting.

Now what was I going to do?

I hadn't seen this idea coming, and I wasn't into it at all. It was the first time Lou had suggested we jump into bed with anyone, let alone a couple. Later on in our relationship, things like this would become almost laughingly routine, and I learned how to deal with it like one deals with a spoiled child, laughing it off and paying absolutely no mind to what he said.

What a card that Lou is, right? Ha ha!

From what I could hear in the living room now, though, there weren't any loud protests being made. In fact, there seemed to be a kind of warm hum to the sound of Ed, Jeannie, and Lou's voices. This didn't sound good for what I wanted to happen ... which was nothing.

But I was afraid to offend Ed. He'd just interviewed Lou, and his article was coming out in a national and well-respected music magazine. I was deeply concerned that if I didn't go along with it, and Ed wanted to, it could jeopardize Lou's career. Is that why Lou was suggesting it? He'd never done anything like this before, so I wasn't sure. Actresses were often expected to sleep with directors to get acting roles; were rock stars and their girlfriends expected to sleep with writers? How far was one expected to cooperate with influential members of the press? I was a novice at all this—I had no idea.

To this day I do not know how, on the spur of the moment, I came up with a plan to break up this little party. As I turned off the light to the bathroom and came out, all eyes were on me. With just the right amount of believable self-consciousness, I hemmed and hawed and, crossing over to Lou's chair, sat down in it—something I'd never before done in front of Lou.

The one time I'd sat in the great 'writing chair,' Lou hadn't been home. I'd brought my notebook and pen, thinking I might write something. Lou hadn't done any writing in it, and I wondered if maybe I could. Was there a curse on it or something? I pushed the great chair back into its reclining position and felt my legs lift out in front of me and my feet coddled by the padded footrest. I didn't get any writing done in Lou's writing chair, either.

But now I crossed my legs as elegantly as I could, took a sip of scotch, and waited, locking eyes with my audience. Lou was sitting between Ed and Jeannie, and when I noticed that I literally felt my blood pressure rise. Despite my increasing alarm, I managed to keep my cool and the timing of my pause perfectly. I arranged myself into a sheepish position, remembering that Meisner said that good acting was always about being 'in the moment' and making one's actions as clear and important as they were to the motivation and intentions of the character one was playing. Believability was of the utmost importance. This meant the stakes had to be as high for the actor as the character he or she was playing.

Suddenly I realized I was being called upon to set a precedent: *this was a test*. The future of our relationship may very well rest on the next couple of minutes, so the stakes were as high as they ever would be, because I had no intention of sharing my bed with anyone but Lou.

I waited a bit longer, then took a huge breath, screwed my face up, and asked, as innocently as I could, 'You know, I've been, like, scratching all night. I heard a couple of my friends at school complain about crabs and I'm not sure how you actually get them, because I've never had them. But does anyone know if you can get them by using the same bathroom as someone who does have them?'

The second lead balloon of the evening fell with a splat into the living room of the Lou Reed household. After a god-awful long pause, things began, once again, to move in a kind of underwater, slow motion. I honestly don't remember much of the details about how Ed and Jeannie extricated themselves, although I was aware that it was very soon thereafter and a rather swift exit, however polite it was.

As Jeannie escorted her husband out the door, she made some soft, reassuring sounds, and as they disappeared into the early morning light, she mentioned almost in passing that they couldn't wait for us to get together again. This was something no one believed, other than possibly Lewis.

As I quietly closed the door behind them, Lou didn't say a word. He hadn't even said goodbye to them. I gathered up whatever dignity I had left, walked over to the couch, tossed the oversized yellow and orange pillows from the corners of our cheap, crushed velvet, tuxedo-styled couch onto the floor, and pulled out the bed. Lewis fell onto his belly in a straight-out, full-length, face-down flop and probably passed out before he landed, dead drunk to the world. He didn't take his clothes off that night, and I didn't pull them or his shoes off for him, either. Nope, not that night.

As I collapsed onto the cold edge of the steel frame of our pullout bed, feeling equally relieved and humiliated, all I heard from Lewis was snoring. A combination of disgust, dread, and fear compelled me to pick myself up and go into the bathroom, brush my teeth, undress, and put on the now laughingly sheer nightgown that hung on the hook of the back of the bathroom door. After getting our blankets from the closet, I sat down on the edge of the too-thin, genuinely uncomfortable mattress.

I was cold. I was also stunned, but I secretly congratulated myself that I had managed, albeit at my own expense, to successfully avoid what could have been a very messy scene. I'd pulled off another superb acting job, although no one would ever know but me. It had been a very close call. I also wasn't all that pleased about having to act in my own home, but I became rather adept at that, soon enough, too. *Don't we all?*

Quickly I slid under the covers and crawled into the clean-smelling sheets, pulled the blanket I flung over us onto my shoulders, rolled over, and curled up, facing the door, with my back to Lewis. As always, I had one foot out, ready to escape. Only Lou was lying next to me, and I could finally put an end to this night's charade. Lou wouldn't remember any of it in the morning, anyway, so if Ed never brought it up again with Lou, we were safe from ridicule. Needless to say, he never did. Later on, after I had had more experience with these kinds of drunken scenarios in different places with different couples—and it wasn't always Lou's idea—I learned how to handle the situation better. But I'd done pretty well avoiding a foursome that night.

A couple of weeks later, Ed McCormack's interview with Lou was published, and he was less than gracious about me, but we knew why. I wasn't interested in sleeping with Ed or his wife. To me, Ed looked like a giant cockroach with entirely too much hair.

I've read and sat in master's degree psychology classes where I learned that, on a conscious level, we really don't have much to do with what sexually attracts us; whether two people fancy each other is largely a matter of pheromones. Ed didn't attract me for several reasons that have increased over the years, particularly after I've heard some of the preposterous stories he's told, in which he attributes an exaggerated involvement in the personal life of Lewis and me.

And I'm not attracted to women. For largely political reasons, during the time I was with Lou, it would have been much more convenient to be gay or bisexual, or at least appear to be, but I'm as straight as an arrow. Ed was a struggling young writer who was trying to make a name for himself, just as Lou was trying to make one for himself.

For the first time, Lou was out there on his own without The Velvet Underground, and that was a little scary for him. Indeed, a great deal of my role with Lewis was about supporting him in his solo career, and some of the works he created during the time we were together have become a significant part of the legend surrounding his genius. Perhaps, in the end, it was worth the cost for both of us.

a surprise engagement........

CHAPTER FIVE

Everything seems so far away when I try to remember some of the finer details about my journey with Lou. Before we moved in together, I often stayed with him on weekends at his parents' house on Long Island. On one such trip, in the spring of 1971, I was riding on the Long Island Rail Road out to Lou's house. As we passed the sign for the New York Equestrian Center in West Hempstead, I thought about how much I missed riding, and felt the sensation of a huge and powerful animal under me, my first memory of riding, bareback, on my father's farm. I wanted to gallop across wide, open fields, the challenge of dodging low-hanging branches and jumping over brush that divided the grazing pastures of another time.

Lewis wasn't a practiced rider, so I was certain that, in order to keep up, he would have to chase me. I loved being chased, and Lou loved chasing me. When we were in my apartment by ourselves, or when his parents were out, we ran around after each other like kids.

The first time we went to the equestrian center, we, like everyone else, were restricted to the corral, while our riding skills were evaluated by the riding instructors. Those who passed the test were allowed to ride on the trails lying beyond in Hempstead Lake Park. Most passed, like me, but Lou didn't; instead, he spent his hour plodding along, around and around on the beaten path inside, and never got out of the corral.

Before I trotted off onto the riding trails, I turned in my saddle to see if he was following me. The last I saw of him, he was slumped over the neck of the nag he'd chosen, looking very disgruntled, his sandy-colored ringlets no longer styled in the usual perfectly coiffed halo around his head.

When it became obvious that Lewis was not going to be let out of the corral, I took off on my horse. Soon we were galloping on the trails and over the fields and streams that lay beyond. When I rose in my saddle to meet the first of the old stone fences on the property, I heard Robert Frost say in his old, cracked voice, '*Something that doesn't love a wall …*'

Although the ride was as exhilarating as expected, I missed Lou. So when I saw my hour was nearing its end, I turned around without any regrets and headed back to the stables. I found Lou slumped in the car behind the wheel in the parking lot. He was grumpy.

'Well, did you have a good ride?' he asked peevishly.

Quickly, I slid over and snuggled up to him to try to calm him down. I could see that he was humiliated by his riding experience—or lack thereof—and I was embarrassed for him. I'd envisioned two lovers riding off into the woods together, but I realized I hadn't really thought through the adventure. It hadn't been my intention to make him feel uncomfortable. I felt guilty, and I worried I'd been selfish.

When I had suggested we go riding, Lou wasn't terribly enthusiastic, but he acted cool about almost everything, even if he liked something or wanted to do it. So how was I supposed to know?

It was dusk, and I thought about what I could do or say to improve his mood. I asked if he wanted to go have dinner; and, if so, where should we go? We hadn't made plans to meet his parents at their club, as we often did, so we were free.

Lewis turned the engine over in his parents' Mercedes, and I heard the soft purr of the car coming back to life. He backed out of the parking space and turned the car around. We drove in silence for a while, my arm through his, my head on his shoulder. After a while, I felt his body relax, and it wasn't long before he turned and kissed me.

'Okay, princess, let's have dinner,' he said. 'How 'bout some Chinese?'

'Yay!' I said, quickly, relieved that he was in better spirits and ready to move on.

Lewis could be a very prickly pear, but having spent the week apart, we were happy to see each other. I wanted us to enjoy this weekend, even if it had begun on a rocky start.

Within fifteen minutes we arrived at Pan's, our favorite Chinese restaurant. I had my usual Moo Goo Gai Pan, and he ordered the broccoli and chicken, but with several Johnnie Walker Reds. I thought this could be problematic, but I knew it was his way of shoving his feelings down to a place where he no longer had access to them. Lou drank until he couldn't think or feel anymore, and then he could be happy—at least that's what I thought then.

I had no idea yet that I was dealing with a bona-fide alcoholic, and absolutely no experience dealing with anyone who drank alcohol. No one in my family drank. The only time I saw my father imbibe was on New Year's Eve, and that was only one shot of whisky to bring in the New Year. I never saw changes in the behavior of anyone in my family because of alcohol.

Unfortunately, it wouldn't be long before I came face to face with Lou's alcohol addiction—a parasite that had invaded him long ago. It was a wily trickster; at first, Lewis was incredibly amusing and charming when he drank, so it wasn't something one necessarily wanted to discourage. Not if you knew the other facets of his personality: moody and very quiet, or vicious and destructive. Ultimately, it would be this wolf in sheep's clothing that would destroy us.

* * *

In the late 60s and early 70s, there were few seatbelts and little concern for driving under the influence. The idea was try to make it home without killing yourself or anyone else—and, above all, not to get caught.

Lou had had only about three or four Johnnies—something he could usually handle. He had an extraordinary tolerance. It wasn't until six or seven whiskeys that Lou began slurring or got sloppy. We hadn't reached that point yet, but when he ordered several rounds of after-dinner Courvoisiers, the thought crossed my mind that perhaps I should worry about getting in the car with him driving. But he'd ordered the brandies for me, too, and I drank them down, meeting him head-on. Soon I was feeling warm and cozy, too.

But I didn't have a driver's license. I moved to New York a couple of months after turning eighteen. Few people who lived in Manhattan drove, including me. But I knew *how* to drive, and was reasonably accomplished. At the age of twelve, I learned how to drive on a John Deere tractor. The fields on my father's working farm in Western Pennsylvania were in the foothills of the Allegheny Mountain Range. They were so hilly that driving lessons from Dad didn't only include learning how to steer the machine and shift its manual gears, but the precautionary measure of where and how to fall off the tractor—between the wheel and the body of the machine—if it tipped over backward going up our steepest climb, Knob Hill. But I hadn't driven a car for years, and all our cars had manual transmissions. The Mercedes was an automatic—something I'd never driven.

Lou got in the car and fumbled with the keys. I slid in quietly next to him and watched him try to find the ignition. I made the decision then to get out of the car, walk around the front, and then open the driver's side door.

'Lewis,' I said. 'Out.'

He looked up at me, and we had what I like to call one of our silent conversations.

'I'm driving,' I said.

Lou saw that I meant business. He turned away from me and then seemed to make a decision himself. Casting a coy smile in my direction, without a word, he got out of the Mercedes and, holding on to it for support, walked stiffly around the back of the car. As he got in the passenger side, I climbed in behind the wheel. We slammed the car doors shut at the same time, saying nothing, and I turned the keys that he'd left in the ignition. The engine rolled over and began purring.

I'd seen Lou's driving, and the automatic gearshift was clearly marked. So I slid the gear into reverse and backed the car out of the parking lot. When we got to the exit, all Lou said was to make a left. I didn't ask where we were going, but I had a pretty good idea.

Lou's favorite bar on Long Island was Jilly's, a gay bar where he had bartended on and off in the summers, home from college. We'd been there a couple of times before, and people knew him there. He was a local celebrity, and they treated him as such.

Usually, we only went there for a nightcap, and we'd sit at the bar and talk to either the bartender or a couple of the other regulars. At first, when they saw us come in, they gathered around Lou to say hello. The gays flirted with him, and he flirted back, but there was nothing inappropriate or outrageous. Everyone knew that I was his girlfriend, and the boundaries were drawn.

Lou's flirting didn't bother me. It didn't mean anything to him. Lou's true feelings ran deep and strong, and I felt secure in his love for me. Underneath all the posing, Lewis was all man—a leader—and particularly courageous about his principles. He walked away from any situation if it meant he was not being true to himself. If he couldn't follow his true course, he would give it all up—which was the main reason he left The Velvet Underground.

Certainly, there were issues with money, power, and control in the Velvets. Gaining control of the copyrights for the Velvets' songs meant the potential for serious money in the future, which Lou wouldn't have to share with John Cale; and, if he could oust John from the Velvets, he could control the direction of the band. He encountered no resistance to any of his suggestions, either in terms of sound or material, from any other member of the band—except from John.

Lou had already fired Warhol because he didn't think he'd done an effective job managing the Velvets and because of how, under his tutelage, Andy had forced Nico on them, which no one in the band had appreciated. Most importantly, however, they had never gained any national recognition beyond rock'n'roll aficionados or writers from the American northeast corridor, which Lou took very personally, and it had hurt him very much.

Because it was mostly about the music. Lou left the Velvets because he wasn't happy with the direction the band was veering toward under Cale's influence, and he was sick and tired of fighting with him about it. He thought Cale was too avant-garde and preventing The Velvet Underground from achieving the huge international success he believed the band was capable of by simply playing good-ol' hard-driving rock'n'roll, along with some of what he called his 'soft songs,' the ballads he'd written. At the same time, this allowed him to push the boundaries of the rock'n'roll genre into the literary arena. As a writer/lyricist, this is what he was determined to do above all else. If he wasn't able to give his best in his chosen field, he wasn't interested in doing it at all.

This was one of the things I admired and loved most about Lewis. He actually was crazy enough to follow his principles in the real world. And because he came from a family who supported him, most of the time, he could. When he walked away from The Velvet Underground, he went back to the family home on Long Island, because he knew it would be a safe harbor for him, personally, artistically, and financially.

I made the drive to Jilly's safely; as we arrived, a guy was pulling out of a parking space in front of the bar. I parallel parked beautifully in the space he left, to which Lou paid particular attention. Turning off the engine, I immediately put the keys in my bag and got out of the car. I was incredibly relieved that we'd arrived without incident.

'Thank you,' Lou said, pulling me to him and kissing me. 'Let's go in for a nightcap!'

I nodded yes and we headed into the bar. I loved gay bars. They were safe for women, and everybody danced. It was early on a Saturday night, but the place was already jumping. As soon as we entered, everybody turned around.

'Lou!' came the cry, up from the bar.

Lou held up his hand in greeting, and several people gathered around him. Tina, the resident queen, was the first to reach Lou. Standing directly in front of him, she draped her arms over his shoulders.

In a very loud voice that was a little *high* up in the registers, and already a bit slurred, Tina asked him, '*Dar*-link!? How! Are! You?'

Tina was in heavily made-up and mascaraed full drag, her strawberry-blonde Rita Hayworth bob topped off with five-inch red patent leather, ankle-strapped platforms. Skintight blue jeans rolled up to just below the knee exposed her shapely, gleaming calves, and a see-through lime-green blouse revealed a black strapless bra.

I suddenly got slammed with one of my blistering headaches and, murmuring some hurried hellos, skirted around everyone and walked quickly to the bar. I was relieved Lewis was engulfed by the crowd because it meant I could take a break from my watch over him.

I got a seat at the end of the bar, and thought I should order a Perrier. Mike, the bartender, looked up at me as soon as I sat down. Without asking, he poured me a generous glass of Chablis and sat it down in front of me. Mouthing my thank you, I took a longer than necessary drink from the sparkling clean goblet, forgetting it was wine, and downed it like water. I noticed my hand was shaking as I put my glass down on the bar. It was, once again, time to fasten my seat belt. It looked like it was going to be a bumpy night.

The opening guitar playing the sweet summer sounds of a dying night rushed over the bar from the jukebox in the back, and one of the great Motown hits from my high school days, 'Reach Out I'll Be There' by The Four Tops, started playing. Jilly's was famous in this part of the Island for blasting out one great Motown hit after another, which was what to often expect in gay bars. Practically everyone in the place danced with wild abandon, and the room rocked to the sounds of Barry Gordy and Motown—some of the best tunes in modern American music.

Oh, this is perfect, I thought, and took another sip of wine.

Lou climbed onto the stool next to me and gave me a quick kiss. He didn't bother to speak, because there was no way you could hear anything anyone said over the music. I watched him as he ordered a double Johnny Walker Red from Mike, who appeared almost instantly.

As Lou spoke to Mike, I looked at him as if seeing him for the first time. He was happy and confident, and he looked like someone I would be interested in getting to know: clean cut, like a normal college graduate—an English major—my kind of guy!

It was fascinating to watch him charming everybody, and I thought, *He really is a first-class performer*! Perhaps I hadn't been wrong to hop on for the ride, after all. If nothing else, I could learn something about the craft of performance.

It wasn't unusual for guys at school or work to approach me with a certain amount of interest. Most of them were good looking. Some of them were smart—often as smart as Lewis. I worked at and went to an Ivy League school; the possibilities existed. But Lou was … *just so cool*! When he cast his spell, all the lights in Manhattan could go out, and no one would notice.

In the end, none of the others made the grade when I compared them to Lewis. He was it for me, and however challenging it got, I knew my heart was in it for the long haul. This was a blessing and a curse.

Lou turned to me and leaned in, and I thought he was going to whisper one of his favorite slightly risqué things to me; instead, he stuck his tongue in my ear, rolled it around, sloshing and slopping all over it, and licked my face. Sadly, I remembered, this was what booze did to him, just before he crashed.

Not surprisingly, by the time we left it was four o'clock in the morning again. I'd danced most of the night. Sometimes Lou danced slow songs with me, but mostly I was just one more in a packed crowd of hot, sweaty people dancing our hearts out. By the end of the night, my hair was a mess. When I walked, my clothes stuck to me in all the wrong places. I probably smelled. My feet were wet from my socks soaked in perspiration inside my riding boots. But I'd had a great time!

Lou had had far too many. He wasn't falling-down drunk, but he was close to it. As I got him into the car, he was morose, mumbling and grabbing onto me, like he was trying to tell me something important. But he was totally unintelligible.

Obviously, there wasn't a discussion about who was driving, let alone about anything else. I'm not even sure Lou knew he was in a car. I strapped on his seat belt and, by the time I got behind the wheel, he was in total blackout.

See, the problem was, I didn't know where we were. I had no idea how to get home. I'd never driven in Long Island. All I knew was Lou's address in Baldwin, Long Island. At this hour, nothing was open in town except for the bar.

It was dark, but for the streetlights. I was afraid this was going to be a very interesting ride. I strapped on my seatbelt, turned over the ignition, and the car started up instantly. I felt entirely alone and looked over at Lou for some reassurance, if not directions? He was slumped over in the middle of the seat. Nope, no help there!

It's just you, kid. Again.

I found the gearshift and was just about to pull out of the parking space when I heard a tapping on the car door window, scaring the daylights out of me. I stared straight out in front of me, sliding my eyes to the left to see who was there.

As he leaned his face in my car window, Mike's face came into view. From the streetlight above, I saw him motion to roll down the window. I sighed with relief, and rolled it down.

'How's it going in here?' Mike asked.

I looked at him and smiled faintly.

'Well …' I began, and then paused for a minute. 'I have no idea how to get home.'

That's when I turned off the ignition and began to laugh. It just came bubbling out of me. The situation was ridiculous, and laughing was the most appropriate, sane response.

Mike smiled and began laughing, too.

'When I saw you two leaving, I thought I'd better come out and check on you,' he said lightly. 'Where does he live?'

'Baldwin,' I answered. Then, looking out into the empty street, I asked, 'Do you know where it is?'

Suddenly the bar door swung open and Tina staggered out. She was alone and walking with some difficulty. The door slammed behind her, and she immediately bent down and unbuckled one of her outrageously beautiful but now scuffed, platform heels. Grasping the heel from behind, she pulled off a shoe. When she bent down to repeat the action, I was sure her head would meet the sidewalk with catastrophic results. But Tina only walked to the car in her stocking feet and sat on it.

'Oh that was so much fun,' she said, really loud but to no one, rolling her head back.

Illuminated by the streetlight, I could see her long legs splayed out in front of her. One of her shoulders was exposed. Her eyes were two black holes in her face. Her lips were puffy, almost purple. She threw her hair back and swerved her head sharply over her right shoulder to look at me. Tina's every move was calculated for effect.

Mike stood up and, sounding rather annoyed, said, 'Will you get off the car, Tina? It's German. I can already hear them screaming from the other side of the Alps.'

I smiled at Mike's sense of humor.

'*Loooo* doesn't mind, does he?' said Tina, starting to cackle.

Just then Lou began snoring. It was the perfect response. Even when he was dead out drunk, he was cool.

Hold on, you still need directions to get home, I thought.

Mike peeled Tina off the car and strapped her onto his side.

'Look,' he yelled, and started shouting some long, involved directions back to Baldwin. 'You know the address, right?'

'Yes. Can I write these directions down?'

'Yes. You got a pen?'

'And a notebook,' I answered. 'Let me get it.'

After I wrote the directions down, I turned on the ignition. The last I saw of Mike in the rear-view window, he was waving good-bye.

Nice guy, I thought.

Suddenly there was movement on the seat next to me. Snorting, Lou sat up. 'Where are we?' he asked, very loudly.

Briefly, I wondered if the excessively high volume at which everyone was speaking was the result of hearing too much Motown—if that was possible—at extremely high decibels for hours, perhaps days.

'In bed,' I replied, in a dour, but normal tone.

'Oh, okay,' he said, falling back over onto the seat.

'Goodnight, princess,' he mumbled.

'You owe me,' I said to the snoring man slumped in the seat next to me, and drove off into the early morning Long Island mist.

* * *

It was the plastic on the couch sticking to my back that woke me. I opened my eyes and began to squirm. The vinyl squeaked as it took its time peeling away from me. Mid-morning sun streamed through the slats in the blinds of the small windows, high and vertical in the corner.

I didn't have any covers on, and I was lying there in only my bra and panties. Fortunately, the door to the TV room was closed, so I wasn't exposed to the entire Reed family. My mouth was bone dry. I tried to find my eyes so that I could rub them awake, which is when I saw that my riding boots were still on.

What the … ?

As I rolled onto my side to go to the bathroom, I almost stepped on Lou, who was lying next to the couch. He was curled up tightly in a ball facing me. I caught myself just before I stepped on his face. Fortunately, my legs were long enough that I was able to step over him. Dazed, I looked around for my clothes. They were on the easy chair near the TV on the other side of the room. I pulled on my jeans and sweater and opened the door a crack to see if Lou's parents were around. But the lights were out and I didn't see them in the dining room, or in the living room beyond. His grandmother was probably in her room, because she wasn't in her rocking chair. It sat still and empty, with only her pillow on its seat.

I streaked as quietly as I could on my tiptoes through the dining room and past the kitchen, into the bathroom. I ran the cold water until it was ice cold and, cupping my hands, splashed it onto my face. Reaching for the hand towel nearby, I dried off my face and looked into the mirror. I could almost see myself clearly, but I moved in closer for a better look. It was a scary sight, so I opened the medicine cabinet where I kept my toothbrush, and squeezed out some toothpaste.

As I closed the cabinet, my image, reflected in the mirror, jumped into view. That's when I remembered seeing Lou sleeping, fully dressed, with his boots on.

What was he doing, sleeping on the floor?

I thought of his mother, who always made up the couch for me before she went to bed. In the mornings, she often peeked in on me.

Why didn't she make up my bed last night? Oh, this was great!

Lou's mother had probably already seen Lou asleep on the floor next to me—and me, splayed out on their couch in my underwear and riding boots!

I knew they were aware Lou came home very late, sometimes falling-down drunk, and I'd been at the dinner table when they had tried to confront him over his drinking. All I could do was hope she realized this was Lou's influence, not mine. Because I knew they counted on me to keep him straight.

After another drunken night with Lewis, I wasn't in the best of moods. I went out to the kitchen, opened the refrigerator, and poured myself a glass of orange juice. I got another one to take back with me to the TV room. As I entered, I saw Lou sitting in the easy chair, facing the door. His elbows were propped up on both of its arms, hands folded in his lap, calmly staring straight ahead. Our eyes locked and I stopped for a moment, then stepped inside the room and closed the door.

'You're up,' I said, as I walked past him and sat on the end of the couch farthest away from him. I started taking my boots off.

That's when Lewis began speaking.

'Princess …'

But I didn't look up at him, nor stop what I was doing. After I removed my boots, I peeled off my soaking wet socks. Then I placed my boots neatly next to each other near where my pillow should have been.

'*P-ewww,*' I said, holding my nose, exaggerating. Lewis didn't say anything, so I draped my socks over the tops of my boots to dry, and decided to tackle the obvious.

'Why were you sleeping on the floor?' I asked.

'I wanted to be near you.'

That didn't make any sense, so I ignored it. He could have just climbed in next to me. Maybe bring some blankets?

'And my bed wasn't made up,' I continued. 'What's that about?'

'Now, *that* I might know something about …'

'Yeah?'

'I wanted it to be a surprise!' he said, pretending to pout.

I continued to look at him, waiting for his answer.

'But it's not exactly working out that way.'

'I got that.'

'It'll make you very happy,' he said, hopefully. 'At least I think it will.'

'Do you?' I said, with little commitment.

'I'm hoping!' he said, brightly.

Well that sounded nice, but I remembered being lost and frightened last night. I was getting sick of all the drunken scenes when everything was left up to me to get us home safely.

Not my job, I thought.

'Lewis, just tell me what's going on. Then you can tell me the surprise, okay?'

He smiled—a little too coyly.

In response, I stared back at him in Scandinavian no-nonsense mode. I'd already said all I had to say.

'All right, don't get upset,' he said, putting a finger to his lips to shush me.

I was in no mood to be shushed, so, grabbing one of my socks, I said, 'I'm leaving.' But as I started pulling one on, I learned that putting on a wet sock is neither easy or fun. Carrying on anyway, I said, 'Your parents aren't home, and your grandmother is probably asleep in her bedroom at the other end of the house. She can't hear us from there. So why are you shushing me?'

He got up and walked over to me.

'I'm sorry,' he said, pulling off the wet sock I'd managed to get half on. 'You're right. I just don't want you to get upset. You're not putting these on, and you're not going anywhere, don't be crazy.'

He stuck both of my socks, wet, into his pockets. I let him.

'Okay, if you don't want me to leave—with or without socks—talk to me.'

'Princess,' he began, as he did.

'Oh, I'll princess you,' I said, and started to get up.

He moved closer to me and put his hand gently on my shoulder to stop me from leaving.

'Okay, Bettye, I told my mother she didn't need to make up the couch for you this weekend.'

Now what did that mean?

I didn't say anything, however, and waited for an explanation.

'She understood, so didn't,' he added. Then he held out his arms for me to put my hands in his. I didn't move, so he reached out and took them.

Easing me up, he pulled me close to him and wrapped his arms around me in that deep hug of his, which always melted me. What was I going to do? I loved and believed in this man very much, no matter how crazy it got. I put my head on his shoulder, shoving my nose under his chin.

In a muffled voice, I said, 'Okay, what's going on?'

He looked at me and began smoothing my hair. We stood in silence for a while, holding on to each other.

Breaking the silence, I said, 'You drink too much.'

There was the truth. It lay between us like a rock.

'I know,' he replied. 'I'm sorry. But sometimes I need to. It helps me handle things.'

I didn't say anything in reply.

I really want to hear this.

'Like … what I'm thinking … worrying about,' he continued. 'Sometimes it's too much, and it just relaxes me, makes it easier. That's why I do it.'

'I know it's been tough,' I said, 'but the drinking is getting out of control. I can't handle it on my own anymore. I didn't know how we were going to get home last night!' I could hear my voice rising, but I couldn't control it. 'I don't even have a driver's license! *I could have been arrested*!'

Okay stop. You're hysterical.

'Oh, they wouldn't have arrested you—they just would have given you a ticket, if you even got stopped. They'd see my condition and understand why you were driving.'

I'd managed to control myself somewhat. 'That's not the point,' I said. 'I was really frightened, Lewis. I don't like feeling frightened.'

Oh, no. I can feel it—the panic. It's rising again. Come on, Bettye—hold on—you can do it!

After a time, I said quietly, 'Things seem to be spinning out of control.'

He held me tighter, and said, 'I am sorry, princess. The last thing in the world I want to do is scare you. I love you so much, and know you don't deserve this. I want to do right by you. I've been doing some serious thinking the last couple of weeks, and I think I've made a decision about what to do.'

I didn't look up or speak. I didn't want to do anything to stop him from talking. But I did want him to stop depending on me to take care of him. I wasn't his nurse or his mother, I was his girlfriend!

I want the man I fell in love with back!

'I mean,' he continued, 'I had cut down, and I was feeling pretty good about that, but then ... the poetry reading at St. Marks ... it set me off again. And happy time at the OK Corral!'

He shrugged his shoulders but managed to chuckle, too. 'It's been a rough couple of weeks.'

He was talking, which he didn't do much of. Gratefully, I could stay quiet.

'Listen ... princess?'

I lifted my head and looked at him.

'Okay … Bettye,' he said, 'will you sit down with me for a minute?'

We both sat down on the couch. He took my hands in his.

'You know how much I love you …'

He was having enormous difficulty expressing himself. I wondered what could be so important. Maybe the big surprise? But I was determined to wait for him to speak on his own time.

Was I beginning to see the man I love again? Was he here? Because when Lewis was sober, the quiet, serious, sensitive man—the man I fell in love with—came back to me.

'Bettye, I need to tell you something,' he finally said. 'Well, actually, two things. I love and adore you. I don't know what I'd do without you. You make me feel like I can do anything I want.'

Suddenly, my heart leapt. This is what I wanted to hear from him!

That he was capable of doing anything he wanted to.

After clearing his throat, he said, 'I've made a decision about what I'm going to do.'

'Yes?' I asked quietly.

I knew what decision he was talking about: the one he'd been struggling with for months, which was whether to continue with his music or pursue his writing as a poet.

After another pause, he said, 'I'm going to keep going with my music.'

My heart fell a little, but I wasn't surprised.

'Great!' I said, with a fake cheerfulness.

Liar, I thought to myself.

'They're not going to let me be a poet.'

I think I may have sighed a little, however quietly—or maybe it was him? Neither one of us wanted to open that Pandora's box, but I felt it would be better if I just … let in a little bit of light.

'Is this because of what happened at St. Mark's?' I asked.

I could hear him struggling with his feelings, but all he said was 'Yes.'

'So that's it?'

'I also really love rock'n'roll.'

'I know.'

'So I'm going to go that way. I can't throw everything away that I've worked for all my life. It'll take me years to get accepted as a poet. I'll never make any money. I can't live off my parents forever.' He paused, looking for the words. 'The St. Mark's poetry reading was good, in a way, because I saw what throwing my music away would do to my life. If nothing else, that poetry reading helped me make this decision.'

I looked up at him. 'Are you sure?'

'Yes. It's time to move on. Get back to my music.' He squeezed me tight and, rocking me in his arms, he added, 'And I want to take care of you!'

'Oh, Lou, you don't need to worry about me,' I mumbled. But I loved hearing him say it. It was about time he took care of me, for a change.

'I do worry about you,' he said. 'You're one of the innocents. And so vulnerable. It's a tough world out there, kid.'

I didn't say anything. He was right about my vulnerability, but I was embarrassed. It made me sound weak.

I laughed, and said, 'The important thing is that you made a decision. And I'm glad for you, whatever it is!'

He sat up some, and I shifted my position.

'Will you come with me?' he asked.

I didn't understand the question. 'What do you mean?'

He sat up a little more, so I did, too, and then I looked at him.

'Will you marry me?' he asked.

I was so surprised that I felt like someone had reached down inside and pushed all the air out of my lungs. That there was no oxygen in the air to breathe. I didn't feel real. I didn't seem to be completely grasping what was going on. Wasn't I supposed to feel overjoyed? I was taken back by the surprise, and I must have been pleased, but all I remember feeling was like I was floating into some unknown space and time. That I had neither beginning nor end. *Maybe it was too soon.* But all I managed to say was, 'I don't understand the question.'

The way he looked at me, I thought my heart would break. He took hold of my arms.

'Marry me!' he said. 'I need you.'

Oh, if he'd only he'd said, 'I want you!'

Trying to buy time, I asked, 'Now?'

'Why not?'

'I can't.'

'Why not?'

I struggled, again, to find the words. I realized I didn't know how I felt. This was confusing, because I always know how I feel. My daily challenge in life was *not* to react to my feelings. Great for the stage; in life, not so much. But instead, I said, 'It's too soon.'

He seemed taken aback. 'Too soon for what?'

I took a beat, and then looked up at him.

'Lewis,' I said, 'I'm too young!'

This was true.

'In my family, we marry late,' I continued. 'I'll only be twenty-one at the end of the year!'

Good. Until you find out how you feel, sound practical.

Lou held my eyes for a long time. Neither of us spoke. He looked like I'd ripped his heart out.

'Does that mean you don't want to marry me?' he asked, quietly.

'No!' I said. 'That's not it, at all!'

Watch out—you can't hurt him! He's not strong enough yet!

'Oh, don't think that, Lewis!' I said.

Time! I need more time!

'It's probably that I just need more time. This is coming so ... unexpectedly for me.'

'It's not for me,' he replied, as quietly as before.

I tried to make light. 'Well, I would expect not! You must have been thinking about this … haven't you?'

'Of course!' he said. 'It's all I've been thinking about for weeks—months!'

'Do you know why?' I asked.

Yes! That's what you need to know.

'Yes!'

He looked at me for a very long time, completely exposed.

'When I'm with you I feel whole.'

'Oh!'

I took his hands, which were gripping my arms so tightly it hurt, and, instead, put them around me.

He's holding on to you for dear life! Is that what you want?

I put my head back on his chest.

But this is where you belong. He feels like home, and always has, right from the very beginning.

'That's lovely, Lou. I think I understand.'

But …' and then I began struggling to find the right words.

The man was a genius. Everybody said so! American music had never heard or seen anything like him or his work!

'I probably just need more time to think about it,' I said. 'That's all. This really is quite a surprise!'

My real concern was a nagging feeling I'd been having with more and more frequency:

What if he's just mad?

I reached up and brought his face closer to mine, and rubbed my cheek up against his. His early morning growth prickled my skin.

'Just give me more time,' I whispered to him. 'That's all I need.'

Then I kissed him.

'I do love you,' I said.

perfect day.................. CHAPTER SIX

I dashed out of the cab on 89th between Columbus and Amsterdam and flew up the ramp of the Claremont Stables, before realizing I'd left my riding boots at my last call, an audition for an independent movie. I was in a hurry to get to the stables to ride in Central Park before meeting Lou for brunch in the park, and I was only wearing sandals—not ideal footwear for horseback riding. I hadn't asked Lou to come riding with me since our last excursion, and learning how little he cared for it.

I managed to make our way on horseback onto the busy New York City streets to the entrance of the Park, several blocks away. I was looking forward to riding on its beautiful trails, which wound through the woods and around the lakes and reservoir. As we entered the green of the park, the usual calm settled over me. It offered peace and respite from the chaos of the city, and it always had a healing effect upon me. It was a Saturday, and the weather was ideal, warm with a slight breeze.

Central Park was decked out in the bright green of early summer, and it seemed that every hippie and flower child in the city had descended upon Sheep's Meadow. Couples sunbathed or walked casually, holding hands and enjoying the scenery; Frisbees sailed through the air as dogs, playing catch, chased them; toddlers clung to their parents, blissful miniature marionettes in tow. Someone was playing Steven Stills on a lone guitar, and the elegiac sounds of the strings could be heard softly in the distance. Occasionally, the sweet smell of pot drifted by on a puff of light wind, caressed by the graceful willows clothed in yellow bloom dotting the meadow.

I was wearing my white jeans and a light, sleeveless top, but within minutes I'd already worked up a sweat, because today there were too many people on the riding trails even during the designated times when only horse and rider were supposed to be on them. Certain intervals, especially around the reservoir, were a bottleneck of bands of teenagers and bike riders crowding the trails, and I was forced to decide whether to charge on, hoping everyone scattered safely out of the way—neither reasonable or advisable—or dodge and weave my horse around all the traffic, which required considerable concentration and some frustration.

Lewis seemed especially keen when he suggested we meet for brunch in the park that day, although he didn't mention anything in particular; by his offhand manner, however, I suspected he might have something special in mind. With Lewis, I'd learned that the more casually he mentioned something, the more likely it was special or important to him.

It had been a hectic time recently. We'd decided it was time for Lewis to move back into the city from Long Island, and had spent several weekends looking at apartments together. We'd talked it over with his parents and, since I was moving in with him, they'd approved.

A friend of his insisted we look on the Upper East Side, because she said that was where everyone rich, important, and successful lived. To me, these were stupid reasons for choosing which part of town we should live in. I preferred the Upper West Side or the Village, where I first lived when I moved to New York, and Lou had only lived on the Upper East Side once, for a short period of time, but he wanted to take her advice, although why wasn't made clear. He was hungry for success and fame right from the beginning, so I guessed that was why. I didn't dislike the Upper East Side enough to protest, so that's where we'd looked. We'd decided upon a small, modest studio on East 74th

Street and First Avenue, which Lewis thought we could afford. We'd moved into it only a couple of months earlier.

Plans were being made for Lou to record his first solo album, to be produced by Richard Robinson, and he was busy getting the material together for it. This was in 1972—two years after Lou left The Velvet Underground—and his solo album was highly anticipated. Much of the material was old unreleased Velvets songs that he'd reworked or simply planned to re-record as a solo artist, but there were a couple of news ones that he'd been working on, including 'Going Down' and 'Berlin.'

Lou had already told me that, ever since we'd met, I'd inspired his writing. But he knew I wasn't interested in taking any credit, and I was aware he didn't easily share the spotlight. Other than music, his writing was, first and foremost, important to him—except for me, now—largely, I feared, because I facilitated his access to them.

Lou was intent upon becoming successful as an original artist, and he believed that garnering as much credit or praise as possible for himself as a songwriter would help him obtain that goal. He rarely, if ever, talked about where his material came from, but if people thought they'd 'picked up' on something in his lyrics, he didn't expand. He wanted his audience to relate to the songs personally, so he rarely talked about his personal writing process.

Lou wrote under a kind of extreme cyclical personal pressure—in spurts, usually overnight, and after thoughts and feelings had built up in him so intensely that they came pouring out, often fully formed. He didn't believe in changing anything once it was written down, however, because he had already moved on. His writing process was cathartic, and it allowed him to reach his most authentic truth, and truth in writing is the most important aspect to produce good—if not great—writing, which he treasured most. Sometimes he reworked a lyric slightly—changed a name, dropped or added a phrase—on old songs that reappeared on subsequent albums.

Our relationship had flourished since he left The Velvet Underground and went out to live with his parents on the Island. We had a particularly strong bond because we first got together when he was making his break from the band. It was a seminal point in his life and career as a songwriter and musician, and I was there with him through it. From our very first date, he had voiced his hopes, dreams, and frustrations about his writing and career, along with his feelings about the band. I was his friend and confidant right from the start.

Lou believed that I understood him, and it was apparent to him that I had no interest in gaining anything materially or otherwise from being a part of his life. That is why I believe he trusted me with his thoughts, feelings and, later, his love, as his first mate.

Lou was excited about his reemergence as a solo artist but, understandably, he approached it with considerable trepidation, which he hid rather successfully from everyone but me. He'd spent almost two years reevaluating his career and past experiences in the music industry, and he believed that he was finally prepared to make his comeback. He'd learned that to succeed as an international star—and that was his ambition—it was integral that he pay attention to the business side of his career, and to cull and massage important contacts. He'd struggled with, and had finally made the decision about, the path his career would take. But now, with me by his side, he felt he was emotionally strong enough to launch his solo career. He'd cut back on his drinking, too, even though he had occasional bouts of drunken episodes, but we'd usually only end up at Max's till the early hours of the morning, and I'd gotten to know many of the people who regularly hung out there, so I had begun to feel safer there.

* * *

It was toward the end of that afternoon's ride in the park that I came upon an isolated stretch of riding trail, and a group of teenagers riding their bikes directly on the trail came upon me, alone. One of the kids in the front of the gang laughed loudly and, shouting and gesturing to the others, yelled, 'Watch this!'

Aiming his bike right at me, he rode up so close that he was able, in passing, to slap the neck of my horse with such force that he reared, screaming, and I was almost thrown from the saddle. Struggling with the reins, I managed to bring him down and stay in the saddle, but the poor beast was so frightened by the blow and unwarranted aggression that he bolted into a full gallop.

My noble steed cut through all the trees and bushes that lay in his path, while all I could do was crouch down close and low on him to avoid low branches, holding on to his mane with all my strength. Charging out of the park, I was on a runaway horse galloping at full throttle against traffic. New York City streets are usually congested most of the time, but on Saturdays they are bulging with delivery trucks and cars of afternoon shoppers. I feared we'd be struck down in the streets, as he galloped over, around, and through the harrowing gridlock. Drivers laid on their horns, and the ensuing racket startled the horse even more. But all I could do was hold on to his mane—reins loose and flying— wrap my arms around his neck, and pray for our lives.

Finally arriving back at the stables, head down, the horse charged up the ramp and galloped into the corral enclosed inside the barn. He reared again on his back legs, this time, and I was thrown to the ground. Two instructors immediately dropped what they were doing and ran over to see if I was all right. I lay crumpled in a heap, dazed for several minutes.

As they began helping me up, they started yelling, 'What's the matter with you? Don't you know how to ride a horse? Do you think this is a circus, galloping into the stables? You could have been killed!'

But I was, after all, in New York, New York. People yell when they're scared here. I was grateful for their help, so I kept my mouth shut. Collapsing on a bale of hay, I ran my hands over my body, checking for broken bones or serious injuries. My ankles were bleeding, chaffed by my stirrups, but other than being sore and frightened out of my wits, I appeared to be whole.

* * *

I wasn't terribly late meeting Lou at the outdoor cafe in the park. He was already at a table, tucked in a corner where we could be alone, and our first pitcher of sangria had just arrived at the table. As I walked toward him and he saw me, he jumped up and gave me one of his huge bear hugs, kissing my hair, cheeks, even my nose.

Lewis was dressed in jeans and a black T-shirt, hair coiffed, smiling and happy. I probably looked bedraggled after being thrown from a horse, but I'd gotten some sun on my face and arms during my ride, so I looked healthy, at least.

While Lou was busy ordering lunch from the waiter, I took three extra-strength aspirin. I was sore all over, and my white jeans were blood-stained at the bottom, but I rolled them up to a fashionable mid-calf length. I didn't want him asking questions, only to share with him our afternoon in the park together or the fantastic mood he appeared to be in. We'd been through a lot together, and deserved to celebrate our union, which was what I assumed was his intention this day.

Lewis was a take-charge kind of guy, and he always made me feel safe and secure. In his arms I finally relaxed, after my harrowing ride. Wordlessly, I let him know how happy I was to see him.

We talked about going to the zoo after our late lunch, and I suggested maybe afterward we could walk to our favorite cinema, the Paris, where the latest Buñuel film, *The Discreet Charm Of The Bourgeoisie*, was playing.

As we sipped sangria and ate our delicious green salads, we talked about our new life in the city. Lou had insisted upon paying the rent for our apartment, but I wanted to contribute to it. My grandmother sent me a check every month to cover my living expenses at school, so

I could help with the bills. Lou said that if it made me feel better, that would be fine. We were living on a tight budget, but that didn't worry us. We were a young couple, and he was starting over in a solo career, so we expected it.

In December 1971, Lou signed a contract with RCA for his first album, and he was beginning his comeback. He was on his own now, without The Velvet Underground backing him, which made him a little nervous, but it was better than trying to resolve all those issues he had with the band. Frankly, the band was now a mess, but he had a lawyer working on obtaining all the copyrights to The Velvet Underground songs, which he began on his own, typing and filling out all the forms when he was employed at his dad's firm. Once he quit the band, he wasn't looking back. He just wanted to get out on his own and back to his music.

We were looking forward to a bright, but very busy year. Lou's manager, Dennis Katz, was already talking about dates for a US tour to support the album, after its recording in London. I knew that he wanted me to go with him, but I didn't know how I could manage it, what with school, rehearsals, and the rounds of auditions I'd be expected to make, even as a full-time student.

Naturally, Lou launched directly into the topic I least wanted to discuss.

'Are you looking forward to the tour?' he asked. 'They're tough, you know. I want to warn you.'

'Sure,' I replied, not knowing how I could ever work out my schedule to go with him.

'You promised,' he reminded me, sensing some reluctance.

'Well, I am at the Playhouse full time in the fall, but when do you think it'll begin?'

'Right after the album is recorded,' he said, in a heartbeat.

I didn't say anything. I looked down, searching for the right words to respond. Lou noticed my hesitation and seemed to decide to brush past annoying facts like specific dates and such.

'Look, let's not worry about details now,' he said briskly. 'We can do that another time.'

'Oh, that would be great!' I said, relieved. I wanted to change the subject, too, and I saw that we were back in sync once again.

'Let's just enjoy our day in the park,' he said. 'I've missed your beautiful face! How did the audition go today?'

'I think it went okay.'

'What was it for?'

'Oh, just some independent movie in the city, but I doubt I'll get it. I just go into these things hoping for the best, preparing for the worse—you know.'

I laughed and brought his hands to my lips. Looking at him, full of hope for the future and his new career, I thought about how happy I was for him and how much I loved him. He looked so clean, young, and full of promise. I knew he'd be the success he was determined to become and, in that moment, I felt lucky he'd come into my life, despite all the difficulty of the last year or so.

He's worth it all, I reminded myself.

'I love you,' he said, bringing my hands to his lips, kissing them, 'You look so healthy! Did you get some sun today?'

I laughed lightly. *If only he knew* …

'Who knows,' I said quickly. 'I'm out in the sun for a minute and I turn beet red.

'We're going to the zoo afterward?' I asked, changing the subject.

'Whatever you want!' he replied. 'I just want to enjoy the day with you, and be together! I can't even remember the last time I was at the zoo! Which animal's your favorite? Mine's the tiger, of course.'

'Yeah, but he's in a cage, and I always wonder … how happy could he be?'

'Hey, most of us are trapped,' he joked darkly.

'I like the polar bears,' I said. 'They're huge, with so much raw power. At least they can roam around on the rocks, and take a dip in the pool, where they are. They're a bit more free.'

'Yeah, but not really.'

'It's better than a cage!' I exclaimed. 'All that poor cat does is pace, back and forth … and he's such a beautiful animal! They're my favorites, too, but he looks so sad and unhappy!'

'Oh, don't worry about it,' Lou said. 'They pump them full of drugs. How bad could that be?'

I looked at him but laughed anyway. 'Leave it to you, to point out the benefits of drugs!'

'It's not *benefits*, Bettye,' he said. 'They're just easing his pain.'

With that, I gently took my hands away, after laying his down on the table between us. I reached for my glass, and taking a sip, smiled and looked at him.

'Well what do you say,' I asked. 'Shall we go? If we don't get going, we won't have time to do everything we want today!'

'You're right,' he said, taking his hands away, and pulling out his wallet.

'Sir,' he called to the waiter, who was, fortunately, rushing around close by. 'Can we have our check?'

'Yes sir!' yelled the waiter, over his shoulder, as he hustled off.

'One thing,' said Lou, rising. 'Will we have time *after* the zoo to drop by Tiffany's to look at rings? Or should we go *before* we hit the zoo? What time is it, anyway?' he continued nonchalantly, looking at his watch.

I sat back down in my chair and looked at mine.

'Four,' I said, weakly. I was fighting for breath again.

'So, maybe we should go now?' He looked at me for the first time.

I couldn't find my words, so began with, 'Lewis …'

'Yes, Bettye?'

'Lou, didn't we talk about this? You can't afford a ring right now.'

'Yes, I can,' he said softly.

He pulled out his chair, sat down and again reached for my hands, which I was clutching together—hard—on the table in front of me.

'Look, Bettye, I've been saving. A couple of royalty checks have come in the last several months, and my father's an accountant. He takes care of my money.'

'But, Lou …'

'*What?*' he yelled.

The waiter hadn't come back yet with the bill or cleaned the table. I noticed there was some sangria left in the carafe. Lou folded his hands and made a bridge with his fingers, waiting for me to speak. I pulled his glass over, and poured some sangria into it, then pushed it back in front of him. I poured some for myself.

'I do love you,' I said.

'Okay …' Lou said. But all I could see were drunken scenes, rushing in my mind's eye. Dragging him out of one bar after another, stumbling, inaudible, helpless. I felt my stomach roll over.

So many bars … so many nights … how many more drunken early mornings could I take?

'Lou, I—'

'Yes.'

He could see I was weak. How could he not have, I was probably turning green. This wasn't exactly the response most girls gave after an invitation to shop for a Tiffany's engagement ring. But I was so frightened.

'You're not going to tell me we still need to wait, are you?'

'No, I just—'

'*What?* What is it, Bettye?'

He picked up his glass and took a drink. A long one, in fact. Then he sat his glass down and moved it over to mine. He touched the rim of his glass to mine, toasting the glass, and then took another drink. As he sat it back down in front of him, I looked up, and into his eyes.

'I love you,' I said.

'But ... not enough ... to marry me?' He looked me straight in the eyes. 'Have you changed your mind?'

'No. Lou, it isn't that. I want to marry you. I do.'

'Then why don't we just go and get your ring?'

Lou didn't like not getting what he wanted. He was demanding an answer. I had to tell him my reservations. It was time.

'What's the *problem*, Bettye?'

'It's your drinking,' I said, after a moment.

'What about it?'

'It has to stop,' I said finally. It was the first time I'd told him he needed to *stop drinking*.

'I can't do that—right away. I can try. But it will take a while.'

All I could think to do is repeat myself. 'It has to stop.'

'What does that mean?' he asked. Are you giving me a deadline? Like, by a week, a month—what?

I just shook my head, *no*.

'Then what do you *mean*,' he asked again, almost angrily.

'I don't know!' I cried. 'I don't know, I don't know, *I don't know*! All I know is that I can't take it anymore. I can't be responsible for you anymore! I feel like you're using me. I don't know if you love me or just *need* me—to help with your comeback. *Your* career, *your* music, *your* writing—it's always about you, you, you! *Where am I in all this?*'

'All right. Just a minute. I love you. You do know that, don't you?'

'Not really. I don't know if you love me or need me.'

And then, dammit, I started to cry. Quietly. Big fat, undeniable tears slowly began making their way down my face. Shit!

This is not right. There's something wrong. I should be happy.

'Okay, look, Bettye—what do you need from me?'

'I just told you.'

'I can't stop just like *that*,' he said, snapping his middle finger and thumb together for emphasis.

'Can you … get help?' It was all I could get out.

'What kind of help?'

'I don't know,' I said, my voice rising. '*Ask your mother!*'

I'm not your mother!

This last part I practically yelled. A couple in the cafe turned around and looked at us, startled.

'You're making me cause a scene,' I told him.

I hated scenes. People from trailer parks make scenes. Right?

'I can't make you do anything,' he countered.

'*Really?*' I cried.

The hell with the couple.

The hell with everyone.

'Do you know what this feels like to me?' I asked him.

'No,' he said. 'Why don't you tell me. Go ahead!' He paused. 'I mean it. Fuck *them*.'

I think I might have smiled, but those damn tears were still coming, so I lowered my voice.

'I'm afraid to make that kind of commitment to—a—*drunk!*'

Oh, Lord, I just spit it out there!

'No, wait, I'm sorry, Lou,' I said, continuing quickly, 'that's not what I mean. I don't want to call you that.'

'But that's what *I am!*'

'*What?*'

'That's what I *am.*'

No one was better at taking the wind out of anyone's sails than Lou Reed. I did not appreciate it.

'I've been doing some reading and talking to a couple of my friends who have met you.'

'*Yeah*? And what do they say?'

'That you're an alcoholic.'

'They're right. I am.'

He did it again. Now I was pissed.

'*You know*?'

'Yes!' he said.

'Well … so …' I was sputtering. I hated it. *I hated him.*

'*So … what do you plan to do about it*?'

'I don't know.'

'Well, that's … just … *lovely*.'

I was furious.

'What do you want me to say, Bettye? I don't know how to stop.'

'I can't do this anymore.'

I stood up so suddenly that my chair shot out from under me.

'I am not your mother. I am not your nursemaid. I am not your personal, private cop. You are not my beat. I can't watch over you, anymore. I'm done.'

'What, are you breaking up with me?'

'I don't know, Lou, isn't that what you want?'

'No …'

'Really. Could have fooled me. The way you act? So that's what you're getting.'

I picked up my bag.

'I *was* your fiancé.'

He looked up at me standing over him. I turned my back on him and started walking. I had no idea where I was going. I put one foot in front of the other.

'*Bettye! Where are you going*?' he shouted.

I didn't answer him. I kept on walking. I heard him call my name one more time, and then I was too far away to hear anything anymore.

I got to the Hans Christian Anderson statue and stopped. I looked around at the park. It was so beautiful. The sun was beginning to set. *The light!* My favorite time of day.

I've ruined everything, I thought.

* * *

The cat was pacing back and forth, back and forth. His tongue was hanging out of his mouth, and he was panting. He looked thirsty. I was watching a little girl holding on to the fence separating us from them. The caged animal, pacing, was going a little crazy. I took another bite of my ice cream.

Soon I guess he'll be getting his drugs. Just like Lou said.

Maybe he can pass out into a grateful darkness. That's probably why he's thirsty. The drugs! Of course.

They'll knock you out, too, you poor beast.

Someone sat down next to me on the garden bench. At first I ignored him. The cat was panting harder. His tongue lolled out, almost to his knees. He lay down in a lump and put his giant head down on his gigantic paw. He blinked slowly. The black parentheses over his eyes wrinkled. I noticed the man on the bench had slid a little closer to me.

Oh, I am in no mood for this right now. I am not getting picked up by anyone in Central Park today!

I steeled myself and turned around to face him, about to bite his head off. But it was Lewis. I was so surprised that I simply sat back and looked at him, blankly staring. He didn't say anything but reached for my hand. I suppose a faint smile must have crept across my face, despite everything that had happened, because he started smiling at me. And then he was beaming.

I didn't say anything to him.

I do love this man. He is brilliant—maybe a genius. He is beautiful. He has so much to give. He is so incredibly warm and loving—when he wants to be! I have given so much to him already …

Gently, Lou picked up my hands. They were in my lap, and he brought them to his lips, held them together in his, then blew on them.

'Make a wish,' he said.

'I have,' I said.

'Okay, you don't have to tell me what it is.'

'Well, aren't you clever.'

'I knew you'd be here.'

'Oh, would you please, just … shut. *Up!*' I said.

He threw his head back and roared.

He had to get help. I couldn't do it for him. It wouldn't work. It had to be him. He had to do it. He had to want to do it.

It's not going to work any other way.

But I was still angry. The son of a bitch had forced me to be mean. I couldn't stand hurting him … although, he didn't look all that hurt. And he was … laughing.

Laughing!?

'What's so funny?' I asked.

'You.'

'Oh. Well, that's wonderful! I'm glad I could provide you with so much amuse—'

He cut me off, took my face in his hands, and kissed me.

'No, *you* shut up,' he said softly. 'I'll quit. I promise. I'll get help. I'll ask my mother …'

I looked at him, warning him not to push it.

'I mean, I'll ask my doctor. How will that be? I have a doctor. I'll ask him what I have to do.'

I didn't say anything.

'We don't have to get married right away. I can wait.'

I still didn't say anything.

'I promise I'll stop. At least cut it down—way down. Till I can drink like a normal person. How will that be?'

I didn't answer his question.

'Bettye, I don't want to hurt you anymore. I'm glad you told me how it is for you. I am sorry. I can be a selfish bastard. And I will fix it.'

I waited a long time before I said anything.

'Okay, Lou.'

'Okay, what, Bettye?'

'I believe you.'

'You do?'

'Yes—don't you?'

'Yes, yes, of course I do! I will—*I will fix this*. Okay?'

'Better.'

'So, do you want to go to Tiffany's, now?'

'We can't. It's closed.'

'Okay, another time?'

'Maybe. *If* I see significant improvement.'

'*Significant* improvement …'

'Yes, *significant* improvement! Otherwise—*forgedaboudit*!'

'Okay. Done. Now, you wanna go take a look at the polar bears? Time for the big cat to get his shot. That's just going to make you sad, so come on,' he urged, rising, extending his hand out to me. 'Let's get out of here.'

He helped me up, picked up my purse and put it over my shoulder.

'Then the movie, afterward?'

'That would be good,' I said.

'Great! What's playing?'

'Something French. Your favorite.'

'Oh, I can't wait!' he said, laughing, and so did I, because I knew how he felt about French films.

But I was working on it.

on the road, part one........ CHAPTER SEVEN

In 1971, at the start of Lou's career, life on the road was good. He was focused and disciplined. Although he was still drinking, he'd substantially cut down, as he'd promised me. We knew that launching his solo career was going to require intense, hard work. But he wasn't starting from scratch; he already had years of experience in the music industry, which would serve him well.

Lou got a record contract with RCA that same year and, in London, recorded his first solo album, *Lou Reed*. By now, he had returned to the city, after living with his parents out on the Island, and we'd moved in together. I set up house on a limited budget in our sparsely furnished first apartment, a small studio on East 78th Street and First Avenue. Our only furnishings were a pullout couch, his writing chair, a Formica barista table with two chairs, a portable TV, stereo system, and his grandmother's rocking chair.

The rock journalist Lisa Robinson introduced Lou to her husband, Richard Robinson, an A&R man at RCA, who was to produce Lou's album. They got along well. Richard was smart; he listened to Lou about how he wanted his first solo album to be a straightforward, unadorned rock'n'roll record introducing songs he wrote while he was still a member of The Velvet Underground, only now Lou would record them on his own. A couple of new ones, like 'Berlin,' were also going to be included.

Lou knew going out as a solo artist would be tough, but he was ecstatic to be brought into the Robinsons' inner circle, as they were influential movers and shakers in the music industry, and he told me privately that he couldn't believe he'd been given such a 'golden opportunity.' If Lewis got Richard to produce his first solo album and it sold at least a respectable number of copies for RCA, he would be on the road to success.

Lou acquired an attorney and a manager, Dennis Katz, who negotiated his first contract as a solo artist. Dennis was a VP at RCA, and was instrumental in getting the label to sign Lewis. He had enormous contacts in the music industry, which Lou knew could only help him in his new career.

Dennis considered himself an intellectual, and he was, indeed, perceptive in recognizing Lou's original talent. But he was also a bit in awe of Lou. This was the perfect combination to solidify Lou's interest, and Dennis soon left RCA to manage Lou's solo career and become his attorney.

Initially, Lewis liked Dennis, and they got along very well together. Of course, their burgeoning personal relationship was in Lou's best interests, of which he was well aware. Privately, he complained to me about how much money Dennis was spending, and why we weren't seeing more of it. Dennis insisted we stay in the very best hotels, where Dennis would stay, too. But Lou thought he spent money—which he consistently pointed out to me was money *he* earned—like water.

When Dennis arrived in London with his wife, Anne, while Lou was recording, or showed up on the road for a gig Lou was playing, he wined and dined Lewis and me like royalty. It's all very well spoiling us, Lou thought, but ultimately it was coming out of his pocket. This splurging was a foreshadowing of their future relationship. Lewis would sue Dennis for mismanagement of funds; Dennis would countersue; and nearly a decade later, after the birth of my second child during my second marriage, I would be subpoenaed to testify in a pretrial hearing for the latter suit.

Back in 1972, Lou needed a band to go on tour to support his album, which was scheduled for released in the spring. The advance he received from RCA wasn't substantial enough to cover the expense of hiring experienced, professional musicians, however. Instead, through his brother, Steve Katz, the guitarist in Blood Sweat & Tears, Dennis found Lou a personal manager, Fred Heller, who in turn connected Lou with a high-school garage band—which is how The Tots became his first solo band on the road. They were regular guys from Yonkers, a middle-class neighborhood in Westchester, the moneyed county just north of the city.

Rehearsals for their first US tour took place in a recording studio in Dobbs Ferry, a small village nestled on the banks of the Hudson River, a half-hour north of the city. Lou and I traveled up to the rehearsals together for weeks; he wanted me by his side, so I freed up my life from all commitments to join him.

The studio rested high on the hill, its windows looking out over the waterfront and the majestic Palisades beyond, across the Jersey side of the Hudson. As I gazed out of the windows onto the bucolic scene below, I was reminded of our first days together, when Lou and I spent many weekends in my apartment on Morningside Heights, looking out on the beautiful river.

As Lou took the Tots through the songs they would be playing on tour, I noticed how happy, positive, and patient he was with these high-school kids who didn't have any real experience and were, in fact, only two years younger than me.

They were nice guys, but I never got to know them personally, because once rehearsals were over, Lou had little to do with them. He thought they were adequate at best, and while he was cooperative with them in the beginning, that was only so they would learn his songs.

At this point in his career, he was only really using them because he couldn't hire professional musicians.

I heard the songs so much during rehearsals that I picked up all the lyrics and music. Later, this would prove handy when I took on the job of lighting director on the road across America. Dates were soon lined up for the tour, and in April, Lou and The Tots debuted at the State University of New York (SUNY) in Buffalo, New York. The Tots pulled through, and Lewis was satisfied with their performance. We were going on the road, and I was excited, as I had only toured briefly as an actress. This would be my first experience with a band playing live across the country.

After the first couple of shows, Lou was beginning to feel a bit more confident about both his performance and The Tots' playing. One night, we were at the hotel bar after the show; Lou was getting pretty plastered, but we had an early start the following morning for the next gig in another town. I was trying to get him back in the hotel room, and I was exhausted.

'Come on, Bettye, stay and have one more drink with me,' he pleaded.

'Lewis, we need to get to bed! We have an early morning!'

'Come on, princess, talk to me.' He raised his hand limply, and called loudly for the waitress. '*Two more, over here,*' he shouted from the table.

Our waitress was standing at the end of the bar, not far away. We were the only ones left, and I just wanted to get out of there. My instinct was to cancel Lou's order, but I didn't want to rile him. He could get a little testy if you kept him away from his scotch. He was in a reasonably good mood, and the show had gone well, but he seemed to want to talk about something. About what, I had no idea; I couldn't really understand him, because he'd begun slurring. So I decided to humor him; if we had only a couple of sips of scotch, I thought I could convince him to go back to the room and into bed. Maybe I could get an hour of sleep.

The tired-looking waitress sauntered over to us and slammed our drinks down on the table. Lou raised his glass and dove his nose into it, missing his mouth entirely.

All right, I'd had enough. I got up and reached into Lou's pocket. It wasn't difficult, because his leg was slung straight out, and he was primed to slide off onto the floor at any moment. Pulling out a wad of bills, I counted out three tens and a five. Leaving them on the table, I helped Lou up, and put his arm around my neck, hoping I could get him up to the room, where I could sling him, if only sideways, onto the bed.

I was grateful that we were the last to leave. The star of the show shouldn't be seen in this condition. But I was troubled, because I hadn't seen Lou like this in a long time. He drank steadily, but not into this kind of stupor—at least he hadn't, so far. It worried me, and then I remembered that he wanted to talk to me, which he wasn't prone to do, at least in public.

As we labored out to the elevator and I pushed the button, he started mumbling.

'What?' I asked, leaning down close to his mouth, near his shoulder, so I could hear what he was trying to say.

Suddenly he stood upright and found the elevator button, which he leaned on indefinitely.

'I SAID,' he shouted, over-pronouncing each syllable, 'We. HAFF … To. Get … RIDDDID. Of. Th—EM!'

I was startled, but I managed to ask, 'Who?'

He looked at me like I was a bug on the wall.

'THE *TAUGHTS*, Sil-LEEE!' he shouted.

Okay. Now I understood who he was talking about. Whispering close to his ear, I made an effort to demonstrate how he could lower his voice.

'Why?' I asked.

'WHY?' he replied, and then he started laughing in that high cackle of his.

'Lewis,' I said, 'calm down.'

I tried to arrange him into a standing position.

'Stop!' I practically hissed.

Lou lurched forward, looked over his shoulder, and put his index finger to his lips, pursing them.

'Oh. *Kay*! You *shhh*!'

He giggled, and then, mincing, covered his mouth with his hand at a private joke only he was smart enough to understand.

'They're … just … so …'

'Yeah, okay, what?' I asked hurriedly.

The elevator doors opened, and I started dragging him inside. After getting him in, I turned him around and pushed the elevator button for our floor.

'They're … just … SO … UGLY!' Lou shouted.

Oh my god!

He'd read that stupid review about our last show. I thought I'd been successful in hiding it from him. But apparently he got it from someone, somewhere. I was learning that you couldn't keep Lewis away from any review about any show, ever. A real detective, this one.

God, please help me get this man into bed, I silently prayed.

The elevator groaned up to our floor.

'UG … LY!' he shouted again, as the elevator lifted us heavenward.

Lou was convinced The Tots had broken his cardinal rule: *One could, at the very least, be good looking.*

At first the band moved their own equipment. Later, Barbara Wilkinson became our road manager, and a couple of roadies were hired. We were on a very tight budget, and in the beginning Lou and I flew coach from one venue to the next, sometimes leaving within twenty-four hours of arriving. The roadies drove The Tots and the equipment to meet us, leaving straight after the show, in order to arrive on time for the next one.

We were out of town and on the road for weeks, sometimes months at a time, without any real breaks. It was hard going, but Lou and I worked well as a team. I gave him confidence and constant emotional support, and I was always by his side, preempting what he needed so that he was always in top performance condition to keep the show on the road. Otherwise, our days were full of radio interviews or meetings with journalists, either at a hotel or for lunch or dinner in town; we were almost always working.

Lou took to heart possibly the most valuable advice Andy Warhol ever gave him: *Work as hard as you can, for as long as you can.* As the child of immigrants, Andy had bought into the American Dream. Work hard and you will be a success. It had worked for Andy. Why wouldn't it for Lou?

Lewis bought into the dream, and brought me along with him. The trouble is, I had no idea what I was in for, accompanying Lewis across the US on tour. Because Lou was an addict, and he could become abusive— with himself, and everyone around him—especially those close to him. If you were the woman in his life, you were as integral to him as an arm or a leg, and would be treated with as much respect and abuse as he treated himself. That's just the way it was.

When we did get a chance to fly home to New York for a couple of days or a week, we crashed at home, exhausted, before starting the next leg of the tour. In New York, Lou also attended meetings with management; the record company; met with musicians, singers, and other songwriters; went to their concerts; and did interviews in town, many of which I went with him to.

Much of the time, I wasn't seen as a person but as an appendage— which is how Lou, I came to understand, regarded me. This was often the case, meeting music industry management executives, record company executives—'suits,' as they were called in the industry—along with studio engineers, whom I was introduced to, however briefly, when I sat in on Lou's recording sessions. Often, I wasn't introduced at all; like the imaginary white elephant in the room, I went completely unacknowledged. I was rarely spoken to, and my opinions were never solicited. Most of the time, I just smiled sweetly at the music-industry men around us. As Lou's significant other, that was my actual job.

* * *

At the beginning of the US *Lou Reed* tour, we'd stay at a Holiday Inn or a similarly low-budget chain on the road. By any stretch of the imagination, life on the road was not glamorous. Lou's college buddy Garland Jeffreys, an exceptionally talented singer-songwriter, was the opening act for a large part of the tour. He was a friend of ours, so Lewis relaxed around him, and we spent our time with Garland laughing, which was light relief for me.

Lou was pleased—grateful, even—to be on tour. He was finally able to get his Velvet Underground songs, which most people had not yet heard, out there. With their prior management and record companies, not getting the necessary exposure they needed was one of the VU's major problems, if not their largest, so this came as a great satisfaction to Lou. The promotion for the *Lou Reed* album was working, and his music was finally being heard nationwide. And his performances—at least in the beginning—were spellbinding.

When Lou was in top form, he possessed extraordinary power and stage presence, despite his limited vocal range and guitar playing at that time. And the more he did his job, the better he got. He loved what he was doing, and he devoted his entire being to its success.

Lou felt an enormous amount of pressure to succeed, not only for his own sake but for that of everyone else who depended upon him. Every day he was on the road he was surrounded by people involved in the show who reminded him of this responsibility. It weighed heavily upon him. But, as with the Velvets, after a while, he viewed this responsibility as a burden—albeit one that was apparent to no one else but me.

My job included keeping an eye on the amount of alcohol he consumed, which could be excessive. At first, it was not a real problem, but as the tours went on, it became the largest issue, and Lou's drinking began to consume more of my time than anything else.

After the first stretch of the *Lou Reed* tour—where, as his girlfriend, I functioned as Lou's personal assistant—I wasn't especially keen to go out on the road again. It had been really draining, looking after him twenty-four hours a day with no respite. I wanted to get back to my own acting career, and I didn't want to resent him for taking me away from it.

As the next phase of the *Lou Reed* tour grew closer, Lou started talking about what he thought worked, what didn't, how things could be improved—that sort of thing. This is when I realized I didn't want to go out on the road again. But I also knew I had little choice; he didn't believe he could do it without me.

I wanted to support Lou's return to his chosen career because I believed in him and his music. But the rest of the job came unnaturally to me, and it made me deeply uncomfortable. I was beginning to feel used, which I resented, and I didn't think our relationship would survive the experience.

Inevitably, that conversation occurred. We were coming home, and he was turning the key in the lock of our new apartment.

'What do you mean, you're not coming out on the road with me?' he shouted, whirling around and looking aghast at me.

'What I said.' I was trying to remain calm.

'I don't understand, you're not coming out on tour with me again?'

'No.'

'*What?*' he yelled. 'And you're telling me this *now?*'

'Yes.'

'And when were you going to tell me?'

He shoved his keys in his pocket and put his hands on his hips, like he was talking to a three-year-old.

I'm actually taller than you in heels, so that's not working for you.

But all I said, as calmly as before, was, 'When it came up. Like now.'

'Bettye, I can't do this without you,' he exclaimed, throwing his arms up into the air around him.

'Yes, you can!' I replied firmly. 'You have a road manager. Your band is together, the songs are down, the show is polished, and you guys sound great! You've got roadies, and your own sound technicians— you'll even have your own lighting company on the road that Dennis just hired! You're going to be a great success! You don't need me, Lou!'

'You're wrong,' he cried. 'I can't do this without you!'

'Baby,' I said, going to him, trying to soothe him, 'you'll be fine. You can do this—I know you can! You need to believe in yourself, without me. It's always been up to you, you know that. And now you've proved you can do this! You don't need me!'

'No,' he said, grabbing me until it hurt. 'I do need you!'

'Yeah, but I don't want to be *needed*. I want to be *wanted*, Lewis, that's what *I* need,' I said, as softly and as gently as I could.

'Oh, come on, princess, you can't leave me now,' he said. He took my face between his hands and looked into my eyes, lowering his voice. 'Yes, I do need you, and I admit it. But I also want you.'

I didn't say anything. I'd said all I had to say.

'I do!' he said, fervently, kissing me.

This is supposed to convince me … how much?

I wasn't buying it, and I decided to tell him my plans.

'Look,' I said, 'I called Bill Esper and set up an appointment for an interview with him this week to see if I can get into his Advanced Acting class at his new acting studio. I've got a chance, because he knows me from the Playhouse. He always liked my work, I think—but I can't be sure. I need to go through the process.'

'Oh, my god, you're serious!' he exclaimed. Smacking his forehead, he broke away from me and strode into the kitchen. I heard the ice tray leaving the freezer, the slam of its door. The sharp crack of ice into the glass, the trickle of sly scotch sliding over ice cubes.

I dropped my bag on the entrance table and slowly moved into the dining room, where I sat down at our sleek, shining clean, glass-and-steel dining-room table. This apartment was much larger; the table was the one thing I'd wanted that, from our tight budget, he'd allowed me to buy, and I loved it. But as I listened to the preparations in the kitchen for the drinking to begin, I felt my stomach roll over and I started feeling nauseous. What time was it, anyway? Two or three in the afternoon?

Oh, no.

Our new apartment was furnished more like a home than our last. We'd finally gotten a bed, and in our bedroom, I'd hand-treated the window shades and hung the curtains my grandmother made and sent for our engagement present. The delicately embroidered Belgian lace cast gossamer shadows from the light of the candles I lit every night to remind me of her.

My grandmother was the only one in my family who I told that I was living with Lewis, because she wouldn't freak out. To her, it was practical. When I was an adolescent, she once told me, 'You wouldn't buy a pair of shoes without trying them on, would you?' When my grandmother was a young woman in Norway, it was the norm for betrothed couples to live together before they were married; in olden times, it was even a legal requirement.

This apartment, our second, which we'd only recently moved into, was a one-bedroom apartment and much nicer than our first, that cardboard box of a studio on 78th Street—which had been a dump, really. But this was a real home in an old, established, more respectable apartment building. It had a canopied entrance, along with the requisite creaking elevator.

The apartment, on the third floor, came with an entry foyer and parquet wooden floors throughout; it had a separate dining room with a large living room that got great light. We had our breakfast in a small but efficient eat-in kitchen facing East 73rd Street, between East End Drive and First Avenue.

Although Lewis insisted we hold on to the cheap living-room furniture from our studio apartment, I loved our bedroom, and this place. We would be married here, only a year later. *Transformer* and *Berlin* would be written in this apartment, and it was here that we experienced the battles chronicled and fictionalized in *Berlin*, along with our divorce, reunion, and final split.

I'd wanted to make our bedroom a restful and relaxing retreat where we could enjoy our time off, after running around town, or back at home, off tour for a few days, and I'd succeeded. Lou loved it. But now all I could hear from there was Lou yelling at someone, probably Fred, his new manager. He'd starting yelling recently on tour. I put my head in my hands.

* * *

Our latest home wasn't much, but it was far more comfortable than our old studio. Lewis continued to be very conservative about money, but this was all right with me. It made me feel secure knowing he watched over our finances.

Sister Ray Enterprises provided us with a check, expressed to us each Monday from management to cover expenses. It was somewhat generous—certainly more than we had been living on a shoestring before—but it was still no-frills. Management paid our rent and utility bills. We were living a little better than we were before, and a private car was hired to take us around the city or back and forth to the airport. We no longer needed to hail taxis at all hours of the night and early morning when we went out.

We often ordered take out or ate at a small, quiet restaurant, the Duck Joint. It was a couple of doors up the block below street level, and was one of our favorite places. It was very private and beautifully lit—sparse but elegant in its simplicity. We acquired a serious taste for their escargot in a scrumptious garlic-and-butter sauce, which was served without us having to order it, accompanied by a nice bottle of chardonnay. I developed a preference for *Pouilly Fuisse*.

I heard Lewis slam down the phone, and the tinkling of the scotch in his glass, as he came out into the dining room and sat down at the end of the table.

'What do you want?' he asked quietly, folding his hands in front of him, his ever-present scotch within reach.

'Hmmm?' I asked, slowly turning to him.

Is there any way on God's green earth I can calm this man down?

I slid him a coaster, and he carefully put his glass down on it.

'What do you want?' he asked. 'To go back on tour.'

I looked at him, then said, very quietly, 'I don't want to go on tour, anymore.'

'I need you to be with me,' he said, reaching for my hand.

I let him take it and rested my head on my other one, propped on my elbow.

'But, Lou—'

'No, what do you want,' he asked, for the third time. 'How can I get you to come with me?'

'You mean, how can you get me to do what you want?' I replied, running my gaze over the fine features of his face. His cheekbones had softened, and his face had filled in, from the drinking.

'Yes, if you want to put it that way,' he answered.

'Lou, I—'

'Isn't there something I can do or give you that would bring you back on tour with me?' he asked.

I sat and simply looked at him. It took me a while to answer.

'All I do is take care of you.'

'I'm sorry. I told you it would be tough out there.'

'Yes, but I didn't agree to that. I'm not a nurse, and I'm not a cop, Lewis. I hate it.'

'Well, is there something else you'd rather do?'

'Yeah, if I had a real job on the road.'

'Like what?' he asked.

'I don't know.'

'Do you want to do publicity? You can write.'

'I don't need to go on the road to do that.'

'Well, is there something you'd like to *do* on the road?' he asked, his voice rising a little.

I could see the skin around his mouth tightening. He was talking through nearly clenched teeth.

'I don't have any training for what you do,' I said. 'The only thing I'm trained to do right now is work on a stage.'

'Well, I work on a stage.'

'Yes, but what can I do on your stage?'

'Isn't there something you like onstage that you could do, *other than act*?' he asked. His voice rose even higher.

'Like what?' I asked. 'All that would interest me, I guess … might be lights. I like lights. But you've got your own lighting company now. I'm assuming there's someone running that show.'

'Wait a minute!' he nearly shouted. An imaginary light bulb flashed on, above him.

Oh, no.

'How about running the lights? Wouldn't you like to do that?'

He was visibly excited.

I wonder if he's acting, I thought.

'How would I do that?' I asked. I don't know anything about lights.'

'Yes you do. You're an actress.'

'Yes, but there's the plots the lighting designer draws up. It's all very technical. I don't know how lights work or how to light a rock'n'roll show.'

'What if I got one of the lighting guys to teach you?'

Really? Now that might be interesting.

'Could you do that?' I asked.

'Sure I could.'

'How?'

'I'd just ask them.'

'What if they said no?'

'They're not going to.'

'How do you know that?' I asked.

'Because I'm the boss. They work for me.'

'Really,' I said.

This is true, I thought. *Don't we all?*

'But wouldn't they resent that?' I asked. 'I mean, surely, that's something they'd like to do. Isn't that why you hired them?'

'Not really—we hired them for their lights, but they don't know the songs like you do! It'll take them a while to learn them. But you already know them!'

'Okay, but I'd still need to learn all the technical part.'

'They can teach you that!' he said. 'Don't you think you could learn it?'

Throwing down a gauntlet, eh? Nice.

'Yes, I think I probably could, but when would I do that?' I asked.

'On the road.'

'*On ... the ... road.*'

'Yes, on the road,' he said, as slowly as I had.

Well, maybe that could work, I thought. *That would be a job. I'd actually love to learn lights. It would also help me, as an actress. In that sense, he's right: I do know something about lights. And I know all of his lyrics and am very familiar with his music.*

Maybe I could light him! The music would probably tell me how, and maybe I could even highlight his lyrics. He's always complaining no one pays any attention to his lyrics. Maybe I could do something about that?

'So, what do you say?' he asked.

'I'm thinking,' I said.

'Well, how long is that going to take you?' he asked excitedly. 'All you have to do is say yes, and I'll call Dennis, get him to call the lighting people, and tell them what we want.'

'That's all it'll take?'

That went right over his head, I thought. *Good.*

'Yes. Just say the word, princess, and I'll make the call.'

on the road, part two........ CHAPTER EIGHT

At Lou's request, it was written into his contract that a bottle of Johnnie Walker Red and another of Courvoisier be in the dressing room of every venue we played. Although he was never drunk onstage in the beginning, the late 60s and early 70s were wild times, and drug and alcohol abuse was rampant in rock'n'roll. So I never questioned Lou's behavior too much on tour—until it became problematic.

Lou guzzled more scotch back at the hotel after the shows, and before and during dinner, topping it all off with a couple of more Courvoisiers before I could finally get him up to the room in whatever condition he was in and into bed so that he could get some sleep and be ready for the next show, either the next day or a couple of days later.

The sheer volume of scotch he was consuming alarmed me. In the last three years alone, Janis Joplin, Jimi Hendrix, and Jim Morrison had all died from drug overdoses. Like Lou, they were also famous for drinking excessively, and their drinking certainly contributed to their deaths. Although Lou wasn't using drugs at the beginning of the tour, it would only be a matter of time before they were thrown into the mix, too. We lost one of these greats every year. I was at Lisa Robinson's house when she got the call from Jim's girlfriend, asking what she should do? Jim was dead in the bathtub.

I didn't want to lose Lou! His drinking scared me silly, but there was nothing I could do except monitor him as best I could.

At first, he seemed to be handling it reasonably well. But then he began to lose control. By the time we finished dinner each night, he was slurring his words. Despite my attempts to keep the number of scotches he swigged down, a couple of times he began slurring during performance, although he hid it by changing his delivery or engaging in stage antics. And a couple of times he completely forgot lyrics, but he was able to bluff his way through those lapses, too.

As the tour went on, his behavior changed in direct proportion to the amount of alcohol he consumed. Along with slurring and memory loss, he became short-tempered, easily irritated, and belligerent. It was hard for me to watch his deterioration, but I blamed a lot of it on all the pressure he put himself under to succeed in his new career, which, coupled with our nomadic lifestyle on the tour, was quite stressful and disorienting.

Around this time, Lou slowly began gaining weight. At first, it wasn't apparent, because he wore his T-shirts out over his pants and could hide his burgeoning belly from everyone but me. But when he split his pants onstage because they were too tight, and we had to buy a larger pair for him, he couldn't hide it anymore. He laughed it off like it was nothing, and everyone humored him, laughing along with him. Everyone except me, because I also shared his bed. I also started getting pressure to do something about his weight.

He became less cooperative with me about his drinking, and when I tried to distract him, he realized what I was doing. This made it more difficult, because Lewis didn't like anyone maneuvering him. I didn't want to run the risk of him resenting me, because he'd only drink more, in defiance.

Telling Lewis 'no' about anything outright was, frankly, never a successful tactic. I walked on eggshells for days—weeks—at a time. When we were out for long stretches without going home for a break,

I was exhausted, and I became tense and quiet, holding all the pressure I was feeling inside. I smiled at everyone and pretended like everything was okay. *Not to worry, I can handle him.* But I was getting seriously worried I couldn't.

As Lou's drinking got worse, nobody could get through to him except me. My constant watch over him evolved into becoming a conduit between Lou and everyone else, and the go-between with him and management. I'd been successfully assigned the role of bad guy on the road. No one dared to bring up his drinking with him; unfortunately for me, it was my job to monitor and try to prevent his inclination toward excess. If I was unsuccessful, I felt the heat.

Then somebody on the road started supplying Lewis with cocaine. Initially, I assumed that it had something to do with the breakdown in his tolerance for alcohol, and I'm sure that was a factor. At first, he only snorted a little before the show, to give himself some energy before performing, and then afterward, to wind down and forget about it. But his drug consumption increased as the tour continued.

With my manic schedule, Lewis could see that I was exhausted, so he suggested I try some. I noticed that everyone walking around sniffling with what appeared to be an incurable cold got a lot of work done. They were wide awake, productive, and in positive spirits due to this drug. So I gave it a shot—and, indeed, it worked. It kept me awake and alert and gave me energy for my incessant watch over Lewis, as well as my work as lighting director. But I prefer being in the driver's seat of my life, and I get real anxious if I'm not. I get little lasting pleasure from anything I become dependent upon, and cocaine is notorious for the dependency its users rapidly develop. I didn't use it when I wasn't on the road, and throughout our relationship, Lewis and I never used it when we were home alone. Then, Lou only wanted me.

Despite finding the tour more and more unbearable, I had made a commitment to do the lighting job. I couldn't get out of it, and nor did

I want to—I loved it, and I was good at it. Just as Lou had promised, the lighting guys taught me all the technical aspects of the job, and soon I could design Lou's lights to highlight his performance onstage, using the music and lyrics I knew by heart to instinctively guide me.

* * *

When we returned home on breaks from the tour, Lou started working on the material for his next album. This would become *Transformer*, the most commercially successful album of his solo career, which propelled him to international stardom. He jotted down his thoughts and ideas about *Transformer* in his notebook, which he always carried with him, even on the road. But Lou was usually too distracted to write when we were on tour. Much of the material in *Transformer* had already been written—these were songs he updated or revised from his time with the Velvets—so he didn't feel pressure about generating new material. But there were some new songs he was working on that he said were about me, including 'Perfect Day,' which he wrote about our day in Central Park.

David Bowie was integral to this next chapter of Lou's life. He ended up producing *Transformer* for Lou when he came to New York to negotiate a record deal with RCA, which Lou was instrumental in helping him get. We'd already seen David and his wife Angie in London, during the recording of the *Lou Reed* album. David's single-minded, steely determination and disciplined approach to his career impressed me, and I encouraged Lewis to get to know him better, because I thought he'd be good for him. I also thought he was the coldest person I'd ever met in my life.

During this period, David was consumed with becoming a star, as was Lou. But despite being somewhat distant when he met new people, he was always very gracious with me, and deferential to Lewis, as they huddled together, talking excitedly about their careers.

David was new on the scene in New York, a rising star. He was brilliant—a genuine original artist—and a great fan of Lou's. He knew Lou was starting out all over again in his solo career, and he deeply admired Lou's writing and work with The Velvet Underground. David genuinely wanted to help Lou succeed as a solo artist, but he also knew that being associated with Lou and his legendary cult status with the Velvets would, by association, bring him cachet and prestige himself, too.

Although it wasn't receiving an enormous amount of attention in the US yet, David's latest album, *Hunky Dory*, was doing well in the UK. We heard it when we were in London and discussed it at length. I loved the album, especially 'The Bewlay Brothers,' and Lewis agreed that David's writing had taken on new heights.

Lou began touting David to management at RCA, and to whomever else would listen. Behind closed doors, he'd already been in talks with his management about David, because Lou desperately wanted David to produce his new album. He figured that if he brought David into the fold, it would only make them closer. Producing the album was something the two of them had been discussing for some time.

Soon, we heard the good news that David was interested in producing *Transformer*. At home Lou was ecstatic about the news, although he never let anyone else know it. He played his usual cool— especially around David.

We had various meetings with David. One day we met Angie and David at the Park Lane Hotel on Central Park West, where David usually stayed when he was in town. While the boys exchanged ideas about their music and careers, Angie, Lou's manager, Barbara Wilkinson, and I went to see *The Godfather*. Then Angie and I met Lewis and David back at the hotel for dinner; afterward, the four of us went out to a party.

Lou and David ended up spending a considerable amount of time alone in a back room, with the doors shut. Angie started banging on the door, demanding to be let in. I danced, distancing myself from the scene Angie was making. I wasn't worried about David and Lou being alone together; they were probably continuing their conversation of that afternoon. They were both obsessed with their careers and ideas for their next albums.

But I also knew Lou wasn't particularly enamored with Angie, and thought she was loud and obnoxious; she was David's wife, though, so Lou was always respectful to her. In fact, I thought it was possible they were trying to stay away from her. Although Angie was confident, and everyone knew she was instrumental to David's career, she was pretty wild. This was not terribly unusual for many in that crowd, but David was quite the opposite from the madness around him; he was quiet, watchful, and extremely disciplined about his career, and right now, he and Lou were talking business.

I liked Angela, and I knew the challenges we shared in the difficult role as the partner of an up-and-coming rock star. Women were generally not treated well in the music industry, and Angie and I were no exception—we both took a back seat to our other halves, despite being the backbone of their careers. Often we were ignored and dismissed by the people around us as nothing more than bimbos. Of anyone, musicians were more likely to treat the girlfriends and wives of their fellow musicians with a modicum of respect. But other than an artist's management team—who knew the invaluable help the partners of musicians gave in managing and organizing them—women were not respected in the music industry, which was notoriously misogynistic.

Women were clerical workers, 'gofers,' or 'groupies'—tantamount to whores. They were treated as underlings or used for amusement, then tossed aside after they served their purpose, like used tissues. There were few female artists and musicians in the industry then, and even they struggled with being treated like second-class citizens.

To celebrate David's signing with RCA, we attended a dinner at the Ginger Man restaurant in New York, with David, Angie, RCA executives and their wives, and members of Lou's and David's management team.

As we got ready for dinner, Lewis spent a great deal of time on his hair but did little else. He wore jeans, a top, and his usual black leather jacket, but he didn't especially dress up. It wasn't his style; especially if someone was important to him, as was David, who, however covertly, Lou was courting. David made it known to the powers that be that he was very interested in working with Lou, but the more Lewis wished to impress someone, the less he acted like he cared. Girls were the only exception. He was polite, shy, and almost behaved like a high-school kid. It was how you could tell if he was really interested in you.

Lou mentioned a dress he thought I could wear, which surprised me. He never told me what to say, how to act, or what to wear. He always told me I looked great, whatever I wore. He had complete confidence and trust in me, and he let everyone around know it. It was one of the great things about being with him. But I hadn't dressed up in a long time, and I loved pleasing Lewis. It made me feel like a girl again. Working on the road, I hadn't felt like one in a long time, so I was looking forward to getting gussied up.

The dress Lou was talking about was one I had bought in London, when Angie and I went on a shopping spree on the Kings Road. It was a 1930s white, beautifully draped, crepe floral dress with padded shoulders and a gathered waist that I cinched with a broad, red leather belt. I wore my red stiletto platform heels (which we called 'fuck-me shoes' back then) to match.

I assumed Lou had suggested the dress because David had commented on it when Angie and I dressed up in the clothes we'd bought earlier. Angie wore a purple boa draped over a sleeveless pink top and lavender silk pants. She walked around, posing with cigarettes in a long holder, like she was Zelda in an F. Scott Fitzgerald novel.

We were driven in the private car organized by the record company to the restaurant. Lewis was serious; he hadn't talked much while we were getting dressed. I wasn't concerned, though, because that was how he usually was before we went out to important events for his career, as well as before he went onstage.

After the driver closed the door behind us, Lou slid over next to me and put his arm around my shoulders. He pulled me to him, and I put my head on his chest. It had been a long time since we'd been treated to luxury. Going out on the road made you feel like cheap, dime-store characters driving cross country for a long goodbye in a beat-up 1956 Chevy Bel Air, with empty bottles of booze piled up and rolling around on the coupe's rear floor. No matter how many showers you took, you still felt grungy.

Riding through Central Park to the restaurant, we talked not about the significance of the meeting but about the weather. That's what people do, isn't it? To fill the unspoken thoughts between them.

'I love New York in the rain,' I said. Drops were beginning to spatter on the side windows. They were so clean that, as they smacked the glass, I pulled back at first, because they looked like they were going to hit us.

So you're a little stressed, after all, I noted.

The driver turned the windshield wipers on. They whooshed rhythmically in the silence.

Lou kissed me.

'I love you,' he said quietly. 'There are no words to tell you how much.'

He leaned his head on mine.

'You'll find them,' I said, snuggling closer.

Lewis could be as tender and gentle as he was, at times, obnoxious and overbearing. I was content to cuddle quietly, because for now, the man I loved was back.

The Kronstad family homestead, Mt. Jackson, Pennsylvania, 1950. *Top row*: my uncles, Harold (aka Babe) and Knut. *Middle row*: a family friend; my grandmother, Gudrun Jensen; and my grandfather, Haavard. *Front row*: Mom, Bettye Saylor; me, age one; and Dad, Gudmund Haavard.

LEFT Me at age three, Mt. Jackson, Pennsylvania.
ABOVE Me at age two with Uncle Babe.
BELOW Dad, just before he shipped off for D-Day, with his dog, Tyler, May 1945.
OPPOSITE PAGE Two photos of Mom, taken after she lost custody of me and relocated to New York.

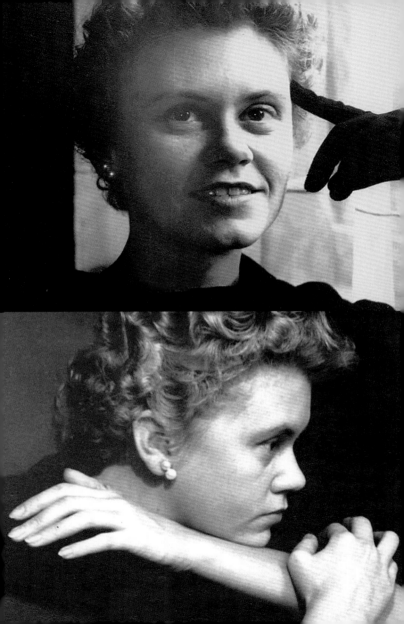

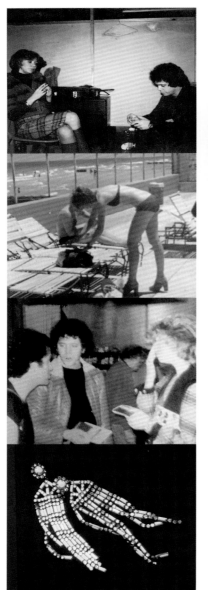

ABOVE Lou and me on our wedding day in 1973. **LEFT, FROM TOP** Snapshots of our relationship, 1971–2: backstage in Philadelphia; sunbathing in Miami; with road manager Steve; the antique earrings Lou bought me in London.
OPPOSITE PAGE Lewis looking pensive in a London hotel room during the promotional tour for *Transformer*.

Lou and me at the after-party following his concert at Lincoln Center, New York, January 1973.

ABOVE Lou, Mick Jagger, David Bowie, and Lulu (*standing*) at the Cafe Royal, London, July 1973. **LEFT** Lou onstage at the Carre Theatre in Amsterdam, September 1973. **BELOW** Me and my daughters, Krista Gudrun and Samantha Anne, in 2006.

We rode in silence for a while when suddenly, out of nowhere, he said, 'Do you know how proud I am to be seen with you?'

The darkness of the night and interior of the sedan enclosed us in our own little world, gliding over the glazed, wet streets of the city.

'Don't be silly,' I responded, smacking him lightly on his chest.

'The other day I read in one of our reviews the journalist called you statuesque. I thought, after I'd read it, you *are* a tall drink of water.' He laughed and pulled me closer.

'The guys I played basketball with at Riverside used to call me that,' I said.

'Yeah, well, they know,' Lou said.

'You're just jealous,' I teased.

'I mean, just how long are your legs,' he asked, laughing.

'I don't know,' I said, sighing.

He's nervous, I thought. *And directing his attention to me, to take his mind off it.* That's okay. I'm a girl and could use a compliment now and then. Most of the time I felt like just another one of the guys.

This was a major night for him, and I wanted to do everything I could to make sure he enjoyed it. Lewis loved my red 'f—me', stilettos, and tonight I'd worn them just for him. I thought pairing overtly sexual shoes with such a ladylike dress was a gas.

'I am a very lucky man, and tonight, when I walk in with you, everyone in the Ginger Man will be jealous. They'll all wonder, *Now, how did this short Jewish kid from the wrong side of Long Island end up with that tall, gorgeous blonde?'*

'Everyone already wonders how I snapped you up,' I shot back, laughing.

'They're all jealous,' he said, 'and don't you ever forget it.'

We rode quietly as the rain beat down on the leather rooftop over our heads. Occasionally, a car horn blared around us, but otherwise it was unusually quiet, or maybe it was just the rain dulling the usual chaos of New York City traffic. It was the dinner hour, and everyone was probably just sitting down to their martinis after making another Manhattan million.

Since we'd been on the road, Lou and I were so far away from this world, it was a comfort to know it was still here. Miles of truck stops, turnpikes, airports, and cheap motels were all we'd seen for months. We'd traveled endless stretches of lonely roads, crisscrossing the great middle land of America, making our way, back and forth over it. Back home, we were surrounded by sharp, beautifully dressed, insistent, ambitious people, armed with enormous drive and egos, determined to make it big. It made our dream of Lou making it closer to reality, and this world was a relief after the endless, empty farmland stretching out over the land of my childhood—and from where I had come only four years ago.

I always knew Lewis was destined for great things, and I wanted to be by his side when he made it. It was why I worked so hard and tolerated things I probably wouldn't normally have. I believed in this man and his work.

Lulled by the gentle movement of our car, I fell into a half sleep, and began dreaming about a morning somewhere in the distance. We'd wake up early on a Saturday morning, eager to get ready for the regatta we were registered to compete in at Larchmont, New York. I imagined our J-27 yacht, lined up and poised at the starting line with all the gazillion dollar yachts and, once the starting horn sounded, we pushed forward, a veritable knife in the water. Despite the fickle wind of the Long Island Sound, because of our crew's astonishing boatmanship and our crafty racing tactics, we drove first over the finish line as the winning boat in our class, once again. We won!

Now that would fun, getting Lewis on a sailboat. Almost as much fun as on a horse.

I chuckled at the thought, and he looked down at me.

'What are you laughing about,' he asked sternly, pretending to be gruff. Then he squeezed me harder, pressing me closer to him.

'*You*!' I said. Then I leaned into his ear and whispered, 'I'm here, baby.'

'And, *Jesus*, this Jew thanks you!' he said, kissing me, again.

For the rest of our ride, other than complimenting me, Lou was a bit closed off and serious, no doubt thinking about how the rest of the evening should go. Both Lou and I knew how important this meeting was for his career, and we were both determined not to make any wrong moves or say anything that might jeopardize the impending deal of Bowie producing *Transformer*, which was what Lewis desperately wanted and knew he needed for his solo career. And to say goodbye to The Velvet Underground forever.

At the Ginger Man restaurant, David was dressed in an attention-grabbing flamboyant outfit. So was Angie, who wore her hair in a short, spiked 'butch' haircut. With David's hair, long and flowing over his shoulders, and his loud, flashy clothing, the entire restaurant turned around when they walked in. David's desire to create attention and be noticed had worked.

During dinner, I was quiet and smiled a lot. I was respectful and attentive—perhaps even more so once I saw and observed how respectful and attentive Lou and David were to each other. Each man knew the other would be extremely helpful in his career.

Everyone congratulated David on his new alliance with RCA, and those responsible for the pairing were very pleased with themselves. But in truth, it was a quiet dinner, and nothing spectacular happened. Angie twinkled brightly and loud, but that was her usual behavior, so no one paid her much attention, really. As we were leaving, people shook hands, congratulating one another and extending good wishes to all. Lou and I went out to the car, ready to drive over to the Robinsons' house for the party.

* * *

Soon we were back on the road to complete the last leg of the *Lou Reed* tour. Newspaper reviews of the shows began to mention the lights. I smiled to myself when I read the Boston review that gave Andy Warhol credit for designing them. 'White Light/White Heat' was mentioned, during which I lit Lou with a single downstage white light from directly overhead. The song's opening chords began in total blackout, and then a single white spot hit Lou front and center as he sang the first line of the song.

The contrast with Lou, dressed in his black leather pants and jacket, was striking, and created an ominous star presence onstage. Dennis commented somewhat critically that he couldn't imagine how Lou could tolerate so much blinding white light, but Lou loved it. He knew I'd also designed them to reflect the first lines of his song: '*White light goin' messin' up my mind / Don't you know it's gonna make you go blind …*'

When I told Lou about Andy being credited for my lighting design, he laughed and said, 'You see, kid, I was right. You're a natural!'

Lou thought that any way Andy Warhol could be tied to his solo career was only to his benefit, and that it would add prestige to the show. He brought up his association with Andy whenever possible. I'd heard him mention Andy in articles, interviews, and comments to the press hundreds of times for that very reason. I took Andy's credit for my design as a compliment, and I was happy that I was contributing positively to the show.

When I agreed to design Lou's lights, I didn't know what that job entailed, or that it included directing them during every show. The venues we played across the US ranged from clubs to large venues, and from a hundred to thousands of people. Directing the lights included 'calling' the spots from a headset, through which I told the technicians operating them which spots to use when, and in which color and intensity. Often the venues we played didn't have enough lighting technicians to operate the board for the stage lights and run the spots, so I learned how to operate the boards at every venue, running them during the show as I called the spots from my headset.

I gave the house technicians—seasoned professionals, mostly middle-aged men, and all members of a union—copies of the lighting plot, and reviewed all the lighting cues before the shows. Many expressed surprise at the number of cues, and occasionally they moaned at all the work. Some of them looked at me strangely, but then I realized they'd never met a female lighting director before. And I wasn't a member of the union, so I tried to get along. I was the boss's girlfriend, yes, but I was also good at my job.

In many of the venues, the lighting board was set up in the balcony, surrounded by the audience. The crowds Lou attracted were notorious for getting wild and were always loud, if not insanely so; even with headphones on, hearing was difficult. At many shows, members of the audience jumped all around me—screaming, high on alcohol, drugs, and Lou's music—so operating the board was often a real challenge.

I was happy doing my job, despite the fly-by-the-seat-of-your-pants nature of it, and Lou was very pleased with my lighting direction. In San Francisco, he conducted a live radio interview, which I attended. The interviewer mentioned how unusual it was for a rock star's girlfriend to direct his lights and asked Lou how I got the job.

Lou put his arm around me and replied that he didn't see any reason why I shouldn't. I had a theater background, he said, and he thought I'd be great—that's why he recommended me for the job. I proved to be a natural at it, and he was very happy with my work. Then he reminded the journalist that The Velvet Underground had a girl drummer—the only one in the business—and that Maureen was one of the best.

My name began appearing in the reviews of more of his shows as his lighting designer, along with the lights, all very positive. If I was backstage before the show and members of the audience caught sight of me, they started calling out my name. At first, I was startled; I smiled, waved, then hurried off.

I didn't want to upset Lou. He could be a bit competitive about who was in the limelight—and he wanted it to be him. I was more comfortable being in the background in these circumstances, so I made an effort to stay out of sight.

I was backstage before each show, anyway, because Lou wanted me there, both in his dressing room and in the wings, before he went onstage. He wanted me by his side at all times, and I was aware everyone else did, too. At the hotel, I would be reminded, 'Bettye, it's time to get Lou to the venue.' When it was time for the performance to begin, 'Bettye, get Lou onstage.'

At first, a routine had developed whereby I would escort him onto the stage before every performance, and he would kiss me for good luck as he left the wings. But now that I was calling the lights for the show, this routine was not possible. I had to leave him so the show could begin, and get up to the lighting booth as fast as I could.

One night, Lou landed onstage drunk. He began slurring, and he couldn't remember some of his lyrics. I'd been dealing with a lighting issue that surfaced before the show began, and I wasn't able to be with him in the dressing room, or in the wings before he went on. Apparently he drank far more than he should have, but nobody noticed it or said anything, until he got onstage. After this incident, I heard from everyone, 'Bettye! *Where were you?*'

From then on, Lou's reliance on me being around him at all times became intense. But I didn't know how I was going to be able to be backstage, and call the lights for the show. I didn't know what to do, so I went to Lou.

'Lou, I can't be both places at once! The show can't start until I'm in the booth!'

Lou looked at me like he didn't know what to say.

'Well, you wanted a job! Now that you've got one, what are you complaining about?' he cried in frustration, throwing up his hands in disgust. 'I need you backstage with me. It's obvious, isn't it?'

He shook his head, looked down, and put his hands on his hips. He seemed conflicted and annoyed, but I didn't know if it was with me or himself.

'Isn't there something that can be done?' I asked.

'I don't know,' he said.

We were back in our room at the hotel, after that calamitous show. He'd had time to sober up. He began pacing, seriously stressed. I started getting worried, because the last thing I wanted to do was upset him.

I wanted to call the show and be backstage with him, because I always managed to keep him calm and in a positive state of mind before he went onstage. But I didn't want to lose my job on the lights. It was the only thing keeping me sane on the road.

He looked around for something to drink, but there wasn't anything in the hotel room. We had just got in, and hadn't ordered anything up to the room.

'Don't we have anything to drink?' he asked.

'No, I don't think so, but don't you think you've had enough for one night?'

He looked at me like I'd slapped him. He was caught off guard, and I'd hurt him.

'What do you mean by that?' he asked, challenging me.

His tone and demeanor immediately changed to one of a disapproving parent—or a boss.

'Nothing, other than—'

'You wanted a job,' he repeated, slowly.

Yeah, I wanted a job, but I was also hoping you could start taking care of yourself, big guy!

I went over, and put my arms around him.

'Look, all I'm saying is, you don't want anything like what happened tonight, happen again, do you?' I asked, trying to console him.

'Of course not!' he cried, 'I can't afford that! But I need you with me. You keep me calm and focused.'

'Surely there must be something we can do,' I replied, brushing his hair out of his eyes. It was wet and flat, plastered to his forehead.

'Yeah, there is! I can ask the guys to take over the lights for you! They've got the lighting plot, they can do it now! Do you want me to do that?' he asked, looking up at me.

'No …' I said.

Neither of us said anything for quite some time.

'Or,' he continued, 'maybe the guys could play a little, after they tune their guitars, before the lights go up.'

He looked away, waiting for my answer.

'That'll work,' I said. 'I'll just have our guys ghost the stage till I get up to the lights, and then you can come on, and the show can start. We'll just work on the opening. Shouldn't be a problem!'

'*After* you give me my kiss. *Then* go to the lighting booth,' he added, looking back at me.

I got the message.

'Do you want to come out as we raise the lights, or do you want to come out in dim, take your place, then we raise the lights?' I asked.

'You're the lighting designer. What do you think?' he shot back.

'No … what would you prefer? You open with "Sweet Jane," now, don't you?

'Yes.'

'That's not a problem. Let the guys play the opening chords of "Sweet Jane" before you come out. That'll be the signal I'm in place. Our lighting guys will bring the lights down onstage, and that'll be your cue to enter. I'll dim just enough so you can see to get onstage, they'll keep playing. When you're ready, they'll get louder, as you join in with them. We'll bring the lights up full then, you'll be onstage ready to sing, and the show will begin!'

Lou thought about it, then quickly said, 'That'll work.'

'Great!' I responded.

I put my arms around his neck and kissed him.

'You're such a sweetie,' I said.

'Really?'

He held me for a bit, then said, 'Hey, why don't we just spend the night here?'

'You mean order up? What about the rest of the guys downstairs?'

He started nibbling my ear.

'You want me to call down to the restaurant?' I asked, giggling.

'In a minute,' Lou said.

transformer, part one............

CHAPTER NINE

The time we spent in London, while *Transformer* was being recorded, was one of the most enjoyable periods of our relationship. After all the hard work touring *Lou Reed* and preparing for the next step in his solo career, when Lou wasn't in the studio we finally had a chance to relax, socialize, and have a good time. Within a couple of months of its release in December of 1972, this album—the most famous of Lou's career—suddenly rocketed him onto the world stage, where he would remain for the rest of his life. Only two years after walking away from The Velvet Underground, and not long after the commercial flop of his self-titled solo debut, we had succeeded in launching his solo career.

When David Bowie, hot off the success of his chart-topping *Ziggy Stardust*, entered the scene, producing *Transformer* with guitarist Mick Ronson, suddenly the world was Lou's oyster. Other than Andy Warhol, who 'discovered' The Velvet Underground, and, by association, gave the Velvets fame and notoriety, David Bowie was the single most important piece in Lou's play for international stardom in his solo career.

Lou's lyrics on *Transformer* discuss taboo topics about drag queens, drugs, and sexual acts that had never been heard on the radio before. But Lou wrote about them so subtly, and Bowie produced *Transformer* with such style and polish, that when the first single from the album, 'Walk On The Wild Side,' slid slyly onto the airwaves, gliding past first the 'suits' at RCA Records and then the radio censors, it made *Billboard*'s Top 100 and the Top 10 in the UK charts. Suddenly Lou had the hit that had always eluded The Velvet Underground—and it brought him worldwide fame.

Flying to London for the recording of *Transformer* was light-hearted in comparison to all the hours of meetings with record company bosses solidifying contractual obligations in preparation for its recording—and a genuinely welcome break from the grueling *Lou Reed* tour across America. On the road, my 24/7 personal responsibility for looking after Lewis had slowly but inevitably evolved into the part of our relationship that I most hated. Here in London, though, it felt like Lou and I could finally have fun again.

David and Angela Bowie welcomed us into their London social circles. Angela rented a house for us in Wimbledon, but we didn't live there because Dennis had booked us into a luxurious suite at the Inn On the Park Hotel, overlooking London's Hyde Park, where he was staying with his wife, Anne. I spent most of my days with Lewis at Trident Studios in London's SoHo district, as *Transformer* was being recorded with Mick Ronson, Herbie Flowers, Klaus Voormann, and other studio musicians who occasionally sat in, including the Thunder Thighs—the female trio who provided the backing vocals to 'Walk On The Wild Side.'

Transformer took little more than three weeks to make, start to finish. The Inn On The Park, now known as the Four Seasons Hotel London at Park Lane, was right by Hyde Park Corner, and 'swinging London,' which began in the 60s, was still in its heyday. Ever since the British Invasion, London had become the most 'groovy' city in the world, topping even New York and Paris.

Dennis and Anne wined and dined us at the best restaurants in London, and Angie and David took us to some of their favorite haunts like the Cafe Royal on Regent Street. We all loved Chinese, so we often had dinner at the best, Mr. Chow's in Knightsbridge. When Lewis was working in the studio at night, I went to the theater with Anne and Dennis, or with Angie, to the West End on a girl's night out. As an acting student at the Playhouse, I'd attended Broadway plays regularly, and had seen some great British actors onstage, including Richard Burton and Anthony Hopkins, but when Angie and I saw Sir John Gielgud in David Storey's *Home*, I was overwhelmed by his legendary prowess onstage and the brilliance of acting in British theater.

After Gielgud's play, Angie and I met Lou and David at the Dorchester Hotel for a photo shoot. Iggy Pop had also turned up, which I was happy about, because I always liked Jimmy—as I knew him. But during this period Lewis tended to distance himself from Jimmy because he was struggling with a drug problem and wasn't in the best of shape. Lou liked to surround himself with successful people, and he had decided that Jimmy was a loser—and he was a little rough around the edges then.

One of Lewis's least attractive qualities was that if he thought you were going through a difficult period in your life, he didn't want to be associated with you. He could easily shut down or cut you out of his life completely—as though he had no struggles of his own. I'd seen Lou ignore Jimmy at Max's, at the end of the night or when no one important was around, which wasn't nice. But when Jimmy didn't feel the need to live up to his wild reputation, like Lou, I thought he was a sweetheart. Everybody went through good periods and bad, and Jimmy's struggle with drug dependency was one of his toughest.

When Lewis heard Angie and I raving about the play and Gielgud's performance, he told me he wished he'd gone to see the play with us, as he enjoyed good theater. But he had a job to do, and the photographs taken that night proved to be worthwhile for Lou, David, and Iggy, as they were published all over the world, and were terrific publicity for Lou and the soon-to-be-released *Transformer* album.

Lou and I went shopping with Dennis and Anne on Portobello Road Market. On one of these excursions, Lou bought me a pair of beautiful 1920s lapis blue earrings. Long and dramatic, and studded with tiny, hand-cut crystals, he thought I could carry them off, and despite the price, he insisted on buying them for me. They remain one of my most treasured pieces of jewelry, not only because of how unique and beautiful they are, but because they represent the first flush of success in Lou's solo career and our relationship at its highest, most positive peak.

Dennis nearly convinced Lewis to buy a suit of armor in Knightsbridge, after Lou fell in love with it. Although it carried a price tag of thousands of pounds, Lewis was entranced with it. Few know this, but Lewis was enamored by the concept of courtly love, and Dennis had almost convinced Lewis that the suit of armor was going for a bargain! It didn't sound like one to me, and when Lou saw the price of the total package, once the shipping and insurance costs were added to the purchase—at the last minute—he decided not to spend the money. Later on, back at our hotel suite, he expressed regret for not buying it.

'Well, why didn't you?' I asked him.

That's when he whirled around to me and cried, 'We can't afford it! Who do you think is paying for all this luxury?' he asked, waving his arms, and gesturing around the room.

'This ridiculous suite of rooms! I mean, it's nice, but we don't need all this, do we?'

'Not really,' I said.

'And what about Dennis and Anne's equally luxurious suite? And all the dinners they're taking us out to around town, which Dennis will write off as a business expense? Who do you think's picking up that tab, even though Dennis is signing all over the town for everything now? *Us*!

'Of course Dennis wanted me to buy that suit of armor,' Lou continued, practically ranting, 'because then he could point to all the ridiculous luxuries *I'm* spending piles of money on, and he wouldn't look like the schmuck he is, running through all our money like it's water! We've worked like dogs for everything we've got, Bettye! And Dennis is throwing it away on what? Luxurious hotel suits nobody needs or wants, the best restaurants, shopping, West End shows—and a full body shining knight's suit of armor? Even though I really wanted it, it's not gonna happen, because I'm not that stupid! They're living off of us because they don't have any talent themselves, don't forget that.'

He had a point, which I kept in the back of my mind, but I began to watch Dennis and Anne as they took us to all the best places around town, and I saw that they were also using this opportunity to show off their sophisticated taste and superior cultural status to the likes of us rock'n'roll ruffians. Little did they know that my *grandmother*, a fine sculptress in her own right, had, as a young woman, worked as a designer in the store where the royal family of Norway bought the material from which their clothing was made before she came to America. But of course the occasion never came up for me to say that or anything about my background, really. Lewis opened my eyes to a lot, and some of it hurt, but it didn't matter to me in the end, because I knew Lou and I had each other—we were going to be a great success. It was already happening, only a year after he began his solo career!

I will always remember the night Angie brought Lulu, Petula Clark, and Dusty Springfield to our hotel suite—all at once—to meet Lou. 'Walk On The Wild Side' was getting a lot of coverage on the radio in London and climbing the UK charts. They all wanted to meet him.

This may have been one of the few times I saw David and Lou overwhelmed by the sheer power of the female wattage in the room—the place was agog with goddesses! Neither Lou nor David acknowledged it, but Lou flirted outrageously with them. I thought it was cute, because I'd already died and gone to heaven. I'd been listening to these three incredible women sing since before I wore a bra.

David seemed overwhelmed to be in the same room as all these famous women, and he left as quickly as possible soon after they arrived. Just as he was leaving, he suddenly turned around and looked me up and down, paying particular attention to the 1920s white floral English dress I'd picked up antique shopping with Angie. But instead of simply paying me or the dress a compliment, he abruptly turned around to Angie and said, 'Why can't you wear a dress, like *her*?' before stalking out of the room. The joke was that this was probably the first time I'd been in a dress for a year.

Both Lou and I noticed there was some tension between David and Angie, but we didn't dwell on it. They had an entirely different relationship to us, and they drew very different boundaries around their marriage than either Lou or I would be comfortable with—an open relationship with lovers. But they made a great team; as a married couple and parents to their young son, Zowie, they were obviously committed to one another.

It was clear that Angie was the key player in David's quest for stardom in a different but equally powerful way as I was in Lou's career, at this point. But Lou and I were both painfully aware of the toll this could have on personal relationships, so we were the last ones to pass judgment on theirs.

* * *

The *Transformer* period was a great time in our relationship. After the album was recorded, we toured constantly in the US and Europe. But when we were back home, our lives were filled with openings, industry gatherings, and parties, followed by late nights at Max's Kansas City. The New York press fawned over Lewis, and I became used to light bulbs popping when Lou and I turned up in public in New York and London. Our names were noted in newspapers, while lots of women— and men—aimed their attributes at him and opened fire.

It was a heady time, filled with extraordinary possibilities, and the future looked exciting. Lou and I were a bit startled by all the fuss, but he rose to the occasion. I had my hands full making sure he was in the right condition to make whatever commitments he had the following day.

From the beginning of our relationship I told Lou in no uncertain terms that if I saw a needle anywhere near him, I would—without fail—leave him. Hard drugs were his Achilles' heel, and I knew they would destroy him if he started taking them again, as he had before we starting going together.

With the pressures from the record company and management booking us on such a heavy rehearsal and touring schedule, the lethal combination of hard drugs and Lou Reed could only lead to disaster. I'd already left my own career to concentrate on his, and I refused to have anything to do with him throwing away his career. His alcohol consumption was difficult enough to monitor, and it had already become almost a full time occupation for me. And now I had to try to keep him away from cocaine, too.

I was totally unaware of the uphill battle I was fighting. Lewis had a weakness for drugs and he couldn't stop drinking alcohol if it was around. I gave him my ultimatum about hard drugs, and we never snorted cocaine or even smoked marijuana at home when we were alone—it never even came up between us.

After we returned home to New York, following the recording of *Transformer*, Lewis was on a fantastic high from his work in London and the growing success of 'Walk On The Wild Side.' The album was climbing the charts on both sides of the Atlantic, and sales in Europe had begun to rise. Even sales of Velvet Underground albums had increased since Lou's solo success. Dennis was scheduling the US *Transformer* tour, and my relationship with Lou was probably at its all time best.

* * *

Soon, Lewis asked, once again, if we could become officially engaged, suggesting again that we go to Tiffany's and choose my engagement ring. He saw that I was becoming more mature and confident—hence, probably, more attractive—and he wanted to secure our relationship in everyone's eyes. I was his, and he wanted everyone to know it. He also didn't want to lose me, as he truly didn't believe he could achieve the success he so desperately wanted without me.

Lou never considered any other store to buy an engagement ring but Tiffany's—in his mind, that was it. I hadn't really thought about it, but once he started talking about it again, I agreed to go with him the following Saturday and look around.

The truth is, I didn't grow up pining for an engagement ring or marrying the perfect man, although most of the girls I went to school with did. I was expected to go to college and become a teacher—at least that's what my grandfather had always wanted for me. He took out an insurance policy the week I was born to ensure funds would be available for my college education. Outside of New York and maybe Chicago, back in those days, girls in the US had basically three professional occupations to pursue—if they didn't get married directly out of high school, which most did.

In 1970—the year I would have graduated from college, had I begun directly after high school—only 8.2 percent of women in the US had college degrees. But my father's older sister, my aunt, obtained her bachelor's degree from Penn State in 1945, the year my father was fighting in World War II. My grandfather got his engineering degree in Germany in the 1920s. Both of my uncles obtained degrees in engineering as well. It was something that was expected of me, too. But the options open to girls at that time, generally, were going to business college, which I seriously disliked the idea of; getting a degree in nursing, for which I had no aptitude or desire; or becoming a teacher in your favorite subject, which seemed most likely for me. At that time in the US, teaching was still considered an honorable profession, and girls who were a bit artistic or creative, like me, were encouraged to enter that field. The fact that I had wanted to be a writer since I was nine years old was never even discussed. What kind of living could I make as a writer to support myself? I couldn't depend upon anybody to support me, and I wasn't raised to expect a man to, so I needed a profession that could. Writing? Poetry? I never even mentioned it, although all my English teachers encouraged me to pursue it.

Getting engaged had never been a goal for me, and I'd never even thought about what kind of engagement ring I'd want. Jewelry wasn't something that meant a great deal to the women in my family. Land, a substantial home, and quality of life was what I was brought up to value—get a good education, a job you loved, and make something of your life. When you were ready, marry a good man and raise a family together—in that order! But it was clear Lou wasn't going to let go of the idea of getting my engagement ring, so we took the train to 59th Street and then walked over to Tiffany's.

As Lou and I were shown one classic diamond solitaire engagement ring after another, my heart fell, although Lou was very happy and encouraged me to try all of them on. I did, but only half-heartedly. I realized that Lou was buying a ring to please himself, but it felt somehow off to me. If he was determined to get me an engagement ring, shouldn't he at least ask if there was some place I would like to go to look for an engagement ring? Of course, thinking that only made me feel like I was being ungrateful, but I didn't see any rings I liked, anyway.

Shopping in Tiffany's did not accurately reflect our relationship, because it was all about the cost, and it made me feel like I was some kind of commodity. I believed our relationship was—or should be—an equal investment in a partnership. Wearing something flashy and expensive on my ring finger attesting to Lou's commitment to me just wasn't how I was raised. I was taught to value investments that reflected solidarity, stability, and permanence, and a Tiffany's engagement ring didn't reflect any of these things to me. A simple band of gold was what my grandparents wore, as did all the members of my family. It was exchanged between a couple as a symbol of love and commitment in quietly personal vows before God in a church they attended in their own community, surrounded by members of their family. Large, blown-out weddings were unheard of and, frankly, in our culture, they were viewed as vulgar displays of wealth—in a word, gauche. I was old-school.

Knowing how important all this was for Lewis, I happened to see, in passing, a silver locket threaded with a thin, black satin ribbon with delicate edging. It caught my eye, and I suddenly stopped and asked the saleswoman if I could see it. It was made to wear around the waist and large enough to hold a keepsake or photograph inside, and it was what I asked Lou to buy me. He was disappointed that I hadn't seen a ring I liked, but he gladly bought me the locket—if only to buy me *something* from Tiffany's. He tied it around my waist, and I wore it out of the store.

As we made out way down 59th Street toward Sixth Avenue, we came upon an old but well-established antique store displaying some beautiful estate jewelry in the window. I stopped and suggested we go in and see what they had. I knew that Lou wanted to buy me an engagement ring, and I guess I just felt more comfortable with antiques. Perhaps they represented permanence to me; I've always preferred them.

Lewis was not the kind of guy who frequented antique stores, but he humored me, hoping perhaps that I would find something in there I might like. The place was filled to the ceiling with all the glorious old antiques one expects to find in these kinds of shops near Fifth Avenue: fine furniture; extravagant crystal chandeliers gently shaking and tinkling as you walk by; crystal glasses and fine vases shimmering on glass shelves in the fading afternoon light.

Beautifully bound leather books lined the walls all the way to the back of the store, good oil paintings and delicate watercolors hung on the walls. It was a place that reflected back to a time and way of life I adored and grew up reading about in all the novels I voraciously consumed. There were rows of watches on the wall behind the glass case used as the main counter—and jewelry! Splendid, insanely beautiful, highly crafted necklaces dripping with diamonds, emeralds, and rubies—delicate diamond bracelets, bejeweled hat pins, grand old brooches with indecent diamonds in intricate filigreed silver and gold settings. And then I saw the rings of the estate jewelry discreetly displayed in beautiful blue velvet trays under the glass counter where an elderly looking, beautifully groomed gentleman stood and asked quietly if he could help us.

We walked over and smiled, and I looked down and quickly started scanning the jewelry laid out on the trays. I was an antique store aficionado; they were like gorgeous invisible magnets, pulling me in, and there was barely one I walked by alone without entering. I was expert at homing in on what I was looking for in less than a minute after walking in the door.

And that's when I spotted it. It lay on the end of the top row of rings with far more glamorous stones. A simple gold band, in which a single, deep red medium size round ruby lay embedded, with two garnets and small diamonds set on either side. I immediately pointed to it and asked the gentleman if I could see that one. It looked small—I wore a size 5½, and it fit perfectly. Solid and relatively modest, I could see the ruby, set in simple gold points, was a good stone. In its simplicity, it was a very beautiful ring.

Lou stepped up to the counter and took the ring from the old gentleman.

'Here let me,' he said, slipping the ring onto my finger. It looked lovely. I watched Lewis as he looked at the ring. He held onto my hand and turned it slightly this way, then that. I saw him register the varying shades of deep vermillion the stone turned as differing grades of light hit upon it. The two tiny diamonds on either side winked sharply, and the garnets drew your eye in softly before it rested once again on the smooth, round surface in the deep burgundy of the ruby set in the center.

Lou raised his eyes to mine, and I could see that he already knew. I didn't have to say it, but I wanted to humor him.

'I think I've found the ring.'

Lou said he thought it was lovely; it was not the sort of engagement ring he'd imagined buying me, but it looked very beautiful on my hand. He liked its simplicity, and the deep color of the stone. I could see that he liked it, too.

'It suits you,' he said, kissing me. 'The ruby is gorgeous and the setting is subtle—classic. I should have known Tiffany's wouldn't have been what you wanted. I see you here, among these fine things, and it's where you belong.'

'We'll take it,' he said, looking up at the elder gentleman waiting on us.

The man nodded and asked if he would be writing out a check.

Lewis told him yes, then turned to me and said, 'Let me look at it a moment.'

I took the ring off my finger and gave it to him. He studied it and then looked at the gentleman behind the counter.

'This is a ruby, right?' he asked, holding the ring up.

'Yes,' the gentleman replied.

'A very good one?' Lou asked.

'The finest,' the old gentleman replied. 'I have the paperwork right here …'

'That'll be fine,' said Lewis. Then he reached out and took my hand, and slowly put the ring back on my ring finger. He pulled me to him and whispered in my ear, 'Baby, always remember how much I love and need you. You are my princess and I will always love you, no matter what happens.'

I was so happy. This is, finally, how I wanted this to happen, even though I'd never imagined it. It was private. No one was hustling and bustling around, showing us flashy diamonds to impress our neighbors and best friends, quoting the carat content, the quality of color and grade of stone, or how much the darn thing cost. We were in a beautiful antique store surrounded by precious artifacts, fine books, paintings, and jewelry, and there was no one else in here but us, except for the courtly old gentleman behind the counter, who looked away discreetly so we could enjoy our moment together, alone.

Lewis was holding my hands and, yes—looking deep into my eyes.

Finally, turning to the man behind the counter, he said, 'We'll take the box with us.'

'Of course, sir,' the salesman responded. 'I will wrap that for you. It looks lovely on her, a classic choice. I hope you two will be very happy.'

'We will,' Lou said.

I was very quiet, looking at the ring on my hand.

This is real, I thought. *I'm going to marry this man.*

The thought sent shockwaves through my body, but then I suddenly looked at Lou. He was looking at me with eyes filled with love. I could see that he did, indeed, adore me. He wanted to make me happy. He scared the hell out of me, but I knew he was doing what he thought was the right thing by pushing everything and anything for his career. He was doing it for us. Even in a world full of craziness, I saw the man I loved. He was here, right beside me. So I leaned over and kissed him.

'Thank you, Lou,' I said. 'I love this. It is simple, and classic—special to you and me only.'

'And the original owner,' Lou reminded me.

'I hope you don't mind me saying anything,' the old gentleman interjected from the other side of the counter, after clearing his throat, 'but I know the lady whose estate that ring comes from,' he said.

'No, of course not,' I said. 'Can you tell us something about her?'

'She was from Upstate New York,' he said, leaning back and folding his arms in front of him. 'Her husband was an ambassador to India or someplace like that. He brought this ring back for her when she was very young—probably about your age,' he added, nodding in my direction. 'From what I see, I think she would approve of you owning it. It is very beautiful, and it looks lovely on you. It's even your size, and fits perfectly, like it was made for … belongs to you!'

'It does,' Lou said, at the same time as I asked the gentleman, 'What happened to her?'

Lou and I looked at each other and started laughing at us talking at once. Then I looked back at the old gentleman, because it seemed like he had more to say about the woman who once owned the ring that now symbolized my promise to marry Lewis, and I wanted to know as much as I could about her.

'Not too long ago, she passed on, and I acquired the jewelry from her estate, along with a couple of other things. We'd developed a relationship of sorts over the years,' the gentleman said. He stopped and picked up a soft cloth on the counter. 'She was lovely, and passed on after living out a peaceful retirement with her husband on a small farm they bought up in Orange County. I'd been up there a couple of times, and she had me for tea. I also met her husband.'

Slowly, he began wiping the counter in front of him with the soft cloth, removing dust and fingerprints from its surface.

'What was *he* like,' I asked. 'Could you tell us?'

'Well, I only met him once. He came in just as I was finishing up my business with his wife, and was about to leave.

'Yes?' I said.

The older gentleman looked at me, and then glanced at Lewis.

'He was devoted to her.'

'How lovely,' I said.

'Yes,' the man replied.

He finished polishing the case with one last swipe, and set the cloth aside.

'A month after she passed, he followed her,' he said, and then he looked at Lewis and asked, 'Shall I box and wrap up the ring, or will she be wearing it?'

Lewis looked at me, and I nodded.

'She's wearing it.' he said.

'Of course,' the salesman replied, pulling out an old leather box from the shelf behind him to give to us.

Lou wrote out a check, and after the men shook hands, we left the store.

A couple of steps further toward 6th, we passed Steinway's, the great artisans' 59th Street display store.

'Oh, look,' I said. 'Let's go in!'

'Yes!' said Lou.

'You play, right?' he asked, as he opened the door for me.

'I can only remember a couple of things that I used to play on our piano back home,' I said, somewhat surprised by his question. I didn't remember talking about playing the piano with Lou, and didn't even know he knew I played.

'I've never heard you play,' he said. 'Will you play something for me here?' he asked, as we walked into the store.

The array of pianos sitting on the huge display floor in the cavernous front room was amazing. The grands took my breath away. We wandered through the first room, marveling at all the beautifully crafted instruments. Lewis ran his fingers over several of the ivory keyboards he passed as we made our way into the next room, where more pianos were displayed.

I was speechless—in awe of the many varieties of Steinways on display—the very finest of these artisans in this country. There were no signs that cautioned customers against playing any of the pianos, so Lou stepped up to one of the black grands and bent to pull out its bench.

Bowing at the waist in that courtly manner of his, Lou said, 'Play something for me on this one?'

I sat down. The instrument was breathtaking. I played a couple of chords to hear how it sounded, and the tone was clear, deep, and resonant, striking similar chords in me. I began tinkling on the keys, thinking about playing one of my favorites, a tune I'd taught myself to read from sheet music. I'd played it for hours, growing up in my father and stepmother's house. Other than homework, playing the piano was virtually the only time I was left alone, away from housekeeping, preparing meals, and rearing my half brothers and sisters, which had become my job after they rapidly began appearing a year after my father and stepmother were married—five in eight years. I loved my half siblings, but it had been a great deal of responsibility for someone so young.

After I'd played the opening chords, Lou said, 'That's Gershwin! I didn't know you knew Gershwin.'

'Oh, I don't,' I said, 'Just this one, really. We sang this musical in my high-school chorus and I learned how to play it from the sheet music we were given to take home and memorize.'

'So you can sing it, too?' asked Lou.

'A little. I think I can remember the lyrics,' I said, smiling slyly.

'So sing it for me,' he said.

'Why don't you?' I responded. 'I'll accompany you.'

'No, you sing it,' Lou said. 'You know I love your voice.'

'Okay,' I said, and started singing.

'*Summertime …*'

Then I stopped, but continuing to play, I said, 'Come on, Lou! Join me. You know the words!'

'Who doesn't?' Lou asked, and we both started laughing.

Lou moved closer behind me and put his hands on my shoulders as we both sang, *'Fish are jumpin'* …'

I'd jazzed it up over the years, but Lou had no trouble following me.

' *You're going to rise up* …'

I felt Lewis shift his weight behind me and kiss the top of my head. Then he bent down and put his cheek against mine.

'So hush, little baby / Don't you … cry.'

I let him sing the last line alone.

till death do us part....... CHAPTER TEN

'Marry me.' Lou said, waking me up.

'What?' I asked, slowly rolling over to face him. The sun streamed in through our bedroom windows behind him. For a cold, December day, it was very bright.

Blinking and squinting, I could barely see him, but he was lying on his side, head propped on elbow, watching me with a calm, serene look on his face. He reached up and tucked my hair behind my ear, then kissed it.

'Oh, come on, Lou, I'm not even awake yet,' I said from under the covers I had just pulled over my head. It was way too bright and early for this discussion.

'Better yet,' said Lou, pulling down the covers from my head.

I rolled onto my back, and Lou, uninvited, climbed onto me, pressing his body, full length, onto mine.

'Lou, it's too early,' I protested, groaning.

Lewis shifted his weight. He was in his briefs, and nothing else. I wasn't in anything. I threw my forearm over my eyes, closing them gratefully. Below his highly pronounced breastbone, his stomach was beginning to balloon.

Crikey, I thought, imagining Lewis as a full-blown fatty.

Hold on, it may not be long …

Rather than have a conversation about marriage, which I really didn't want to have now, I said jokingly, 'Okay, tell you what—if you get me a glass of V8 with a slice of freshly squeezed lemon, I'll marry you.'

'Done,' he said, pushing himself off and padding into the kitchen.

'Don't forget the fresh pepper,' I called out after him.

Surely that will do it?

I expected him to return momentarily, grumpily crawl back into bed, and pull the covers over his shoulders, back facing me. Because Lewis never served anybody anything—except if I was nauseous in the morning, although that had gone away. I felt my head start to pound, and my heart sink into that vaguely familiar but broken, almost bottomless place.

I heard the refrigerator door open and the sound of Lou uncharacteristically bustling in the kitchen. He dropped something.

Probably the half-gallon of blood-red V8 all over the white sink and floor.

'*Shit*!' he exclaimed.

Oh, please.

I pulled the covers back over my head and waited for him to climb back into bed. But he didn't.

Oh, no. He's getting my V8, after all.

Now, listen, Bettye. You wanted to wait until he achieved success … well, it's happened. Transformer'*s going to make him a star!*

By now, Lou had already had his first solo hit with 'Walk On The Wild Side,' and there was no question that he was on his way to international stardom. For almost three years, this is what we'd been working toward, and now it was actually happening.

We were still touring *Transformer* at the time. We'd started in Amsterdam and continued north through England, then on to Glasgow and back to London, before flying home. A couple of stateside shows were scheduled as a warm-up for his Lincoln Center debut at the end of January, a little over a month away. We'd just come back from Cleveland; next was Philly; and now we were off for a month before the Lincoln Center show. No wonder Lewis was thinking about finally marrying, now that we had some spare time.

'*Shit*!' I heard from the kitchen again.

I hope he hasn't cut his guitar-picking finger off slicing my lemon. I'd never hear the end of it from Dennis.

Even my grandmother said it was time to make it legal—although she had never met him. Lewis couldn't find the time to stop off to see her when we were in Cleveland, which was only a little over an hour from her. That had been very hard to accept at the time, but I had just about got over it.

You're too easy. You've sacrificed too much for him.

My grandmother had practically come right out and said as much last week, and she never came right out and said anything. This had been troubling to me. My grandmother was the mistress of the understatement; however much I didn't always like what she said, I adored how she said it.

'I'm sorry, Ma, I can't come and see you,' I said into the telephone, holding it tightly up and away from my lips, to try and mask my feelings. 'We have to leave early tomorrow morning for the next show,' I added, bucking up and bringing the receiver back down, so she could hear me.

'Be a man,' I heard my uncle say. How many times had he told me that until I protested?

Be a woman, I said to myself, hearing my uncle, smiling broadly, correcting himself. It took a lot of courage to tell my grandmother the truth that we weren't coming to see her.

Uncle Babe was proud of me, and his standards were high. Not only was he like a father to me, but the man was an original SEAL. This elite arm of the marines began in Korea, when the Americans began blowing up bridges with teams of underwater demolition experts, where he served as an engineer and marine training sergeant.

'If you knew how to build bridges, you knew how to blow them up,' he said.

What would I have done without Uncle Babe and my grandmother in my life? It didn't really matter how little I saw them—they seemed to understand, or at least let me think that—as long as I gave them a call and checked in. Like I was doing now.

'How long have you been in Cleveland?' my grandmother asked. 'I'm not that far away,' she said. 'How long has it been, dear? I miss your sweet face.'

My father and I had always been told we'd inherited her looks. I thought that was ridiculous, because she was a classic beauty. Dad, yeah—he was apparently better looking than Paul Newman. Most women thought so. But me? I honestly didn't see it.

Out of all her children, Daddy, my grandmother's favorite, inherited her artistic temperament and talent. A naturally gifted musician, my father could pick up any instrument and play it by ear, and he would sound as good as any classically trained musician. He played piano, violin, clarinet, trumpet, accordion—but he loved his harmonica best. I grew up hearing him play it on the back steps of our porch, at dusk. Only if you loved what you were playing could you make a harmonica wail like he did.

He was quite a charmer, too, and had 'a way with words.' I was convinced it was a pox on me, growing up with a father like mine—and for the men to whom I was attracted. But I didn't know what to say to my grandmother's subtle plea over the phone to visit her. She was the last person in the world I wanted to disappoint.

After I lost my mother at five years old, my grandmother largely raised me until I left home for good at seventeen. She was, to me, my mother. And nobody knew better than me how lucky I was to have this beautiful, elegant woman in my life, but at the time I hadn't seen her for almost two years! She was alone now, and getting older—probably needed me, not that she'd ever let on. But if anyone understood me moving away from home directly after high school graduation, it was she. She knew I had to get away from the hornet's nest my father and stepmother's home had become—and she could empathize with my plight with Lou because she knew all too well the sacrifices women made for their men. She'd uprooted herself and her two small children to leave Norway, the country of her birth, which she adored, for her husband's professional ambitions in the US, as chief engineer of an international cement factory, supplying the steel industry in nearby Pittsburgh and around the world, which is why we had ended up in this part of Pennsylvania. In his study at home, he gave me a stool so I could draw and color at my place at his drafting table beside him. At the end of his life he'd racked up close to forty patents that my uncle Knut managed after he was gone. My favorite was the one he'd sold to Japan, a vacuum cleaner that utilized centrifugal force. Hovering over the surface of floors, it didn't touch them, gliding effortlessly over carpets, never scuffing highly polished wood. It was awesome.

'Bettye?'

'Yeah, Ma, I'm still here,' I said into the mouthpiece.

I wanted to call a cab, throw the damn phone on the floor, and zoom off into the night to her doorstep. I needed to wake up smelling the giant *fortunea* rhododendron blooming in our front yard from my open bedroom window, and to visit the back yard where I used to feed the comets in our goldfish pond, and stick my nose in the tiger lilies nearby. With the corner of her apron, my grandmother would wipe away the rusty-colored pollen from my nose, wrap me in her arms, and give me the peace and safety I felt missing in my life, which I was craving these last two weeks. I wanted to crawl away and hide from everything forever in her arms.

'What's going on, dear?' she asked.

She always knows.

'We're on tour, and Lewis is playing Cleveland. We're at the Holiday Inn—aren't I lucky?' I laughed, trying to distract her. 'I'm just about to go to the theater, but thought I'd call and tell you that it's not going to work out. Maybe next time we blow through town we can come 'round?'

I said this last sentence with not as much subtlety as my grandmother had taught me, so she ignored it.

'Well, then you better get going,' she said, with absolutely no hint of emotion in her voice whatsoever.

'Ma, I am so sorry!' I said, rushing from where I'd left off. 'I asked Lewis, but he said we didn't have the time, with the show. Then we're leaving early tomorrow morning for the next one!'

'Well, then, you can't come, darling,' she said, nonplussed. 'He probably knows best.'

'Really, Ma?' I asked, almost frustrated with her, 'I'm not so sure about that!'

'Think what you want, just don't say it to him,' my grandmother said.

Over and over, that's what I heard, growing up.

'Yeah, I know,' I sighed.

'He needs you.'

'Yeah, *insanely*,' I muttered.

'That's what they do,' my grandmother said stoically.

'*Seriously?*'

'They need us, dear. It's as old as time.'

'Why?' I asked. 'Everything in the world is geared to them! What are we …'

I stopped myself before completing my thought. But it didn't matter. Ma always heard what I didn't say. And I heard what her silence reminded me: don't explain or complain.

Translation: *suck it up*.

'Oh, heavens,' Ma gently chided. 'They know how important we are to them. It's why they love us. They will always need us. Support him, and he will be a success for you both. That's how it works—you know.'

'I am!' I cried. 'It seems that's all I do!'

'Then you are doing the right thing,' she answered.

'Have you found something for yourself to do, by his side?' she asked, turning the topic to me.

'Yeah, I design and direct his lights for the show,' I replied.
'Do you like it?' she asked.

'Yes.'

'Are you successful at it?' she asked.

'Yes.'

'Then what more do you want?' my grandmother asked.

'Some relief!' I cried. 'I watch over him all the time, when I'm not working for him.'

'You'll always be working for him,' she remarked, almost as an afterthought.

'But, Ma! He scares me!' I confessed on the phone.

'Men are scary,' she said. 'I'd worry about you if he didn't.'

She didn't mince her words—like Lou, she could use them to defeat people, but her approach was dignified and calm. So much saner.

'Ignore it. Eventually, they grow up,' she said, gently laughing.

'Great!' I replied, exasperated.

'When am I going to hear that you've married him?' my grandmother asked, switching the subject back to me, again.

'What?' I asked, genuinely taken aback by her forwardness.

'You know that's coming,' she said. 'He's afraid to lose you. He's not stupid, he knows what he's got: you, dear! You love him, don't you?'

She knows I do. What's her point?

'Yeah, but so what, Ma?' I cried. 'I don't want to marry him! Not yet.'

'Bettye, you need to take care of yourself. Don't be so easy.'

And there it was.

'What do you mean?'

'Well, if you're doing everything for the man, get a ring. Make it legal. Share in the profits, along with your sacrifices.'

'He does talk about it,' I said, feebly.

'Don't give your all away for nothing. You'll lose his respect. More importantly, you'll lose your own.'

She's right, I thought, running my hands over my flat stomach, waiting for Lewis to return.

Curling up, I felt my heart plunging into that dark place again … but then Lewis was back with my V8.

As he handed me the miniature glass on a small saucer, I saw how the sprinkles of freshly ground pepper had created crevices in the lemon oil as it sunk into the bloody colored drink.

He looks like one of the boys who serve at his club. Maybe I should change my order to a Bloody Mary and have it spiked?

No, just do it. Marry him, and protect yourself.

I took the V8 and downed it, then handed it back to him. 'So, when?'

'When what?' Lou asked.

I wiped my mouth on the cloth napkin he'd also brought, laid neatly on the saucer.

Ah, the royal treatment.

A napkin instead of my head on a plate.

'Wait!—You mean get married?' Lewis cried.

I raised my eyes to look at him and handed him back the saucer.

'You do! You mean get married,' Lou said, and then his voice trailed off softly. He put the glass and saucer on the nightstand.

'Let me call Fred and see what he can arrange,' he said, sitting next to me. He gently moved my head and placed it in his lap, then reached for the phone. Just before dialing the number, he bent down and kissed me. '*Then you'll be mine.*'

* * *

The Roman Catholic bishop about to perform our wedding ceremony was actually flirting with Lewis, which of course thoroughly entertained Lou.

Well, this could be a first, but what else is new? Where did Fred get him, again?

'New Jersey,' said Cynthia, Fred's wife. 'He thought it would be appropriate—you being Presbyterian, and Lou Jewish.'

'Really?' I said. 'Fred's got some sense of humor.'

'Here, let me do the clasp on your pearls,' Cynthia replied.

I turned around and stooped so she could reach it.

We were in Lou's and my bedroom, putting the final touches on my wedding outfit—white satin pants, navy blue cashmere sweater, and pearls.

Ma would love this, I thought, smiling—the outrageous simplicity of it all. Especially the Catholic bishop marrying us at home. But she had great difficulty walking nowadays, and there was no way she could make it to New York alone, now that Grandpa was gone.

I decided I'd put on my red platform stilettos when we went out after the ceremony so I wouldn't tower over Lewis—instead I wore my navy blue flats. The only thing I'd had removed from the traditional vows was the line about the wife obeying the husband.

Probably not.

Lewis was in an all-white suit he'd bought shopping with Fred, I assumed, but he'd kept it a secret and I hadn't seen it till today, when Fred brought it with him, along with the priest.

Stevie Wonder's *Talking Book* could be heard from the living room, since we'd agreed it would be the background music while we got married. We'd decided to play the song 'I Believe (When I Fall In Love It Will Be Forever)' just before the ceremony.

When I called to ask my father if he'd fly in for the service, he'd replied, 'I can't. I've got a farm to run.' This was his way of saying he couldn't believe I was marrying Lewis. He'd seen the cover of the *Transformer* album, which I'd sent him, although I doubt very seriously that he'd played it. He didn't approve of, nor, I'm sure, understand Lou's white face makeup, but it had never come up.

The last conversation I had with my mother, which turned into a fight, was when I told her that Lewis had asked me to marry him, a year after we'd been dating. I'd showed her some songs, along with a couple of poems he'd written about me. She'd come to visit me when I was still living in student housing at Columbia.

'He's using you,' she said.

I couldn't believe she'd said that as her immediate response! I'd only seen her twice since I was five years old. How well did we know each other? Why should I believe her? We got into a blowout fight, and I didn't even ask her if she wanted to come to our wedding.

Lou said that since my folks weren't coming, he wasn't going to invite his family, either. So it would just be us at home, the bishop, and two witnesses. His sister, Bunny, was furious at not being invited to the ceremony, he told me, and now she wouldn't talk to us. At first, I was really upset about this, especially since we'd been in her wedding the year before. But what could I do? Bunny was his sister. Decades later, I found out she hadn't been angry but hurt, and that she had cried for two weeks about it. I also learned that it was Lou's practice to deliberately keep the women in his life as far away from each other as possible, even if it meant lying to them. He was expert at compartmentalizing, especially with the people who were closest to him. That way, he could control the stories he told each of us about the others; indeed, this was a perfect example of the control he exerted over the women in his life.

The ceremony was simple, a classic exchange of vows—for better or for worse, till death do us part. We kissed and hugged afterward, and hung on to each other for quite some time. I think we were both a little frightened, taking this major step in our lives without any family present. Then Fred took several photographs with the new Polaroid Instamatic that everyone was crazy about at the time. I thought we'd get more photos at the dinner later, but that never happened.

The dinner was sponsored by RCA and Lou's management, and the managers' wives turned up, as well as a couple of my friends. But there were also many industry people there. To me, it seemed truly odd that business and marriage should be combined so blatantly on our wedding day.

Lou and I just stayed as close together as we could, and he spent as little time with the industry people as possible. Friends of his drifted in from time to time—up-and-coming designers, musicians, journalists. He looked very happy that evening, which everyone remarked on, and those who knew about our wedding that day came and congratulated us. We pretty much sat quietly, holding hands, chatting with our friends who were seated nearby, trying to find some intimacy at this very public dinner.

Lou's solo debut at Lincoln Center was coming up in a few weeks, and he was terribly nervous about it—which, of course, no one knew about but me. To everyone else, Lewis looked confident and had everything under control—other than his drinking, which they looked to me to handle. But I was worried about him. He'd already established a reliable pattern in the past that could reasonably predict his future behavior. To ease increased anxiety and worry, he'd turn to his old bosom buddies, drugs and alcohol. So when we had a moment alone I whispered in his ear that we should go on a honeymoon. We had almost three weeks before his Lincoln Center show, and it would be great for both of us.

'Do you want a honeymoon?' Lou asked.

'Yeah!'

'Because I don't think you mentioned it …'

'I didn't.'

'Ah. You just suddenly thought about it?'

'Sort of.'

'Oh.'

'I also thought it would be great if we could just get away from all this,' I said, gesturing to all the music moguls in suits—smoking cigars, kibitzing, conducting business, wheeling and dealing.

'Maybe you and I just go off somewhere, rest and relax. We've earned it. We just got married, Lewis! Let's go on our honeymoon, honey!'

'Great idea!' Lou said, looking at me. 'I would love to get away from all of this and be alone. Where do you want to go?'

'Someplace warm, tropical, lots of sun … the ocean?'

'Done,' said Lou, leaning in and kissing me. 'I'll talk to Fred and Dennis tonight about it, and have them put it together.'

* * *

The air smelled sweet. As soon as we left the plane, a jolly gentleman handed everyone a sweet drink to welcome us to Jamaica. We had just landed in Montego Bay for our honeymoon, a week after getting married.

Granted, it had taken Dennis a while to get used to the idea.

'Now she wants a *honeymoon*?' he'd exclaimed. Like it was the most unusual idea on the planet.

Yeah, big guy, that's what I want. Deal with it.

Nevertheless, we negotiated a week of relaxation, sun, and fun with which to start our married life. We'd been booked into a lovely set of rooms directly on the water, but we had our own swimming pool to take a dip in whenever we wanted as well. The cabin was isolated, and in its own, small protected cove.

We spent our days sunning on the beach and took a motorcycle ride around the island on the local roads. Lou revved his engine and I followed, weaving all over the road, as I wasn't very adept at riding motorbikes.

'One of these days,' I suggested, 'we should take a tour of the island.' This was something that was readily available—a common tourist activity on Jamaica.

'What do you want to do that for?' Lou asked.

'I want to see the island,' I shot back. 'What do you think?'

'Oh, come on, Bettye, I'm not in the least bit interested in how these island people live.'

Really? I thought. *As if I didn't know.*

Before, when we were in Paris on one of his European tours, Lou wouldn't even go to Notre Dame with me, after I'd suggested it as we passed it on our way back to the hotel. So as soon as we got to the hotel, I dropped him off and told the driver to turn around and take me back to the cathedral. Although I'd been there many times when I was in Paris as a student, Notre Dame was the cat's meow for me. I'd read Victor Hugo in high school, and I thought he was buried there, like how writers are buried in London's Westminster Abbey, at Poet's Corner, where I'd seen the memorial of my all time favorite poet, William Wordsworth. I'd stood on the floor stone of George Eliot, one of my treasured writers, as well as Dylan Thomas's, and T.S. Eliot's, among others. I'd solemnly gazed at Geoffrey Chaucer's magnificent 500-year-old tomb in awe and amazement.

When I saw W.H. Auden on the same plane we'd been on flying over to Europe the year he died, I got weak in the knees. Dennis had come running back to where Lou and I were sitting, exclaiming, 'W.H. Auden's in first class!' Lou looked at me like I was nuts, but I didn't care; I found a reason to walk up and past him, just to see him, although I hadn't had the temerity to interrupt his flight by speaking to him. Sadly, the following year, he, too, was interred in Westminster Abbey.

But Victor Hugo is in the Pantheon in Paris, which I had also visited in 1968. I thought for sure Lewis would go see this great writer's grave, but I was wrong. Lou was not a sightseer.

Nothing touristy—no siree!

In Jamaica, I think he humored me, because we took the private car and toured the lush island, while the driver pointed out all the famous places. It took all day, and Lewis wasn't all that enamored with it. We went to the Green Grotto Caves, Sevilla Nueva, St. James's church, and actually climbed Dunn's River Falls. This, Lou enjoyed. After the day-long trip, it wasn't all that difficult for the driver to convince us to drive to Kingston and visit some of its night clubs.

Abruptly, and out of the blue, Lou suddenly asked the driver where he could get some cocaine. Reluctantly, the driver drove us to a place tucked into a side street, and he and I sat outside in the car while Lou followed his instructions and entered the building. It was very dark, and I thought it looked dangerous; the alleys and backstreets of Kingston had bands of youth roving around, and there was little masked hostility toward tourists. I'd read about the island's poverty and increasing social unrest when I did a bit of research before we left for our honeymoon, so I was concerned. But Lewis made the transaction without incident, returning to our waiting vehicle alive and well.

'Mission accomplished,' he announced triumphantly, slamming the car door and holding up the familiar plastic bag filled with the tricky, delicate-looking white stuff. Apparently the driver's connections had been stellar and safe.

Marijuana was sold openly in the nightclubs, but neither Lou nor I was a pothead. The live reggae music playing at a club we ended up at was fabulous, and Lou encouraged me to go out on the dance floor and dance, which he knew was what I really wanted to do, anyway. He had other activities foremost in his mind, like snorting cocaine as he settled into the deep, luxurious couches lining the dance floor. And drinking the most potent island concoction one could order as he watched me boogaloo till dawn.

On a break, I came back to our table. Thirsty from my wild abandon—dancing with everyone and anyone, and having a great time—I saw he'd passed out. Head back, mouth open, he was sprawled all over the couches holding the plastic bag, now empty, in one hand; his drink in an upright position in his other one, still resting on his knee.

I found our tour guide, who was waiting for us in the car out front till it was time to drive us back to Montego Bay, and asked him to take us home. I got Lou out to the car by myself. The guide helped him into the car, and we were driven back to the hotel.

While Lou slept, I thought about all the impoverished neighborhoods we'd driven through on our tour that day from one tourist attraction to the next. I'd never seen so much poverty in my life, and the conditions—the shacks people lived in, with open and running sewage on their streets—were devastating to see. The children, blissfully running around the streets, clothed in little, climbed all over our car, begging for money. It had been really depressing.

Perhaps this is why Lewis was reluctant to take the day trip.

He'd actually looked angry as we drove through some of the most impoverished areas. He knew how much it upset me, I decided, but while Lewis had enormous compassion for people, at times he could be incredibly cruel to have-nots, like not having was a contagious disease. I wondered if he'd been trying to protect me from seeing the squalid conditions these people lived in. His parents had been here, and maybe they'd mentioned it to him. Perhaps that was a more generous explanation for his behavior than was true in this instance, but I learned over time that protecting me was often his intention, although I wasn't always aware of it until afterward. I preferred thinking this was one of those instances, but for now he was out to the world, and I was only left wondering, as we drove past the lush landscape draped in shadows, rife with strange, unfamiliar noises from the jungle.

When we arrived at our honeymoon cottage, getting Lewis awake, up, and out of the car was a dismal, discouraging task. I was so tired of this, and yet here we were, married, and it was still going on. When would it ever end?

After our guide helped Lou to the door of our cabin, he fell onto the floor of the room as soon as I turned the key in the door and opened it. I hadn't realized that the guide had propped him up against the doorframe, or that it had been his sole support.

That night we had the only disagreement of our honeymoon, although no words were exchanged. Instead, I threw a lamp at him. Thinking back on it later on, I was shocked, because I rarely, if ever, got physical when I was angry or upset. But I'd been drinking at the club and lost my patience trying to get him up off the floor—which I really didn't have the strength to do—and then haul him into bed. I didn't feel comfortable calling the front desk for assistance, so I threw the first and closest thing I could reach—a lamp on a side table—out of sheer frustration, as I struggled with the dead weight of his body.

I was unable to get him into bed, because he was dead out— dead weight—so I left him and the lamp, smashed, on the floor, and crawled into bed. Somehow, I finally fell asleep, but not before calling my grandmother. It was the crack of dawn in Pennsylvania, but I knew she rose early, and that by now she would be having her first cup of coffee.

After telling her where I was calling from, and that we were on our honeymoon in Jamaica, I suddenly began crying. Everything I'd been holding back came babbling out—probably nearly incoherently—as I confessed to her his drinking and some of his drug-taking. I'd never told her all through the years we'd dated and been engaged.

After listening quietly and soothing me, she said she thought it was unfortunate, but that with my help, she believed he could beat it. She'd never steered me wrong before, so I believed her.

Later, after I left Lou, my grandmother told me that her first love had also been a writer—a poet—but he didn't abuse alcohol or drugs. She had never been around anyone who did, and she was as much out of her league as I was, although I hadn't realized it at the time.

Even though I was deeply troubled, I hung up the phone more determined than ever to help Lewis conquer his demons. But I braced myself.

Only time will tell.

transformer, part two . . . . CHAPTER ELEVEN

'Everybody out,' I said uncharacteristically, waving my arms to dispel the crowd in Lou's dressing room at Lincoln Center's Alice Tully Hall.

People turned around and looked at me, surprised and a bit taken back, because they'd never heard me say that before.

Lou was slumped in his chair in front of the bank of mirrors at his dressing table, covered in sweat, head hung down, looking somewhat defeated, which seriously alarmed me. As soon as he heard me, he glanced up and shot me a grateful look. With that, I said, 'Come on, people, let's go! Everything's fine, let's just give him some space. Give us a couple of minutes, will you?'

I held the door open and stepped aside so they could all leave.

I had just got into Lou's dressing room, after pushing through the crowd of people following him as soon as he got offstage from the first set of his 'Phantom of Rock' *Transformer* debut at Lincoln Center.

I had been down front, sixth row center. The show was a near disaster, and that's why I wanted everybody out. Lewis had been drunk, slurring, and even forgot lyrics, although I'm not sure the audience realized it. He may have just appeared tired, but that wasn't good, either. The last half of the show was in an hour or so, and I worried if that was enough time to get him sober.

It was January 27, 1973, only a week after our Jamaican honeymoon.

Lewis had been jubilant, relaxed, and smiling upon our return, but as the momentum gathered toward the show, each day he became more withdrawn. At home, he nervously paced back and forth from room to room, like the caged tiger we saw at the zoo on our day in Central Park. He immediately replenished the scotch glass he carried around with him, pouring larger amounts than ever, until he finally passed out on our bed at some odd, early-morning hour. Then I could pull off his boots and remove enough clothing to tuck him in between the crisp, clean sheets I made certain the cleaning lady put on our bed each night. This was my one indulgence—I adored freshly laundered sheets—and our cleaning lady, the superintendent's wife, lived in our building.

When Lou wasn't drinking until he passed out at home, we attended parties where I saw him steadily drinking more, while snorting increasingly copious amounts of the powdery white stuff. It was laid out on coffee tables or any horizontal surface large enough for the mirrored lines everyone inhaled through tightly rolled Ben Franklins, often rammed up bleeding nostrils.

And that is how we'd ended up here.

Once everyone had cleared out of his dressing room, I firmly closed the door and pulled up a chair beside Lou.

'What is going on with you?' I asked, taking his chin and raising it to look me in the eyes.

'I don't know, what does it look like,' he answered, without a trace of defiance. He was exhausted and disheartened, batting my hand away like an annoying fly.

Undeterred, I said, 'Lewis, you're so blown away, you're slurring and forgetting your lines. I don't know how you got through that set!'

'I don't, either,' he said simply, slumped in his chair. I hadn't seen him look more despondent in ages, and I was deeply concerned.

'Here, let's get you on the couch to lie down,' I said, taking his arm and helping him over to it. After getting him out of his wringing wet black leather jacket, I threw it on the chair across the room. Someone could dry it out with the damn handheld hairdryer, if necessary.

I was seriously pissed, but I couldn't afford to let him know. What was important now was to get him sober for the last set, when all the critics would be sitting on the other side of the lights. So I swung his legs up, plumped up a pillow, and placed it under his head. I found a towel on the vanity table and brought it over, along with my chair, and sat down beside him. I wiped off the wet, mottled white globs of 'Phantom' makeup, black eye-shadow and mascara trickling through rivers of sweat. Next, I'd lay a cold washcloth over his face, get some coffee in him, and see if he would sober up.

'Baby, what are you doing?' I asked him—the same question as before.

'I drank too much, what do you think?' he replied defensively.

Okay, there's some spirit—maybe he's coming back.

I didn't say anything for a while. I finished patting his face and neck dry, then under his black T-shirt, which was also soaked, so I insisted we pull that off, too. I covered him with a jacket lying nearby, then got a wet washcloth from the sink, wringing it only slightly dry. His eyes were already closed, so I laid it out on his face.

Good. I couldn't hold back my tears much longer. Why is he blowing this?

The words were practically screaming inside my skull, ricocheting around the right and left hemispheres between rational thought and hysteria.

'You're here, baby, this is what we've been working for, why are you sabotaging this?' I asked.

That's when he ripped off the washcloth and sat up, looking at me. I turned quickly, wiping my face with my hands.

'I'm not the *Phantom of Rock!*' he yelled, nearly knocking me off my chair.

Righting myself, I reached for the arm bearing all his weight.

'Darling, everybody knows that!' I said. 'It's just a stupid publicity stunt. You know that—forget it!'

He was furious. He was also hurt. I could feel his arm trembling with his weight and pent up anger.

'Here, lay back down,' I coaxed, moving my hand down his body, easing him back again.

I knew he resented all the press *Transformer* was getting, but rather than appear, at best, thankless and ungrateful, he was powerless to say anything to management or complain about the trajectory his career had suddenly taken. It was the album that least represented his work but which finally jettisoned him into his long sought-after fame, and it put him in considerable conflict. It didn't reinforce his confidence, even though he was getting his Velvet Underground songs and his new material out there.

'Look, I'm here,' I said. We were newlyweds, and we had just come home from our honeymoon. I leaned over and kissed him.

He took hold of my hand and held onto it.

'Thank god!' he muttered.

I took the wet washcloth with my other hand and spread it out over his face again.

'It doesn't matter what they call you, baby, just sing your songs.'

He raised his hand to take the cloth off his face to look at me, again, but I stopped him.

'Leave it,' I said. 'Just lay back and relax.'

So he did.

I almost felt like I should sing a lullaby, as I once had for my little brothers and sisters. Lou was so vulnerable, it nearly broke my heart. I almost forgot how hurt and disappointed I felt during his first performance.

But not quite.

He began shivering.

'Here, let me get something to warm you,' I said, starting to get up so that I could throw my coat over him.

'No, stay!' he cried, grabbing my arm.

He slid over, so I moved onto the couch next to him, and put his head in my lap, pushing his hair, soaking wet, off his face.

'I hate these stupid songs,' he said.

'I doubt that,' I said, 'and surely not all of them.'

'No, not all of them,' he replied forcefully, making a fist and hitting the wall beside him.

Okay, he's coming back. Now if we could just get to his incredible will and ambition, he will make it.

'I'm sick of "Walk On The Wild Side!" It's all they want to hear! What about all my other ones?' he cried.

'It's a good song, Lewis,' I replied, quietly.

'It's just a little ditty! I was just playing around and having fun, and now—what? *This* is what makes me famous? Like hell it will!' he yelled, continuing to bang his fist against the wall.

I didn't say anything, waiting instead to hear all the frustration I knew that had been building up in him since the song took off, creating a sensation.

He needs to start fighting back.

'I'm a failure and a fake!' he cried. 'I don't deserve any of this!' he said, almost shouting. 'None of this has anything to do with me or my music!'

'Lew—'

'Bettye, I'm not the fucking phantom of rock! I'm a writer. This is such *fucking bullshit!*'

'I kn—'

'I just want to sing my songs!'

Lou's manager, Fred, was a nitwit with this Phantom of Rock stuff. One of his ideas was to take out a full-page ad in the *New York Times*

using only the *Transformer* cover photo, with no copy on the page other
than the time, date, and place you could see this person—not even Lou's
name! Nevertheless, he had talked Lincoln Center into letting him play
the Alice Tully Hall, which was as unlikely as one could imagine, and
an accomplishment. Lincoln Center was the home of the New York
Philharmonic: Mozart, Beethoven, Haydn, the New York City Ballet.
But here lay the Phantom of Rock after stumbling, drunk, offstage—
singing about transvestites, hookers, and copping a dime bag of heroin
in Harlem.

Now that Lou had begun yelling, I didn't want anyone hovering
outside the door to hear him, although it didn't matter, really. I just
didn't want to give them any ammunition to put more pressure on him.
It was the last thing he needed.

'Oh, come on, Lou,' I said, exasperated. '"Walk On The Wild Side"
means a great deal to many people who've never spoken out about these
things. It's unprecedented! And so are you, by giving it to them!'

Lou just rolled his head side to side.

'You have your others—your VU standards, the soft ones—your
ballads. "Satellite Of Love" is phenomenal, one of the best on the
album. It's a classic!'

As I desperately searched for any way I could get him to connect
back to the peace and quiet of our honeymoon, he started to settle
down.

'Let alone "Perfect Day," baby,' I added, kissing him.

'*Really?*' he cried, furiously, pulling the washcloth off his face. 'It's
not even on the setlist—*it got voted off!*'

'It's just for tonight, what do you care?' I said. 'They'll eventually
hear it, it'll just take time, that's all.'

'I wanted to sing it for you tonight—here—in Alice Tully Hall!'

'Oh, for heaven's sake, silly, you wrote it for me! How many girls
can say they've ever gotten anything like "Perfect Day"?'

'Yeah, yeah,' he said, slapping the washcloth back on his face.

'Wait, let me run some more cold water on it,' I said, taking it and going to the sink.

I'd been hurt when he hadn't played 'Perfect Day,' but I knew management had gone over the setlist with him, which they rarely did. But this was a big night—professionally, it was probably the biggest one in his life.

'Doesn't matter. Sing "Satellite" for me—I'm out there. And I love it!'

'You do?' he asked, pulling the washcloth cautiously off his face to see how I really felt.

I was always honest with him about his work. It is what he wanted, and it may very well be what he loved most about me. We both knew that in the disingenuous world in which we worked and spent our lives, it was what he needed most.

'Of course I do!' I replied, almost as forcefully as when he'd spoken of his worse fears earlier.

'It'll be the next hit from the album. It's already taking off!' I cried.

I leaned down close to him.

'It doesn't matter what they call you,' I said. 'You're no kind of phantom to me.'

He kissed my forehead then looked at me.

'Did I blow it out there?' he asked.

'You've got one more set, Lewis. I honestly don't think it matters. The crowd out there already loves you, no matter what you do.'

'Yeah, but not the press.'

'They're only reviewing your next set.'

I passed my hand over his eyes, letting him know he should close them.

'Come on, maybe you can get a couple of minutes. I'll bring back some coffee. Let's get you straight. It's going to be okay.'

'All right,' he sighed, like he was doing me a favor, closing his eyes.

'Do you want me to throw ice cubes down your back?' I teased.

'No, no, that's okay,' he replied hastily, but I saw the sudden flash of a smile.

'Not if we can help it—maybe if I can just catch a couple of minutes of sleep …'

'All right, then, just lie quiet, maybe get a nap.'

Just before rising, I said, 'We're going to be okay, baby.'

He searched for my hand, then threw his arm over his head and rolled onto his side, facing the wall.

I got up and moved toward the sink on the other side of the room.

'Let me get this cloth cold again. I'll get your clothes dried and bring some coffee back. It'll be okay.'

'Don't leave,' he said, his voice trailing off.

Maybe he'll fall asleep. Let's hope!

'Like you always tell me, Lewis—*fuck 'em!*'

'Yeah, okay.'

'Just sing your songs,' I said, turning the tap on.

By the time I'd turned the water off and started walking toward him, his breathing had become steadier, deeper. His abdomen rose and fell rhythmically. No matter how angry I'd been earlier, I was glad I hadn't voiced it.

I would tell him how I felt later, to be sure, but for now I just pulled his jacket off the chair, picked up his shirt, and went to the door. Quietly opening it, I ran directly into the mob of people working for him outside.

They turned to the door en masse, and I jabbed my index finger to my lips.

'*Shhh,*' I warned them.

Yes, the gorgon has emerged from her cave, folks.

Immediately, the crowd dispersed.

Pussies, I thought. *You want me to do the dirty work? Then back the hell off!*

I closed the door softly behind me.

And let the man who signs all your paychecks sleep it off.

* * *

The tenor of the audiences for the US *Transformer* tour was quite different from before. RCA was now promoting Lewis's 'glam rock' image, with heavy white makeup copied from the album cover, to reinforce sales of *Transformer*. 'Walk On The Wild Side' in particular was getting heavy radio play, which all helped promote this new 'persona.'

At the start of the European *Transformer* tour, Lou wore whiteface and starkly contrasting, heavy black eye makeup. Backstage, I used lots of black liner to encircle his eyes and darken his eyebrows. I brushed purple eye shadow over his eyelids until they were glistening, almost black. Gobs of heavy black mascara and a dab of iridescent pink lipstick completed the look. But back in the US—frankly, as soon as he could—he lost the white makeup. It just wasn't who he was. He was a rock'n'roller, not a glam rocker.

There wasn't a marked difference with European audiences, but in the US, *Transformer* attracted concertgoers who seemed to be expecting some kind of freak onstage, and on the surface, Lou's makeup satisfied their desire. Combining this with his usual black leather outfit, he was quite different from anything they had ever seen—dark, menacing, and coming from a place few had the nerve to visit, however fascinated they were.

That was why they loved him. Lou challenged all previously known rock-star personas. Glam rock was coming to America, and now, with *Transformer*, Lewis had been elected its toastmaster.

The dangerous streets Lewis had written about in his Velvet Underground days, and in the new songs written for *Transformer*, addressed lifestyles that had never previously been sung about on the radio or performed live at rock'n'roll shows. The seats of Lou's shows were filling up with outsiders, the disenfranchised of society. As a result of 'Make Up' and 'Walk On The Wild Side,' gays, bisexuals, transvestites, and transsexuals flocked to Lou's shows, standing for hours in line for front row seats, dressed in the psychedelic outfits of the late-60s British Invasion.

Full-blown hard-core drug users from the streets of major cities across the US invaded his shows, too, wearing clothing that announced their presence—shades, leather pants, deliberately ripped jeans. A generally unclean, grungy appearance was increasingly the look du jour of the *Transformer* tour. Dyed purple and pink streaks ran through deliberately dirty, unkempt hair; tattoos, piercings, and safety pins punctured ears, eyebrows, and cheeks. Glam, gay, psychedelic, and grunge were merging in a clash of unity, reflecting the subsequent emergence of punk rock, which Lou found himself in the middle of. Lou, in fact, would become the Grandfather of Punk Rock.

Lou was being touted as the voice of the gay community, which *Transformer* made crystal clear; the irony, of course, was that Lou and I had just gotten married. Not surprisingly, our engagement or wedding didn't make the *New York Times'* 'Weddings and Engagements' section, nor did I submit our information. Neither our engagement nor our marriage found its way into any of the promotional material, articles, or reviews for the *Transformer* tour. Our nuptials had no place in the market RCA was seeking to capture, promoting Lou as its new, sexually ambiguous champion. Gay, bisexual, transsexual—with his glam rock makeup and *Transformer* lyrics, no one knew for sure what Lou's orientation was. This sexual ambivalence was exactly what Lewis was looking for. Having studied at the feet of one of the best, Andy Warhol, Lou honed his marketing genius, and he knew there was a substantial slice of the retail recording industry just waiting to be tapped.

Both Lou and David Bowie made the most of the hype, grabbing headlines after the famous photo taken in London of him and Bowie kissing. They weren't gay lovers; the shot was taken at a deliberate angle to create that illusion. It was a sensational stunt for the press to help sell their newest albums.

Lewis continued to play his old Velvet Underground songs, as before. Strikingly, his new stage persona played perfectly to these lyrics, even though they'd been written years earlier. The titillating, edgy suggestion of sadomasochism; creative sexual positions and partnerships; shooting and securing heroin and speed in Harlem; all were substantially enhanced by his new makeup and stage persona.

But after the first leg of the *Transformer* tour in Europe, Lewis quickly grew tired of the glam-rock persona. It was nowhere near as popular in the States as it had been in the UK, and it did not reflect who he really was. He also felt uncomfortable portraying something he wasn't. Although he wasn't gay or a transvestite, that didn't bother him much, because he knew what he was, and he didn't have anything to prove or defend. The real problem with the Phantom of Rock persona was that it made him feel like a clown, which worked against him if he wanted his writing to be taken seriously.

Lewis never came out directly and said he was gay, bi, or a transvestite to the public; he just didn't deny it, leaving the topic open for speculation. It sold more albums and concert tickets. He left it up to his lyrics on the album to imply what he was, even though there were a couple of songs on the album, along with ballads composed during his VU days with songs about his relationships with girls, including me, like 'Perfect Day' on *Transformer*; the interpretation floating around that Lewis was singing about heroin was so far off base it was almost funny. He didn't deny it, because it could potentially pump up sales from the drug-buying culture. But when you make a pact with the devil—if only metaphorically—a price will be paid.

Although *Transformer* was the album that launched him into worldwide fame and became the most famous of his solo career, its songs—or, rather, the production of them, however brilliant it was—didn't truly reflect his music. He felt that he was betraying himself, and he began to resent playing some of those songs, which he also considered somewhat frivolous.

Since The Velvet Underground had disbanded, playing the songs he wrote as one of its founding members—a source of love and great pride for him—also had the unfortunate ability to remind him of what he had lost in leaving the band. The crowds he attracted as a solo artist requested VU classics like 'White Light/White Heat,' 'Heroin,' and 'I'm Waiting For The Man,' with which they were already familiar, but this only reminded Lou of the band's failure to achieve commercial success. His decision to break up the VU had caused him enormous conflict and had been very painful for him. Now, every time he played a VU request, it also reminded him of the part he played in the band's demise, and all the guilt, pain, and conflict was reawakened—at every show.

As is inevitable, Lou started getting bored of playing the same old songs. His beautiful ballads weren't given their due—the audience response wasn't what he thought they deserved—and sometimes the crowds became impatient when he played them. Ballads like 'Candy Says,' and 'Pale Blue Eyes,' from his VU days, or even some of the slow ones from *Lou Reed*, like 'Berlin,' 'Lisa Says,' or 'Wild Child,' were songs he loved to perform. But as soon as they ended, and the band began playing his hard rock'n'roll songs, the audience screamed and shouted with enthusiasm. It was obvious to everyone which songs his audiences preferred, especially Lou, and that hurt and made him very angry.

* * *

One of the reasons Lou loved to play 'Heroin' was because through his lyrical writing he was able to express his thoughts about a topic never before addressed in rock'n'roll—resulting in a song which, for that alone, was truly groundbreaking. It was a slow song, and he loved those, because his lyrics could be heard clearly over the din of the guitars.

Lewis's drugs of preference when I was with him were speed and cocaine, not heroin, because he thought it increased the amount of work he could produce. When we were in town, there were countless mornings I found myself sitting, half-awake, on the concrete steps of Dr. Freymann's office off Fifth Avenue at 8am, after Lewis had shaken me awake, insisting I throw on some clothes—*now!*—so we could hail a cab and arrive before any of the doctor's other clients got there to get his famous injection of vitamins laced with amphetamine. Lou loved them more than any other drug he took.

Lewis denied it when I asked him if Freymann was the notorious 'Dr. Feel Good' who gave his patients hard drugs, because he knew I would disapprove. The first time Lewis took me to see him, we waited for two hours, corralled in one tiny waiting room after another—there must have been at least five of them—until we finally made it to the great man's inner sanctum. It was like waiting to see God. After we chatted for a bit—him in his thick Austrian accent—he bent down and smiled at me, flourishing a huge hypodermic needle. I immediately withdrew my arm, because I am seriously not fond of needles, but the doctor laughed, took my arm back, slapped my veins, and tied me off.

'I am going to make you *feeel* like no man has ever made you *feeel* in your life,' he said. And then, very quickly, with me wincing, he shot me up.

After one of these shots, I surrendered to the high. Floating out of Dr. Freymann's office, I felt like I was in my own magical world. Strangers on the street smiled and nodded, wishing us a lovely day. Everything seemed rosy and easily within our grasp.

Once, when I was very ill with a frighteningly high fever for days, Lewis asked Dr. Freymann to make a house call. He was extremely worried about how sick I was, not least because we were soon due back on the road. After the house call and another injection, I was fine, back on the road like nothing had ever happened. Whatever was in that shot, Dr. Freymann got rid of it that night.

I liked Dr. Freymann. He was an excellent physician, and he had a tremendous sense of humor. Years later, when I remarried, I even brought my firstborn to the doctor to have him examine her.

About a month after I left Lou for the last time in Paris in 1973, I received a call. It was Dr. Freymann, and he said that he was calling for Lou. He told me Lewis needed me, and still loved me very much.

'Well, why doesn't Lewis call and tell me himself?' I replied. 'I'll talk to him. And doc—did he ask you to call me?'

'Yes,' he replied, 'but he *iss* a man, he can not do *zat*. Can you not call him?'

'That's probably not going to happen,' I said.

'Do you not still love *heem*?' he asked. 'You two are very *goot* together—you are meant for one another.'

'He wasn't so good for me, doc.'

'I know, but we all know Lou can get—ah—a little cray-zee. He gets a *leetle* nervous. You know. But I will talk to him. He needs you and loves you, *darlink*. He just does not know how to call you and tell you. He *iss* a man.'

'Doc …'

'We are all worried about him. Think about it, dear. You are his *wiffh*. Call him.'

Then he hung up the phone.

going down............CHAPTER TWELVE

With the success that accompanied the release of *Transformer*, Lewis had become a very different man than the one I fell in love with in the beginning of our relationship. That man was quiet, reflective; a writer, a teddy bear. I suppose a superficial explanation for why I married Lewis might be because he wrote 'Sweet Jane.' I always respected his writing, and I loved that song as soon as I heard it—it became a joke between us. But I hadn't bargained for his descent into alcohol and drugs as a way of coping with fame. Success brought back a reliance on all his vices, old friends to him.

He hadn't yet started drinking at noon, but that would come shortly. We rarely went anywhere where he didn't snort barrel-loads of cocaine, which gave him the confidence to achieve the success he craved—and what we traded the sanity of our lives for. But it did nothing to alleviate the nagging feeling Lou had that he wasn't entirely worthy of it.

Looking back, I can't believe how much responsibility was placed upon my young shoulders: trying to keep him out of trouble; providing him with the security and safety to write; keeping him in a condition where he was able to make his commitments for his recording and touring, as well as his obligations to RCA. But I was the only one he trusted, or to whom he would listen. That was the price I paid, as his partner, for agreeing to help him achieve fame on an international level.

By the time we were on the *Transformer* tour in the US, Lou started ordering me a Johnny Walker along with his. I went along with it, because it was easier, and it made him look less like an alcoholic, which I felt a great deal of pressure and expectations to control. I didn't drink before I began seeing Lewis, but I started having a glass of Chablis with him, which then progressed to scotch. It helped me relax faster, and masked whatever resentment I was feeling. His extreme dependency on alcohol and drugs—which, in effect, kept me on a constant watch over him on the road as well as at home—had become a very real burden for me.

When we were out at Max's or at a party, we were surrounded by Lou's friends; there was no one who didn't drink or use drugs. The people that Lou was closest to drank and snorted as much as him. I didn't want to be the odd one out, so I joined in.

Even after we were married, at twenty-three, I was still the youngest person in Lou's social circles. In the beginning of our relationship, I had felt inexperienced—an outsider—but now, after traveling all over the US and Europe, and assuming so many personal and professional responsibilities with Lewis, I had proved my worth. Not only to him, but more importantly, to myself, just as my grandmother advised me. Although there were some people who only accepted me because I was his wife, I honestly didn't care. I moved freely and with confidence in his circle of friends.

I was brought up to be nice to people, but in the circles within which Lou traveled, quite the opposite seemed to be the norm. Lou ran in an incredibly ambitious, passive-aggressive, and sometimes almost creepily predatory pack. Tearing people down and being 'bitchy' seemed to be the high marks of sophistication. Most acted like they were superior to everyone, which was annoying. It seemed like a huge waste of time and energy to me. Why would anyone need to project their superiority unless they felt inferior?

When Lewis was around his crowd, he, too, was bitchy and mean, although not with me. But I saw that people were afraid of his caustic tongue, both at home or on the road—especially journalists. Lou was becoming like an adult child, and he needed me around him constantly. It began to seriously irritate me. Coupled with the responsibility of buoying him up when he got down—which happened with more frequency the longer we were on the road—it was almost more than I could bear.

The longer we were on tour, the more he drank and the more drugs he took—cocaine to get him up, valium to bring him down, scotch to level him off and ease his emotional pain—and the more difficult my role with Lou got. So I began drinking and taking cocaine with him. It created a bond between us when we were on the road or out together, and he could continue to trust me. We were in this together, and I seemed helpless to fight all the drugs and alcohol that permeated the road and our social life. This worried me, but there was no one with whom I could share my concerns. When we were at home alone, we still never took anything, although Lewis always had Johnny Walker by his side.

'Prince Valium'—Lou's name for the drug—became a staple for me. A muscle relaxant, it helped keep me calm during my trying surveillance over Lewis, who seemed to be spiraling out of control. A little voice inside my head kept saying it was time to get off this ride, but I couldn't. Lou was completely dependent upon me, as was management. I was his wife and my vows, which I took seriously, were for better or for worse. It looked like we were entering worse territory, so I took what I had to stay on for the rough ride.

Cocaine was rampant in the music industry, throughout all the arts, and in our social circles. It can be a feel-good drug for a while, but it made me feel bad about myself, because this wasn't me. Like Lou, I felt like a phony, pretending to be someone I was not.

As Lou became more of a liability, my professional responsibilities on tour suddenly ended. One day, returning to the road in Ohio after a break, I went backstage to work on the lights, only to be told by the technicians in our company that they were now handling those responsibilities. This was explained to me patiently like I was a dunce, as if it was a good idea for me just to keep an eye on Lou.

Hey, guess what, Bettye? Now all you have to do is sit back, relax, and enjoy the show!

Life as a blonde, albeit a natural one, is a double-edged sword. Although it may have a superficial advantage, I had become very tired of being conveniently pigeonholed and treated like a dumb blonde; nevertheless, I'd learned how to play the best damn dumb blonde you've ever met, and I used it when I felt that's how I was being treated. But this wasn't one of those times.

When I asked Lou what was going on, he claimed he had given the lighting responsibilities to the other technicians on Dennis's orders. When we got home and I saw Dennis, I asked him, and he blamed it on Lou. I could hardly ask the lighting guys, so it was a *fait accompli*. I was not consulted, nor was it discussed with me in advance. Nothing was said to me—*zip*. It was hardly an appropriate way to remove me from a job I loved and had done successfully. And of course, as his fiancé and wife, I drew no salary.

* * *

As we crossed the US, I saw how the parameters of the *Transformer* tour—the different crowds it was drawing, and Lou's discomfort and boredom playing songs from the album—began to change him. He was physically out of shape, which I was blamed for, because I was supposed to keep tabs on his diet, although everyone knew he was packing the weight on because of the increasing amount of booze he was drinking.

I was doing the best I could to control it—and I was doing better than anyone else could, that was for sure! Without me, he was impossible to deal with. Everyone had already experienced what happened when I wasn't around, and it was disastrous. Onstage, he would stumble, slurring and forgetting his lyrics; offstage he was lethargic, irritable, and distant. He could be a real pill with management, the band, and everyone else on tour—except the people who were supplying him with drugs. That's how I figured out who his dealer was. I talked to management about putting a stop to it, but there was no proof, and nobody was talking, so nothing was done.

I knew why Lou started falling back on drink and drugs: he relied on them to ease the pressure building up in him; by deadening it, he was trying to control it for as long as he could. He was also manifesting symptoms of the 'aftershocks,' as it were, of the electric-shock therapy (EST) he received in late adolescence.

At seventeen, Lou's parents had sent him to see a psychiatrist who prescribed EST for his depression and mood swings. During the summer of 1959, he was treated at Creedmoor State Psychiatric Hospital in Queens, New York, where the EST treatments were administered without an anesthetic in twenty-four sessions over two days. At that time, the procedure involved putting him on a wooden gurney with a rubber block between his teeth. A muscle relaxant was given to him as two electrodes were attached to his head. While two orderlies physically restrained the patient, the doctor administering the EST would flip the switch controlling the electrical current, which coursed through the convulsing patient's body. This was an experience that scarred Lewis for life.

It is commonly thought that EST was prescribed to Lou in order to cure him of his 'bisexual tendencies,' but he never told me this or even alluded to it. I think he told journalists this to be more sympathetic to the gay community, in part to broaden his appeal to that audience, but he never said it to me.

Lou knew I understood what EST was like, as I'd seen its effects on my father, who had undergone at least a year of the treatment as part of his long repair in hospital following the injuries he suffered during World War II. With only a glance exchanged between us, Lou knew I understood his special challenges. It helped calm him down, and was why he listened to me more than anyone else, because he knew that I understood what he was going through on a deeply personal level. I always thought that was significant. He acknowledged and respected what my dad had been through, and he would never violate that respect. It was a major factor in his complete trust in me, but it was also why I was more tolerant of his increasingly erratic and sometimes aberrant behavior, until I realized all the drink and drugs he consumed had overtaken him.

Lewis told me his parents went along with his psychiatrist's decision to give him EST because they 'thought he was crazy.' I know he was extremely angry with them for allowing it to happen, and I don't think he ever quite forgave them for it, although he seemed to place the blame almost exclusively on his father. Sadly, his parents never forgave themselves. But I also saw Lou use this guilt as a way to manipulate them into letting him do whatever he wanted.

Recipients of EST are not terribly resourceful under pressure; one of the regrettable side effects of this therapeutic treatment is that their nervous systems are permanently compromised. I began to see these effects upon Lou on the road, and only later realized that it was what I had seen in him all along. I'd been responding instinctively to him from my childhood experience and memory, rather than what was clearly before my eyes as a very real condition with which he struggled, in addition to his challenges with drink and drugs.

EST affects many facets of the personality. Depending upon the severity and length of treatment, vast periods of memory are erased, and short term memory is compromised, sometimes permanently. Although this was something Lou and I rarely discussed, like my dad, he had memory lapses, which he tried to hide, along with extreme behavior—even when he was completely sober and clean.

Dad turned eighteen the same year that, on D-Day in 1944, he landed on Utah Beach during the invasion of Normandy as a member of the fifth wave, then marched to Belgium for combat in the Battle of the Bulge. After he came out of the hospital to resume civilian life, during prolonged periods of stress he was extremely irritable, impatient, and nervous. You could actually see the pressure building up in him over time. This is when I was most often awakened by his nightmares, where he relived some of the horrible scenes he experienced during the war.

This is why my father sought the peace and tranquility of the life of a farmer. He didn't grow up in a home where farming was practiced; our acreage was rented out to a local farmer. But he wanted to escape from the mayhem of the world he'd experienced during the war.

Lewis was different in that he sought out, rather than tried to escape, the havoc of modern society. This only taxed his already compromised nervous system, thanks to both the EST treatments and post-traumatic stress that inevitably accompanies them, as well as his escalating drink and drug problem.

What I saw of my father's EST experience was the loss of memory and personal boundaries, and the emotional crumbling during prolonged periods of stress. And this is also what I saw Lewis experience.

When Dad totally lost it, he suddenly picked me up and threw me across the room, either into the next one or against the first wall I met. He never swore at me, but he screamed right up in my face. I'd never heard anyone in my family raise their voices to each other, so this isn't something Dad learned at home. It was the EST treatments and what used to laughingly be called 'battle fatigue' but is now referred to as PTSD. I could see he was out of his mind—I was damn well close enough—and that he didn't know what he was doing. He was over the edge.

Lewis would also 'lose it' completely, although he didn't throw me around. He couldn't; he wasn't physically as strong as my father, who was six-two and still in great physical shape, despite his war wounds. Nor would I ever permit it. And by the time I met Lewis, I was no longer a child.

Daddy didn't drink; instead, he got into some furious battles with my stepmother and me, especially during my rebellious adolescence. As we baby boomers progressed through adolescence, even parents without EST in their backgrounds were confused and upset by our behavior— upon which rock'n'roll had an enormous influence. The world was changing. Teenagers were more independent, and it was no longer a case of 'sit down, shut up, do what your parents say.' My generation grew up being taught that the American GI's had turned the tide of World War II. By fighting in the 'good war'—and winning—our fathers gave us the moral conviction and confidence to protest against a bad one, Vietnam, and help to end it.

I always drew a distinction between my father, a decorated soldier who volunteered his life for his country in 'the good war,' and Lewis, who had an addictive personality. Nevertheless, I saw overwhelming similarities in them. Both were deeply ashamed of their abusive behavior, but being different people, they repaired their broken bridges differently. Within a day of one of Dad's episodes, he would apologize for losing control. Lewis would feel so bad that he'd only drink more, which felt selfish to me. Having no background with alcohol, I didn't understand that he'd lost all control of his drinking—or maybe I just didn't want to admit it.

Lewis had given up trying to moderate his addictions by the time we were on the US *Transformer* tour. His behavior had become so erratic that Dennis joined the tour a couple of times to try and exert some control over him. But the more Lou drank and took cocaine—and the more the pressure grew on him to write his next album, with RCA breathing down his neck—the more unstable his behavior became.

He also began to behave abusively toward me, expressing his anger both emotionally and physically, which seriously rattled and upset me. At times he emotionally withdrew from me, and he took refuge in the passive-aggressive silence I'd seen him use against other people; or he was curt or sharp, which he'd never been before. Usually, this happened when he was completely stoned on alcohol, drugs, or both, in private when we were alone. There were times when he would shove me out of the way as he staggered around our hotel room after everyone left at the end of another night on tour, or when we'd come up to our hotel room after hanging out with everyone in the hotel bar or restaurant following the show. This was the worst possible behavior to exhibit around me. It freaked me out, but I was raised in a family that valued restraint, and could repress my feelings. It is also a survival tactic kids learn growing up around abuse, but as an adult, I had very little tolerance for it.

Lewis was angry with Dennis, too: for several reasons, but a major one was that he believed Dennis was skimming profits. This only made Lou more paranoid than he already was. Along with his anger about having a glitter-rock persona imposed upon him for publicity and the fact that audiences didn't want to hear his more finely crafted songs, he was at the point of exploding. This resentment directly impacted his writing. He couldn't write on tour, because it was too distracting. He was between a rock and a hard place, and the pressure to write his next album hung over his head like an axe waiting to fall.

I learned later that he'd also been shooting speed, although he was successful in hiding it from me, because I always said I would leave him if he started injecting drugs, and he believed me. It was my ironclad escape clause. I've always wondered if I was the only one on the *Transformer* tour who didn't know, because I had no experience with hard drugs or how they manifested themselves in varying personalities—especially one as volatile as Lou's.

* * *

After the show at Alice Tully Hall—which despite all the drama was reviewed favorably—we took off for the Upper Midwest, Boston, and on to Buffalo, where Lou was assaulted onstage by a rabid fan who bit him on his butt. This incident is indicative of the kind of audiences Lewis was attracting for the *Transformer* tour. Although Lewis was shaken by the incident, he continued playing after the lunatic was tackled and removed. Privately, he told me it didn't hurt that much—he was, after all, wearing leather—but said it created great publicity, gaining him more attention.

At home, when we had breaks from the tour, Lewis was deeply depressed about not being able to write, but all he would do about it was drink—which now began at noon—and inhale cocaine. Going out to a party distracted him from thinking about writing and kept his fears at bay, but we both knew this was a waste of his time. I was confused and concerned by this, because he wasn't even trying to write. He was under pressure from his management and RCA to get his next album out, but he was acting like he was caught in a web from which there was no escape.

Lou couldn't talk to me about it, because I was too close to him. It made the reality of the writer's block he was experiencing too real for him to face. To articulate his thoughts to me would have required him to deal with it, which he didn't seem to be able to do.

The problem was, he didn't know how to follow *Transformer*. The direction of this glam-rock album hadn't been his in the first place. It was certainly his most successful album—and still is to this day—but while it catapulted him into the international fame that had previously eluded him, the sound and production of it wasn't his but Bowie's—and, during the tour, Lewis had become conflicted about it. He wasn't sure where he wanted his music to go next, but was certain that wherever it went, it would be *his*.

Lou didn't want to crank out music just for commercial success, and he was concerned *Transformer* had thrust him into that rut. Certainly, RCA wanted his next album to be a hit; although *Transformer* was making waves, as of yet, it hadn't made any real money for the label. The label executives wanted him to follow *Transformer* with a sure-fire hit so they could get a return on their investment.

In effect, the progress of Lewis's writing was stunted by the very things he wished for and wanted the most—fame and commercial success—which greatly contributed to the writer's block from which he was now suffering. But watching him trash himself, rather than trying to find the writing I knew lay inside him, caused me to lose respect for him. In the past I had always been proud to be his partner because of his courage, convictions, and principles about his music, but now he seemed to have lost it all, and was only interested in escaping or striking out and overindulging.

He began to pick fights with me, and we were arguing a lot—something we never did before. I was tired of all the drama, and I couldn't find any peace myself. I was unhappy with all the drinking and drug taking, including my part in it. I looked at myself and our life together and I wondered—*where am I in all this?*

One night, after Lewis, fueled by scotch plus equal parts insouciance and rage, purposefully picked one too many verbal spats with me and had started becoming verbally abusive, I got up and left. I told him not to wait up for me, because I didn't know when I'd be back. While he was in the kitchen filling up his ever present scotch glass, I had called a girlfriend from the Neighborhood Playhouse who lived a couple of blocks away and asked if I could crash on her couch. She said sure, come over; we'd have a long overdue pajama party.

I needed to get away from Lou's depression, the drinking, and his ever-present anger at himself. To Lewis, I had always been like an extension of himself, almost like one of his limbs—that was why he always needed me around him. Perhaps without even knowing it, he had begun to constantly project his anger at himself on to me. It looked like it was turning into one of those nights, and I simply didn't want to be around him. I just wanted out.

I returned the next morning around 10am. Lou had a girl in the pull out bed of our living room couch with him. They were both naked, and clearly she had spent the night. I walked in the room and looked at both of them; then, without saying a word, I sat down in Lou's writing chair.

Well, now, isn't this interesting, I thought.

I simply looked at them. I had nothing to contribute—what was there to say? The scene was so obvious it was almost laughable. I felt like I was in a soap opera but, nevertheless, I lived here, and this was my home. Neither of them said anything, except Lewis, who had called out my name in surprise when I walked in.

After a while, it seemed like the girl might be waiting for me to leave the room so that she could get up and put her clothing on and make her exit.

That's probably not going to happen. Why would I try to make you feel more comfortable?

I think she started to introduce herself, and then I just looked at her as if to say, 'Are you kidding me?' She said sorry weakly, got up, put her clothes on, and left. I never took my eyes off her as she dressed. I noted Lewis hadn't taken her to the bedroom and into our bed of freshly laundered sheets.

Even before she'd closed the front door, Lewis was profusely apologizing, telling me he thought I'd left him for good. In a panic, he initially told me that she was someone he picked up; later, he admitted he'd called someone he knew would come running, because it was what he needed. He couldn't be alone, thinking I'd left him.

'She means nothing to me, I—'

'I know that,' I said.

'Nothing hap—'

'*Please.*'

'Okay!' Lewis said, throwing his arms up in the air, sitting up in our pull out bed of our living room. Nude.

Oh, this is priceless, I thought, wishing there was a camera nearby.

'I was at Judy's on 72nd,' I said.

'Why didn't you call?'

'Don't know.'

'Was anyone else there?'

'Yeah.'

'Really? Like who?'

I waited for a bit. He deserved to suffer.

'Bettye?'

All right. Enough already.

'Her roommates. There are three. We had a pajama party. It was great.'

'Oh, yeah?' he answered casually. 'What did you do?'

'We played Dionne Warwick and lip-synced along.'

'Oh, she is wonderful,' he replied, finally looking up at me.

'Yep.'

'Which ones did you play?'

'*Anyone who had a heart,*' I sang, '*could look at me …*'

'*… and know that I love you,*' Lou added.

'*Anyone who ever dreamed could look at me, and know I dream of you …*'

'Knowing I love you ...'
'So!' we both sang.
I should have thanked her before she left, I thought.

* * *

Back on the road, we played Toronto, where we also spent time with the Canadian music producer and keyboardist Bob Ezrin and his family. Bob was courting Lewis to produce his next album, which they talked about in a couple of meetings I attended. Lewis eventually felt comfortable enough with Bob to confess that he was suffering from writer's block. He felt enormous pressure about not being able to meet his contractual obligations with RCA and write his next album, which terrified him.

Bob listened to him, which gave Lou the confidence and space to express his fears out loud. He gave him a deadline, too, for when they could further talk about his ideas, which was also helpful to Lewis.

We had a nice time in Toronto. We went out to dinner a couple of times with Bob and his wife, Janet, and they had us over to their place, where I also played with their young children, who were the same ages as my little half-siblings. When we left Toronto, Lewis felt better, and we went back on the road with renewed spirits.

Lou played with some incredible musicians on the *Transformer* tours, along with Garland Jeffreys and The Persuasions, who opened for him again. Among others, he played with Jeff Beck, Genesis, The New York Dolls, Yes, Chicago, and Peter Wolf of the J. Geils Band, another friend of his from way back.

My experience at the first Scheessel Rock Festival in Germany, in 1973, was amazing. Spread out over these gentle lowlands were 52,000 young people in attendance. It was overwhelming for both of us. On the bill with Lou were Chuck Berry and Jerry Lee Lewis—and they were incredible. Buddy Miles, Richie Havens, and Manfred Mann were also playing, and it was truly a thrill to meet all these legendary artists and hear them play up close from the wings of the stage. Lewis was ecstatic to be talking with Chuck Berry and Jerry Lee Lewis, as they were heroes of his from when he was just a kid.

When I first arrived at the festival and looked out on the sea of thousands, I couldn't believe how quiet the audience was—certainly compared to American audiences. I actually wondered if there was something wrong, but I had no idea what it could be. Then one of the musicians explained that many of them were spaced out on heroin, which he said was very popular there at the time, and when I took a closer look, the crowd did indeed look 'laid back.' I thought it was incredibly sad.

Another standout show was in Miami, where Lewis was arrested during the show while singing 'Sister Ray.' The police had quietly entered the auditorium about halfway through the concert. They lined up, fully uniformed, carrying guns—against both walls of the auditorium. Those in the back by the lobby doors were wearing riot gear.

When Lou got to the line about the '*po*-lice' 'knocking on my chamber door,' the officers walked down both sides of the auditorium, and through the middle isle, billy clubs in hand, and strode onto both sides of the stage to stop the show.

One officer took his microphone away from Lewis and spoke into it, telling the crowd that the show was over. Everyone needed to get up, leave the venue in a respectful manner, and go home. Then he turned to the band and told them to get off the stage, signaling to the lighting booth to turn the lights off—but not before Lewis was taken into custody and handcuffed, where he was arrested for public indecency and drunkenness.

The audience was angry, but the presence of so many armed police officers prevented any riot. Lewis was escorted in handcuffs to the patrol car waiting out front in the traditional 'perp-walk,' otherwise known as the walk of shame. This is the very antithesis of the American judicial system, which claims everyone is 'innocent until proven guilty.'

Lou was placed in the back of the police car, and taken off to jail. Conveniently, Dennis happened to be on the road with us, so our driver followed close behind. I waited in the police station while Dennis went back to the holding cells where Lou was incarcerated. He made arrangements for Lou's bail and got him released.

I was glad Dennis was here to deal with this debacle. It didn't take long, about an hour—maybe less—and soon Lewis was walking out of the detention area with Dennis. As soon as he got to me, he put his arms around me. I marveled at how, for someone who was just coming out of jail, he seemed fine.

We were driven back to the hotel, where we had dinner, as usual, and Lewis got drunk and stoned again. He was exuberant about the publicity the incident created, resulting in substantial coverage in the papers, on local TV, and on the radio, even making some national spots. Lou was happy that the incident could only increase sales of *Transformer*. All he'd actually done was sing 'Sister Ray' in performance, but the powers that be in the City of Miami were deeply offended by him, as the voice of the gay community.

At that time, homosexual activity was still a crime in the US. Lou's lyrics to 'Walk On The Wild Side,' which was receiving heavy airplay in Miami, celebrated what were still considered deviant sexual acts—which were against the law. Evidently, he and his music were so offensive that he needed to be arrested.

I always wondered if it was a publicity stunt; someone must have tipped off the police about the best time to arrest him, because they seemed very well informed about the setlist, and the lyrics to 'Sister Ray,' but no one ever said anything. Before the show, Dennis told Lewis and me that there might be some trouble. Miami was really *Deep South*, and was very socially conservative, compared to New York.

Perhaps it was a coincidence that the police entered at just the right moment so that Lou's lyrics matched the real life scenario. Later, when Lou talked about it with me, he said he'd been shaken by the incident. The police were not pleased with him.

Another show that stands out in my mind was one in Boston. I was onstage when the venue's doors opened and the audience was admitted. The house lights were up, as a couple of guys from our lighting company and I were reviewing them with some technicians, making some adjustments. Suddenly I heard my name and, startled, turned around. In the front row, thirteen gay men who had stripped their shirts off, nude to the waist, stood smiling, waving and blowing kisses.

'Hi, Bettye!' they shouted.

I was surprised, and I wondered how they knew who I was, although my photo had turned up now and then with Lou in the papers, and the lights had continued to get positively mentioned in reviews of his shows. All at once, on cue, they turned around in unison, like they were performing a choreographed move. On each man's back was a single large letter, arranged to spell out the following words:

WE LOVE YOU LOU!

Shocked, but delighted, I clapped, smiled, and waved back at them. They continued to blow kisses.

'We love you, too, Bettye!' they screamed.

Back in the US, I was working the lights again, often surrounded by the audience as I called my cues from the balcony. The crowds were even wilder and more boisterous than on previous tours, if that was possible.

Every time we headed out to the Midwest—Chicago, Madison, Detroit, and especially Minneapolis—we prepared ourselves for these crowds. This was Viking country—my people—and they were the rowdiest of all.

Some of those upper Midwest shows were downright scary, and I was incredibly relieved at the end of some of them to walk away unharmed.

But as I walked through the empty auditoriums, picking my way through the seats and floor littered with needles, liquor bottles, beer cans, rolling papers, tin foil—all the paraphernalia of the drug culture that had now entered the American consciousness—something in me recoiled at the thought that I could be perceived as being a part of what was encouraging this dark turn of America's youth. I couldn't help but wonder what my family would think if they knew about it, or saw all this. I suspect my father *did* know, and that this was, in large part, why he didn't approve of Lewis.

berlin . . . . CHAPTER THIRTEEN

One night not long after our run-in with the police in Miami, Lou had been drinking and snorting cocaine from early afternoon on into the night after the show in a veritable marathon of drinking and drugs. It was now the early hours of the morning, and I was getting him up to our hotel room. He couldn't walk on his own, so I was helping him over to the bed.

Suddenly he turned around and hit me in the face—hard. My glasses flew off my face somewhere onto the floor. Stunned, but more than anything else, hurt and outraged, I cried out.

'Lewis, what in God's name are you doing?'

Lou started laughing hysterically and fell down on his back onto the bed.

Without thinking—it must have been pure 'fight or flight' reflex, because there wasn't enough time for a second of thought—I immediately jumped onto the bed, straddled him, and slapped him as hard as I could in the face.

Now that'll stop your laughing, won't it, buddy?

He didn't swing back.

Before I climbed off him, I looked him dead in the eyes and said, '*Do not ever* hit me again.'

Lou was on his back, looking up at me, his hand covering his face, as stunned as I'd been.

'That hurt!' he cried.

'Yeah, doesn't it?'

With one last horrible look, I got off, found my glasses, and picked them up. Thankfully, they were not broken. I walked over to the full-length mirror and turned on the light to examine the damage.

My right eye was already red and swelling, and there were scratch marks under my eye and on my cheek.

'Look at my face,' I said, turning to him. 'It's already red and swollen. God knows what it'll look like tomorrow!'

Lewis didn't say anything. He just lay there in permanent pause, holding his face and staring at the ceiling.

I walked over and said, 'Get off the bed.'

Slowly he pulled himself up on his elbow, holding his face.

'And where do I sleep … *Princess*?' he scoffed.

'Hopefully, on the floor,' I said. 'There's another bed. I don't care, just get off mine.'

'You're such a *bitch*,' he said, struggling to get up.

'And you're a fucking coward, hitting a woman,' I replied.

I walked toward the adjoining bathroom, pulling my clothes off as I went.

Just before I slammed the bathroom door shut, I heard him get off the bed and start stumbling and crashing into things. I didn't know what, nor did I care.

I was shaking as I examined my face in the bathroom mirror. My eye was turning purple already, and the right side of my face was blowing up. I pulled my hair back with a headband and wiped my face with a cotton pad soaked with my nightly cleanser. Leaning over the sink, I ran cold water over a washcloth, applying it soaking wet to my face.

Suddenly I heard an enormous crash in the bedroom. Wringing out the washcloth and holding it to my eye, I opened the door.

Lou was standing on the far side of what was now his bed, looking at me, shaking with rage. A chair was upended on the other side of the room.

I didn't acknowledge he was there. Naked, I walked over to the bed, pulled the covers back, and slid in between the sheets.

'Turn the light off when you're done,' I said, turning my back to him and pulling the covers up over my shoulder.

All I heard was Lewis cursing and rattling around in the mini-refrigerator, then going into the bathroom. The sound of running water lulled me to sleep.

The following morning, I woke up and Lewis was sitting on my bed, next to me, staring. His eye was as black as mine probably was by now, I noted, satisfied. I ignored him and got out on the other side of the bed, picked my clothes up off the floor, and went into the bathroom. After closing and locking the door, I looked at my face in the mirror.

That's quite a shiner you've got there, darlin'. Oh, this is going to be so much fun.

Disgusted, I turned on the shower and got in. Even though I'd never hit anyone in my life, clearly, my instinct was not to flee.

Later, when I thought about it, I realized that I hadn't been afraid of him for an instant. I'd been on autopilot. I was also incensed beyond any rational thought. In his condition, he could have beaten the bejesus out of me, because he was furious when I slapped him. I'd seen him go wild before, lashing out, throwing things and attacking whatever was nearby—he was definitely capable of hurting me.

But he didn't.

When I came out of the bathroom, Lewis wasn't in the room. I hoped I'd never see him again. I put on my sunglasses, picked up my bag, found the key to the hotel room, and went into the hallway. I needed to get a coffee and breakfast, and figure out what I wanted to do.

As I walked to the elevator, Dennis suddenly appeared, striding toward me from the opposite direction. Before he was near me, he began yelling.

'What did you do to Lou? He's got a black eye! How is he going to go onstage like that?'

I continued to walk toward him, despite his yelling, but when he got to me, I stopped. Then I took my sunglasses off. He gasped and covered his mouth with his hand when he saw my black and blue, swollen face and eye.

He stood silently, staring at me, and said, 'My god, you two are going to kill each other!'

'If he ever raises a fucking hand to me again,' I said, 'he'll look a hell of a lot worse than he does now. Let the Phantom of Rock wear sunglasses onstage, I could care less.' Putting my sunglasses back on, I added, 'One more time, and I will really hurt him—or have someone do it for me. You tell him that, then we can be sure he won't have a black eye onstage, *poor baby*.'

With that, I continued walking to the elevator. I punched the button—*hard*. Dennis said nothing, nor did he follow me onto the elevator.

The son of a bitch didn't even ask if I was okay, I thought, as the elevator doors closed. *Nice.*

But I was right: Lewis never raised a hand to me again. See, that's what you've got to do. Swing back as hard as you can like a kid in the playground, or leave forever.

Because cowards don't fight fair.

* * *

After the *Transformer* tour was over, things started taking off quickly. Back at home soon after our return, one morning around 8am, I woke up and noticed Lou wasn't by my side. Worried, I quickly got out of bed.

Oh, god, now what? Where is he? Wandering the streets, staggering around, lost or lying in a gutter somewhere—beat up or dead?

I walked out to the kitchen, and then, from our entrance foyer, I saw Lewis sitting in his writing chair with a bottle of Johnnie Walker three quarters consumed and a half-empty glass on the occasional table beside him. His guitar was propped up on the floor against one of our giant stereo speakers nearby. He was awake but staring glassily straight ahead. He slid his eyes over when I walked into his eyesight, but that was his only movement.

Spooked, I entered the living room anyway.

'Lewis what are you doing,' I said, 'it's eight o'clock in the morning, and you're awake, still drinking? *I cannot believe—*'

'I wrote the album last night,' he said, breaking in.

At first I was relieved, because RCA would finally have the album they had been pressuring him to complete for months. It was a matter of weeks before it was due, but now he needn't to worry about being dropped by them for not fulfilling his contractual obligations to produce another album after *Transformer.*

Then he tossed his notebook on the floor toward me and told me to read the lyrics, and he'd sing his new album for me. This was the first time he didn't ask me to sing the lyrics of his new songs while he played along on guitar, but that was okay. I was thrilled he was finally writing again.

I'd been through this before with Lou. It is how he wrote his other albums—overnight, all at once, piecing together old material with new songs—so I made us some coffee and then told him he could sing it for me.

He gestured for me to pick up his notebook and sit down on our couch. I was a bit put off that I was supposed to pick up his notebook from the floor like his handmaiden, but I thought—whatever—because I was eager to hear his new songs.

Lou picked up his guitar, and began to sing. He began with 'Berlin,' which I knew well, as he'd recorded it on *Lou Reed* and played it on tour many times. I sipped my coffee and listened. Next, he played 'Men Of Good Fortune' and 'Oh, Jim,' which I also knew, although it sounded like he'd reworked them a bit. Next, I heard 'Caroline Says,' but the lyrics seemed different than I remembered.

I glanced at his notebook lying on my lap, but I decided I'd just listen, rather than follow the lyrics he had jotted down. His writing was nearly indecipherable, anyway. When he started singing the song, 'Lady Day,' he suddenly stopped and asked me to bring him his notebook, because he couldn't remember some of the lyrics. I took it over and put it on his lap.

I asked if he wanted another coffee, but he shook his head no. Glancing at his notebook, he began singing again, so I sat down and listened. He got through 'How Do You Think It Feels,' which I thought was unfortunate, the way he felt, then went on to 'Caroline Says II.'

I listened, stunned, and put my coffee down on the glass table next to the couch. When he finished, he looked at me. Tapping my cup to indicate I was getting more coffee, I left the room.

I made it to the kitchen before I started crying, running the water so he couldn't hear me. He'd included the black eye he gave me in the song, and the time when I put my fist through a windowpane during one of our most bruising fights in the apartment. But I also realized there was a narrative going on and the lyrics really had little to do with me, because he was only taking real life moments and adding them to his story to give it an immediate sense of reality.

Buck up, kid, let's get through this.

I poured myself another cup of coffee, went back into the living room, and resumed my seat. He had just finished the song.

'Are you all right?' he asked.

Oh, no. He's acting oh-so cool. What's that about?

'Keep playing,' was all I said.

The next song was 'The Kids,' and the first lyrics he sang were, '*They're taking her children away / Because they said she was not a good mother.*'

I froze when I heard that first line.

So that's it.

When he sang the line about how '*they're taking her children away because of the things ... they had heard she'd done,*' I abruptly stood up, but he kept on singing. Still as a statue, I kept on listening, because I recognized the line as something I'd said verbatim when I'd told him about how I'd lost my mother when I was five years old.

Only a week or two ago, I'd received a phone call about my mother from someone who said they were from the Queens County Clerk's Office, which had prompted me to tell Lewis the story about how my dad had kidnapped me from her. I'd never told this to anyone before, and it had been a huge leap of faith for me to tell Lewis.

When I heard the line about the waterboy—how the real game is 'not over here'—I sat back down again, because he was right. Yes, the real game wasn't here. The situation he was singing about was mine.

The real story about my parents and my childhood was far more incredible than Lou's lyrics. It was a beautiful love story. How they met at a dance her uncle had escorted her to at the fort where Dad had been in hospital repairing from the war. They were crazy about each other, two beautiful people who had in common the love of swing, big band, singing, and playing music together. Why they parted in a terrible, volatile end was because of Dad's PTSD and his ECT treatments—and World War II was their backdrop. I was in such a state of shock, I felt like I was in a dream listening to Lou singing, but I wanted to hear his narrative, however painful it might be.

When I heard the line about how he was a tired man with no words to say, I recognized it as something I'd told him my father said, the only time he ever talked about taking me away from my mother. Dad brought me back in a Greyhound bus from Lake Charles, Louisiana, my mother's hometown, where Mom had taken me after leaving him. He'd physically threatened her during one of their awful battles. I was three years old, but I remembered standing between my parents legs as they yelled at each other—their legs like bars capturing me—along with the knife she pulled on Dad to back him off. A spirited Irish lass, my mother would never take abuse from a man, no matter how much she loved him. But she hadn't even been home when he stole me and took me back to his family's Pennsylvania homestead.

When Lewis got to the line about how, '*since she lost her daughter, it's her eyes filled with water, and I am much happier this way,*' I got up and left the room, went into our bedroom and sat down on the edge of our bed closest to the door. It was as far as I could walk. Lewis continued playing.

Hearing the rest of the song nearly destroyed me. He was embellishing the story, but repeated the line about the woman losing her daughter. And the fact that the narrator was much 'happier' about what happened to, essentially, my mother—as it was her story that gave him this part of the narrative—there are no words to describe how I felt listening to these lyrics.

You son of a bitch, this happened to me, as you damn well know.

Although my mother traveled to Pennsylvania and fought for me in court, I was awarded to my grandfather in the custody battle. My father had left a couple of weeks after he'd dropped me off at my grandparent's home to re-enlist in the army. But a single mother without any financial support in the 1950s—she'd never asked for anything from Dad, had simply taken me and left without contacting him—couldn't afford an expensive attorney like my father's family. She was denied all rights to see me from the time I was five until my eighteenth birthday, when my grandmother was required to send me her address in Queens, which was where she moved after losing me.

Trying to find her was what brought me to New York in the first place. In the thirteen years I'd been estranged from her, she had not been mentioned once by anyone in my family except my stepmother, who once said disparagingly, 'You're just like your mother!' My father stopped her cold and told her to never sully my mother's name by mentioning it again. So no one did.

My mother might as well have been dead. I'd always felt she was alive somewhere, because I adored her, but I didn't even feel like I could ask. Losing her when I was only five years old, I had gone into a nearly catatonic state for weeks after Dad brought me home to Pennsylvania. But my grandmother stayed by my side night and day, even sleeping with me. Soon, she was able to get me to the bathroom and back. In a couple of days, she was able to take me downstairs to the kitchen, then back up to my bed again. Finally, she got me downstairs and out onto the back porch. I still remember looking up at our old catalpa tree near the back steps, thinking I must be under the canopy of heaven.

After a while, my grandmother took me back upstairs and into bed again, where I fell asleep, exhausted. But she persisted, and a little bit at a time, my grandmother pulled me out of it and brought me back. By the end of the summer, I was well enough to enter first grade, still only five years old.

When I heard the bridge again, I realized it was extraordinarily beautiful. But my heart was broken. I could have picked it up in little pieces from our llama rug beneath my feet. I was completely devastated.

Sitting on the edge of the bed, my hands on either side, holding me up for support, vaguely, I heard Lou walking across the bare parquet floor of the foyer and turn the corner toward our bedroom. When I heard his footsteps stop, I looked up. Neither of us said anything.

Finally Lou broke the awful silence.

'Listen, this is just a song, Bettye.'

I lowered my eyes to my lap, refusing to speak.

'Bettye?'

'Look, it's what came last night,' he continued. 'I just wrote it down.'

'But Lewis,' I said, looking up at him, 'you've taken my story. You intend to tell the whole world how I was taken away from my mother when I was a kid on your new album? About my mother? What she was accused of, which was completely untrue? And losing me? *That's my mother, Lewis.'*

Lou put his guitar down on the floor and leaned it on the bed. Then he kneeled down in front of me and put his hands on my knees.

'It's just what came. It's an incredible story—'

'Yes, but it's *my* story,' I said, 'how could you break my confiden—'

'I have to get an album to RCA. I'll lose everything if I don't, you know that!' he cried. 'It's not about you, princess—'

'Oh, yes it is,' I said, stopping him.

'All right, yes,' he confessed, 'parts of it, but I've embellished it. No one will know.'

'*I will.'*

'Just come out with me, and hear the rest of it,' he coaxed. 'We have to get through this. I don't want to lose you. It's just a story, Princess.'

I had absolutely nothing to say. Words were lost to me.

Anything else you want from me, Lewis? My blood? Well, actually, you took that, too.

It was beyond reprehensible.

'Just listen to the rest of it. I love you, you know that—I can't do this without you!'

But I'd had enough.

Lou took hold of my elbow and pulled me up to him. He laid my head on his chest, resting his chin on the top of my head. It was a familiar way he would hold me, and I was blown away.

I let him bring me into the living room and sit me down on the couch. Then he immediately picked up his guitar, sat down and started playing, 'The Bed.' For this one, he didn't need to check the lyrics.

All right, we don't have any kids.

I was relieved about it in more ways than one.

Maybe he'll leave me out of this.

But then I felt the hair on the back of my neck rise.

Because I lit the candles in our bedroom every night.

Okay, but wait! I hadn't cut my wrists over him, so that part wasn't true!

Nevertheless, the cold, cruel clarity of the song overcame me. I realized it was brilliant storytelling. But he'd stolen my confidence and broken my heart.

Then I heard the line about 'the boxes she kept on the shelf, filled with her poetry and stuff.'

Oh, no.

I kept all my poetry and papers in a box on a shelf in the foyer closet.

I reminded myself, before I seriously started freaking out, that my husband was a writer, and that this is what writers do—especially good ones, which he was. They write what they know; take the truth and embellish it, shaping it into their own narrative.

But where's his respect? Why did he have to use the most painful episode of my childhood and my parents' lives? This was just wrong.

I knew these songs weren't just about me. Nico was in there—and all the drugs. But his misogyny and misplaced anger he'd been projecting onto me for months was unmistakable.

Hang on, don't go over the edge.

He had to get an album out.

He's desperate. Time's running out.

He hadn't been able to write for nearly nine months.

For better or for worse.

How could it get worse? This was the ultimate betrayal.

My blood.

'Sad Song' was next, and when I heard the line about how '*she looks like Mary Queen of Scots,*' I grew wary again, because I thought he was talking about me. When he sang that she seemed '*very regal,*' I was certain, because he'd called me that before.

But then the lyrics went on: '*Just goes to show how wrong you can be.*'

Although I hadn't been able to look at him, as I held on to my cold cup of coffee like it was a weighted buoy in water, I glanced up at him, and our eyes met. But he just … kept singing.

Finally, when I heard the line about how he was going to stop wasting his time—how '*somebody else would have broken both of her arms*'—I got up, walked into the bathroom, and shut the door.

I didn't want to hear anymore, but he kept on playing, and I heard the rest of the song anyway, looking into the mirror, watching myself, dazed, trying to separate story from fact, story from song. It had become seriously confusing.

Hold on, Bettye, this isn't about you.

Yeah, and if I keep telling myself that, maybe I'll believe it?

I held onto the sink and looked into the mirror.

He's desperate, and his back is up against the wall. It's all he can do.

What was really sad about this song was his self-pity. He stopped trying long ago, and all he'd done was drink.

But then I heard his steps coming toward the bathroom, a light tapping on the closed door.

'Bettye?' he called.

I said nothing and started running the water, throwing the cold, clear liquid on my face, over and over again.

'Bettye, come out, let me talk to you,' he repeated, tapping on the door between us.

Finally, I reached for a towel, dried my face, and looked into the mirror one last time.

Time to grab this bull by the horns.

I opened the door and looked him in the face.

'How dare you,' I said quietly.

'It's what came, Bettye! I haven't been able to write in months, you know that! I have to put out an album, *or I'm done!'* he cried, looking into my eyes.

I didn't like what I saw there.

I brushed past him. Walking into our bedroom, I shut the door to dress in private.

No, we're done.

I was done ever exposing myself to this man.

You'll never see my body again, and that will be your loss, because I know how much you love it.

I began dressing in front of our full-length mirror.

I heard his tap, tap, tapping on our bedroom door.

Like a robot or a Stepford wife, I said, 'I'll be out in a minute.'

He's lost me. It will be so much easier to deal with him now.

I heard his boots on the hardwood floor go into the kitchen, and the freezer door slamming shut. The familiar cracking of ice cubes rattling out of their tray, tinkling merrily as he casually dropped them into a clean glass. The unscrewing of Johnnie's cap, and the crack and pop of the cold cubes abruptly changing temperature as the golden liquid flooded over them came next.

You've made your choice.

* * *

A week later, we were at a party at his friend's house—the same blonde woman who told us to get an apartment on the Upper East Side, because that's where all the important and successful people live. I'd always thought that was strange, because she didn't live on the Upper East Side! She had an apartment on Fifth Avenue, around 10th or 11th Street.

The place was packed with people, drinking and snorting coke as usual. I was sitting down, talking to Donald Lyons, the theater critic, when suddenly I saw into the bathroom, as the door swung open, and someone came out. Lewis was sitting on the commode. His arm was tied up with rubber tubing. His friend, bent over him, was shooting him up. Lewis was smiling grimly at her. She looked like a mother giving her baby milk; she was calm, almost methodical, with an odd, ghost of a smile hovering on her thin lips. At the time I assumed it was heroin, although it could have been speed.

I was flabbergasted, but I did not react at all. I didn't want to call attention to myself. Suddenly, the blonde looked up and saw me watching them. Without stopping, she lifted her foot behind her and slammed the door. But it was too late.

I was devastated and appalled. How long had he been injecting?

Some friend you've got there, Lewis!

I'd always known she was crazy about Lewis—everyone did, it was obvious. She'd do anything he asked; maybe she hoped that, if she did, she'd get him? But Lewis never wanted her; he wanted me, and I had always felt her hostility, however much she'd thought she'd hidden it, pretending to be my friend.

I'd never trusted her, but I'd never said anything, not even to Lewis— what was the point? I always thought she was weird, and I had never really given her much thought, anyway. Another one of the minions Lewis kept around to do his bidding, stringing them along with just the right amount of hope—plus a dash of jealousy.

I acted like I hadn't seen anything, and eventually I moved on and wandered over to the circle of people gathered around, snorting coke. I took a couple of lines, then quietly slipped away and out the door. I made it past the spiral staircase and into the foyer of the building. The uniformed doorman was gone for the night, so I ran down the steps, stepped out onto Fifth Avenue, and hailed a cab home.

I heard Lewis come in later, but didn't know what time it was or how long I'd been sleeping. I'd taken a Valium and climbed into our fresh, clean sheets and closed my eyes, resolved about what I would do.

I felt Lou lay down next to me and put his arms around me, shifting my head onto his chest as he lay back. I let him move me, because it didn't matter anymore, and nestled into him like most nights. I'd already decided what the morning would bring; for now, let us have one more night together.

Like a prince in a twisted fairy tale, Lou became the man I had fallen in love with only when he was sleeping.

* * *

The next morning I got up quietly and went into the kitchen for my V8 and coffee. Lou was still sleeping. Silently sipping it, while sitting at our tiny cafe table by the window, I looked out on the shaft of soft morning light hitting the narrow street below. People were walking their dogs, dragged by a leash with one hand and, in the other, holding partially wrapped bagels in the brown paper bags that they'd picked up at the corner deli. Another frantic morning in Manhattan had begun.

I heard Lewis get up. Stumbling into the kitchen in only his underwear, he scratched his stomach, stretching.

'Morning,' he mumbled, opening the refrigerator for his orange juice.

'Morning,' I said perfunctorily.

Slipping behind him, I went into the living room and sat down on our pullout couch. The velvet material was coarse to the touch as I rubbed against its grain.

'Bettye?' he called from the kitchen.

I didn't say anything. I had decided to wait till he came in and sat down beside me.

Then I would tell him. Right from the get-go.

'Princess?' he said, coming into the living room.

He sat down next to me with a glass of orange juice in his hand. He smoothed back some loose strands of my hair with his other.

'What's up?' he asked.

I didn't say anything for a while. I wanted to be certain that what I had to say was just as I wanted to say it.

'Bettye,' he said, 'what happened last night, why did you leave? I looked around and you were—'

Here it was.

I turned and looked at him quickly, interrupting him.

'Lewis, I want a divorce.'

He stopped talking, and his eyes opened very wide.

So now you're awake.

'What did you say?' he asked.

'I want a divorce,' I repeated.

I looked down at my coffee and took another sip.

'*What?*' Lou said, genuinely taken aback.

'I want a divorce.'

He started to laugh, but then he stopped and looked at me.

'You're not serious.'

He took a drink of orange juice from his glass, then put it down on the smoked glass table beside him, turning to me.

'I am.'

'Bettye, what are you talking about?'

'I want a divorce, Lewis.'

'Good one,' he said, snorting and sitting back.

'I saw you last night in the bathroom with your friend,' I said.

'So?' he answered. 'We were just talking, Bettye, nothing was going on.'

'She was shooting you up, Lewis. And you, all tied up, sitting on the toilet, like a junkie.'

'No, that wasn't me, it must have been someone else—'

He's rushing, I noted. *But he's playing this rather well*, I thought, silently congratulating him.

'No, it was you, Lewis,' I said. 'I saw you both.'

'Wait a minute,' he said, scratching his head, 'can we talk about this?'

'No, I want a divorce. I told you if I ever saw you with a needle, I would leave you. I wasn't kidding, you know that.'

'*All right*, she was just giving me one of Dr. Freymann's shots he gave her to take home.'

'He doesn't give anyone those shots to take home, Lewis, you know I know that. The only one who gives those shots is Dr. Freymann, in his office. No need to lie about it.'

'No, he gave some to her, she had some kind of infection—'

'Lewis, stop. *I know*.'

'Bettye, wait—'

'No, *you* wait,' I said. 'Do you want to call Dennis or shall I?'

He got up abruptly and stood over me.

'You're being ridiculous,' he said, looking down.

'Oh, okay,' I said, rising. I walked into the kitchen to pour myself another coffee. Lewis followed me.

'Princess …'

As I moved past him in the narrow kitchen, I looked at him. His face was weirdly collapsed. He looked how I imagined someone would if they had just been shot.

As promised, later that morning, I called Dennis and told him I wanted a divorce. He was as shocked as Lewis and, at first, he began protesting, but when I told him why, he grew silent. He knew I'd always been serious about leaving Lewis if I saw him use hard drugs.

The scene had become too crazy for me. I was becoming someone I didn't know anymore. With Lewis in the condition he was in—and, now, shooting drugs—I was frightened out of my mind, but I couldn't tell anyone. Who could I tell? What good would it do?

Shooting drugs was serious business, but apparently it was now Lou's, too, despite the fact that we'd all lost so many people to overdoses. Every week we'd hear of someone else who'd dropped dead after shooting up, or had been found in the morning, overdosed, cold and dead.

What if it happened to Lewis? The old worry I had right from the start—that his using and drinking could become fatal—reared its ugly head. I wouldn't be able to take it. I couldn't stop him, and I couldn't sit around and watch him risk everything, or us—me—further. Lewis had been reeling out of control, and I couldn't handle him anymore.

I had given up. I was honestly afraid that I would die if I didn't get out of this scene; things had become too dangerous.

He's got his album, now, I told Dennis. He would have to make it without me.

'Why don't you two come into the office today, and we can talk about it?' Dennis asked. 'I'll clear my calendar. When do you think you two can come in?'

'I'll ask Lewis, and he'll call you,' I said, and hung up the phone.

I wanted to honor my vows, but I was a survivor. The man had cheated and lied to me, and with *Berlin*, he'd broken my heart and all the trust I had in him. I wasn't breaking my word—I was keeping it. I had been frightened for so long, and had wanted to leave for a great while. But I had been so pressured by Lewis and his management to stay, because of his total dependence upon me, that I'd made one excuse after another, so I could.

Just goes to show how wrong you can be.

divorce, reconciliation..... CHAPTER FOURTEEN

Lewis refused to go with me to meet Dennis and discuss the divorce I wanted because he opposed it, so I met with Dennis alone. By the time I got there, however, it was apparent they had spoken on the phone. At first, Dennis suggested I get an annulment, which he said would be very easy to obtain. It would be the least amount of stress on both of us, and we wouldn't need divorce lawyers. Everything would go away like nothing had ever happened.

Like me?

Because I'd seen how Lewis could get rid of people and wipe all trace of them away as if they'd never existed.

With an annulment, they'll bury me.

However, there was one problem. Even if they did want to eradicate me, they couldn't pretend I'd never existed, because of 'Perfect Day.' I was the only person in that song who Lou could be singing about at the time it was written, recorded, and then released. The song was written about me.

This beautiful song was an ode to our love and relationship, and the best gift any man could give a woman he loved. Even though Lou never mentioned me or credited me for being the inspiration behind the song for many reasons, he would never deny 'Perfect Day' was written with me in mind. Because it meant as much to him as it did to me; I was as confident about that as I was about breathing. And I was right: he never denied I was the inspiration behind this song, because it captured a moment of our time together perfectly. I knew not only how much Lou needed me, but how much he loved me. Now, however, Dennis was pulling all the strings.

Dennis reminded me that he was Lou's lawyer and couldn't represent my interests, only Lou's, which he did; and if I pushed for a divorce, he would have little else to say to me other than to advise me to obtain a divorce attorney. And indeed, I actually *was* buried, because I was never mentioned or given any credit for all the work I did helping to launch his solo career in nearly half a century.

But I had something that couldn't be bought or sold. In a world run by deals and money, 'Perfect Day' lived in a place untouched by beacons of power. It was where Lou and I lived when we were together. It was seriously good, and anyone who heard 'Perfect Day' could relate to it in their own lives. As it turns out, the whole world has heard it—it is a classic.

I knew that whatever happened, this song would always be mine.

I was also deeply conflicted about demanding a divorce, because I was acting against my heart. I loved my husband, but I also feared for my life. I couldn't continue living our life together as it had become, and I couldn't think of anything else to do but walk away. This was another instance where I didn't think I had a choice. I left Lou to survive.

But I believed I needed to get out fast and get out now, before I changed my mind. If I didn't, I might never escape. Not only did I need to leave the life Lou had created for us, I couldn't continue living the one I'd found myself in. It wasn't only Lou's fault that our lives had become dysfunctional. It was also mine, because I could have left him long ago; indeed, I'd tried. But Lou could be pretty persuasive, and I was fighting considerable odds every time I tried leaving: My feelings for him, and my emotional and professional investment in his career; but most of all the pressure from Lou and his management to stay, because he believed he couldn't function without me. Maybe he couldn't, but that wasn't in our vows, and he shouldn't have been my responsibility.

Perhaps one of the strongest reasons why I stayed with Lou longer than I should have was my belief in his music. He brought the principles of good writing and literature to American rock'n'roll, and writing was as important to me as it was to Lewis. I loved rock'n'roll. The lyrics in Lou's 'Rock And Roll' could have been written for me. I was just like Jenny in the song who was also blown away when she finally heard it on the radio. I started dancing to that fine, fine music in high school, and my life was changed from that point on. I was forever grateful to rock'n'roll, because it saved my life, especially during adolescence.

After I told Dennis that I wanted out, and that I wouldn't ask Lou for a financial settlement of any kind, he began explaining all the papers I needed to sign before Lou would give me a divorce. All I wanted was my salary as his lighting designer and director, as he'd promised, but which I'd never received. Dennis offered me a price, which sounded too low. I told him I would think about it and get back to him.

First, I needed to call Uncle Babe, who always had my back, and talk to him about it.

As Lou's wife, I agreed to sign away all my rights as vice president of Sister Ray Enterprises, Lou's corporation, and all monies that could be gained from it—his record deals, music, and writing copyrights, now and in the future. Even though I was legally entitled to 50 percent of Lou's financial worth—and, considering the work I had done on Lou's behalf, personally and professionally, I was certain both Dennis and Lou were concerned I would ask for at least that, if not more—and probably get it.

But Lewis never liked parting with his money, and it was Dennis's job to make sure he didn't. Lou had also been emotionally and physically abusive with me, and that was probably worth some financial compensation. All I needed was a decent divorce attorney, which I could get. But I decided not to go down that route. Perhaps I was being a pushover by giving it all away, but I didn't think so. Because I wasn't really walking away from Lewis empty handed—he'd already given me 'Perfect Day.'

Dennis set up appointments for me to see several attorneys, all of whom required me to sign papers relinquishing all monetary claims I had as Lou's wife for any income he was earning, now and in the future. So, in reality, this was all what I really had to deal with when I said I wanted a divorce.

Going from one lawyer to another to sign away all my rights was disheartening and unpleasant. The last attorney was a divorce attorney who required me to sign a letter stating he advised me against relinquishing all monetary rights as Lou's legal spouse, which tied me to any of Lou's finances. I hadn't gotten back to Dennis about my lighting fees, because I hadn't spoken to my uncle yet, but that was still under consideration.

So, yes, I read the letter, advising me that signing away all monetary rights as Lou's spouse to his current and any potential future income was against the advice of counsel, but I signed it, anyway. The lawyer was so angry with me for giving up these rights that he was almost yelling by the end of our meeting. He repeatedly told me I was making a terrible mistake. Lewis would undoubtedly be generating money in the future through various avenues, and for me to give that all up when I had a clear legal claim to them, especially as the vice president of Sister Ray Enterprises, was a sorely inadvisable if not blatantly careless and ridiculous thing for me to do.

Additionally, considering all my personal support before and during Lou's solo career, as well as my professional work as his lighting director, his muse, and the emotional and physical abuse I'd endured during our relationship, there were probably additional financial claims available to me.

But I was heartbroken, distraught, and discouraged. All I could see were the last five years of my life gone—*poof!*

I wanted to pick up the pieces and get back to my own career and onto the path I started before I met Lewis. After all, I was still young—I was only twenty-three. I needed to stop living his life and get back to mine, but that took some planning, and it couldn't be achieved immediately.

Leaving a star like Lewis, a knighted son of New York, left me pretty much on my own. Our friends were his friends, really, and, not surprisingly they remained his after I left him. Lewis was a very influential friend for anyone to have, particularly in the music business or the creative arts. My friends were all out of town working, or in summer stock, and I'd lost touch with many of them as I'd become almost exclusively involved in Lou's life and career. Other than relatives who gave me long distance advice over the telephone, I was on my own.

Because of my family circumstances, I didn't have the support I probably needed to sustain me through a brutal divorce battle, unless I moved and went to live with them. But I didn't want to leave New York, because this is where I'd made a life, and I loved it here. I could make my own way in the world, I thought.

I don't need him!

But a young woman in the creative arts, on your own, in big, bad NYC? It's easier said than done.

I called my uncle soon after I left the divorce attorney's office and told him I'd signed all the papers giving up all my spousal rights to Lou's income. I could hear his disappointment.

'I don't want to get paid for loving him,' I told my uncle.

'Bettye,' he said, and then I heard him stifle himself. 'It's not about that, but the time and effort you put into his career during your relationship with him. A wife's time and energy should be compensated for, and why there are divorce laws to protect you. That's why you need a divorce attorney.'

'That's not the only reason why I don't want his money.'

He paused for a moment. He heard there was something I wasn't saying.

'Okay, tell me,' he said.

I just came out with it. It didn't matter anyway, I'd already signed the papers.

'I *couldn't* take his money, Babe!'

I'd told my uncle about *Berlin* and how Lou had taken parts of our lives and my childhood and put them into that album. A week after Lewis wrote it, I'd called him, nearly hysterical. Things always hit me afterward—a protective mechanism children who are brought up around abuse often have.

'Why not?'

'Because of what he said about my mother in his new album!'

My uncle didn't say anything for a while.

'I know that really hurt you,' he said. 'I'm sorry, kitten.'

'I can't take money from a man who betrayed me,' I said. 'It makes me feel dirty and small.'

I started to cry.

'All right, princess—'

For as long as I remembered, my uncle had called me this. Perhaps that's why I didn't mind Lou calling me his princess, although I knew it looked like a conflict in values, accepting it. But it had always been a little bit of home, even though Lou didn't know it.

'Hold on, it's okay. You don't have to take anything you don't want to,' Uncle Babe said. '*Don't* take his money.'

'You wouldn't be disappointed in me?' I asked.

'No, I think you deserve it, but I can see how it might be very difficult to take money from someone who's betrayed and hurt you so deeply. I'd just want him out of my life.'

'That's what I'm trying to do!'

'Okay …'

'But those lawyers treated me like I was an idiot.'

'*Please.* They're lawyers.'

'They made me feel horrible and stupid.'

'Look, kid, they're not known for their sensitivity. What do you care what they think? What matters is what you think. Although …' he said, his voice trailing off.

'What?'

'Well, there are many who would want compensation *because* he wrote about your life. You might even have a libel claim on your hands.'

'Seriously, Babe?'

'I'm just saying. It's possible. It wouldn't be that hard to prove—what happened to you and your mother. What happens in *Berlin*—'

I had to stop him from going on, because not only had I never told him about Lou's drinking and drug taking—although he wasn't stupid, it was just never mentioned—I never told him about the black eye Lou gave me, although he'd approve of me giving him one back. But I couldn't.

My uncle was a marine—an original SEAL. Where he came from, men protect women, they don't hurt them. *Ever.*

'Babe, stop. I'm not going to do that.'

'Why not?'

'*Because I can't, all right?*' I exploded. 'I'm hurt and angry. I can't even talk about it, how could I ever go through something like that?'

'Look, there's no need to get upset, there's a way out of this.'

'*What?*' I cried. 'I've already signed all the papers in the attorney's office.'

'Was that their lawyer or yours?' he asked.

'Lou's lawyer sent me to this divorce attorney.'

'Well, kid, that means he was acting on your husband's behalf. No wonder he tried to make you feel terrible. Did you get your own divorce attorney?'

'No.'

'Why not?'

'I couldn't deal with it! All this pressure about money—I just want out, Babe! He scares me! Not only being around him, but what he could do to me if I opposed him. He's got a lot of resources and knows a lot of people—he can get all kinds of things done! And a divorce attorney could prolong things forever. I don't think I could handle it.'

'Look, I understand you're trying to divorce a man with an enormous amount of support and power behind him. You're on your own up there in New York—and I understand that's where you want to be. But it's going to be okay.'

'How?'

'Just take your lighting design and directing salary you earned that he never paid you. You asked for it, right?'

'Yes.'

'You need to be practical, Bettye. How will you support yourself until you get your life back on track again? Take the salary he owes you. Then you don't have to take anything from him other than what you've earned. You can live with that, can't you?'

'Yes.'

How much did they offer you?

'It's ridiculous.'

'Triple it and don't go below double what they offered. They'll fight you, but just hang in there. They're just trying to get the best deal. You can do it. Bettye, we don't work for nothing, do we?'

'No.'

'Then don't. Take your lighting fees, and take care of yourself. You won't be taking anything from someone who has hurt you as much as he has, and you'll feel better about yourself. I swear to god, I wish I was up there—'

'Okay, Babe!' I said, cutting in. 'I can do that.'

'Good. And get the lighting payment worked out with his attorney.'

'Okay, I will.'

'And tell them you didn't do all that work for *nothing*!'

'All right,' I said, quickly, because he sounded like he was getting upset.

'Okay. And when you get done with your classes—you are going back to your acting classes, right?'

'Yes, I am. I have to call and make the appointment, but that's the plan.'

'Good. When you finish those classes, come down here and stay with me. Unless you want to come now. Do you—'

'*No!*' I cried. 'I want to get back to my life!'

'Okay, okay! We'll get you back on track when you come down here. Don't forget, you're not alone. Your grandmother and I always have your back, although she's getting up there. But I'm not, okay?'

'Okay.'

'That's my girl. I love you.'

'I love you, too, Babe.'

'One thing,' Uncle Babe said.

'What?'

'After you get those lighting fees worked out ...'

'Yes?'

'Then you walk.'

'Okay, Babe.'

'And you keep walking. Don't look back, you hear?'

* * *

After my plane touched down in Santo Domingo, my attorney took me to the hotel where I'd be staying overnight for my twenty-four-hour divorce. It was the easiest thing for me to do, and would get me out of Lou's life as quickly as possible, which is what I wanted. At my suggestion, Dennis arranged it through a contact of his. I told Lewis I'd go, because I wanted the divorce. I also didn't think he'd be able to go through with it, and would try to change my mind.

The hotel was okay, but only a step above a Holiday Inn. It consisted of one story shaped in a circle of connecting rooms with sliding glass doors leading out to terraces looking out onto a central court, where tables were set up for outdoor dining.

Singles, many of them young and around my age, sat outside under the small cafe tables, their umbrellas providing shade from the tropical sun. Many were drinking, talking, and laughing, and seemed to be having a good time. It almost looked like one big party.

Well, in a way …

But I just wanted to read my book, so after checking into my room and getting settled, I went out on my terrace and lay down on the chaise longue. I ordered a tropical drink from room service and settled in to read and enjoy some sun.

I could see everyone, but they were far enough away, and they weren't distracting, just a little cocktail-hour noise tinkling in the background. It was actually somewhat comforting to see normal life going on around me while I was in the midst of madness.

After a while, a man came up and leaned over the hedge that separated the hotel rooms from the outdoor cafe. He asked if he could buy me a drink. I thanked him but said I didn't think so, I wouldn't be there long.

'None of us will be,' he said. 'You're here for a twenty-four, right?'

'Yes,' I said, somewhat hesitantly. It really wasn't any of his business what I was doing here, but it looked like the scene was a little—well, relaxed.

'So am I. So are we all,' he said, spreading his arms out wide, embracing the landscape.

I wondered how much he'd already had to drink. It was something

I'd noticed I thought about more now. I guess that was the remnant of living with an alcoholic. It might come in handy, too. Like now.

'I'm turning in, anyway,' I said. 'It was a long flight, and I need to get some rest for tomorrow morning. At 9am, I'm due in court.'

I got up, and began putting my things away. I dog-eared my place in the book I brought along and picked it up.

'Okay, just thought I'd ask,' the man said, walking away as casually as he'd come over, back to the bar.

So I sat back down again and settled in, reading and slowing sipping my cocktail in the warm sun. I guess I fell asleep for I don't know how long, but when I woke up, it was early evening.

I went back to my room, ordered room service, turned on the TV, and had some shrimp cocktail. I didn't have much of an appetite, but I knew I needed to eat something, and this was light. There was nothing on TV, so I prepared for bed, and read myself to sleep. I was eager to wake up tomorrow morning, go to court and get my divorce, then board the plane and fly back to New York. By tomorrow tonight, I'd be back home in my apartment.

Alone—and free.

The following morning I got an early wake-up call arranged by my attorney's office. I met my lawyer for the first time at the front of the hotel, my bags already packed. He drove me over to the courthouse. I was before the judge by 9am.

The proceedings were conducted in Spanish. My attorney spoke for me and translated when necessary. He asked if there was anything I wanted to tell the judge. I just wanted to drop Lou's surname and resume using my own, I told him.

He told the judge, who nodded his assent and wrote something down.

'It's done,' my lawyer said, turning to me.

I received my divorce papers after we left the courtroom. They were also in Spanish. A huge, bold red ribbon flourished at the bottom of the back page. For some reason my divorce papers reminded me of what I thought the induction papers of the armed services in a Latin American country might look like. I felt like an inductee into the Venezuelan Mexican army. It was almost bizarrely comical.

I thanked my attorney and shook his hand, then went out to the steps of the courthouse, where a private car was waiting for me. I boarded a plane soon thereafter, and by the afternoon I was at LaGuardia Airport. Within an hour, I was home. It was actually rather effortless, however surreal.

I made myself a cup of tea, called my uncle to tell him I was okay, then slipped into my own bed and, for the first time in a long while, fell asleep without a Valium. Later on, when I woke up around 10pm, I ordered up some pizza at the place on First Avenue we always called.

The following day, I called Bill Esper's Acting Studio to see if I could enroll in his advanced acting class, but the summer session had already started. I would need to set up an appointment with him later on in the summer, to be accepted in the fall.

Lewis called the day after I flew back from Santo Domingo. We had an answering service, which was still connected to our phone, and he left a couple of messages, but I hadn't called him back yet. I had no idea where he was living, and I hadn't even asked.

Most of his clothes and things were still here, so I guess we were supposed to sort that out later. I couldn't deal with it right now, or maybe I just didn't care anymore. Perhaps he was living with the blonde woman; maybe she'd finally got him.

In that case, it's what you deserve, Lewis.

My uncle called, and I told him how Santo Domingo went. I said I was fine, that I felt very relieved. I'd flown down and got my divorce, and it was over quickly.

I got my lighting fees as the financial settlement in the divorce, and a payment schedule was worked out as to how it would be dispensed. I'd get a year before having to get a paying job—one year to concentrate on getting my life back together again on my own. It was something I was comfortable with, and I was glad the finances had been resolved.

I told Babe I'd missed the summer session classes, so he suggested I see as many plays as I could. Forget about auditions for now, and just rest, he said. I'd earned it. Afterward, I went out to the corner to pick up a *Times* and check out the theater section. It was early in the evening, and I was thinking about ordering up some Chinese when the phone rang. I picked it up.

It was Lewis. He told me he was downstairs at our favorite restaurant, the Duck Joint, with a couple of friends. Would I come down and meet him?

I thought for a minute, then decided, what harm could there be? I was free. I'd just say hello and have a quick drink. I hadn't returned his phone calls, and felt bad about that.

We could be friends, couldn't we? We always had been, right from the start.

So I said I'd meet him in a bit and threw on some clothes, put on some lipstick, and went down to our restaurant.

Times have certainly changed, I thought grimly, as I walked up to the familiar entrance.

Lewis was sitting at a table in the center in full view of the door with a couple of guys. He stood up when he saw me and came over to meet me, kissing me on the check.

'You look great,' Lou said.

'I've had a lot of sleep,' I said.

Now that you're gone …

We chatted for a bit, but it felt awkward with his friends there, who I hardly knew. They seemed a little too superficial—very attentive about everything that was said—and I didn't actually know what was going on while they were all talking.

Who really are these people, and why are they here?

I didn't think it was appropriate to talk about Santo Domingo, but he asked how everything went, and I said fine. He seemed relaxed and happy to see me. I actually thought he was flirting with me, which felt weird. But I didn't stay long, and I only had one drink. He wanted to know if he could call me and we could go out to dinner—maybe we could talk?

'Sure,' I said, smiling brightly.

It was all a little too civilized for me, and I was happy I was leaving.

'I miss you,' he whispered as he kissed me goodbye. I stopped at the pizza place on First Avenue and got a slice, then went home and read until falling off to sleep, early. I was alone and happy—at peace, and single again.

* * *

The following night I was on the couch, watching television, when the phone rang. I thought about letting the answering service pick it up, but it was early, so I went ahead.

'Hello?'

'Bettye?'

'Yeah, hi Lou,' I said. I was confused but I hid it successfully.

Jesus, I just saw him yesterday—what does he want now?

'I'm at the Duck Joint again, but I'm alone, do you think we could have dinner together?'

'Tonight?'

'Yes.'

'Are you calling from a pay phone?'

'Yeah, I'm on the corner.'

'Well, Lewis, I hadn't planned on going out … I'm just lying here on the couch, watching TV, thought I'd order something up, maybe—'

'That's all right, I can bring something up. What do you want?'

'I don't know, I've had Chinese and pizza already this—'

'Why don't I go and ask the guys at the Duck Joint and see if they'll put something together for me and bring it up?'

'They don't have take out, do they?'

'No, but I think I can convince them.'

I laughed, because he probably could.

I wasn't really happy with the idea, but he was here, and he seemed positive when I saw him last night, so maybe it would be okay. I was feeling lazy, so I agreed.

'Okay, sounds like a plan.'

'Great!' I'll be up as soon as I can get it. What do you want—the usual?'

'Yeah, that'd be great, I haven't had that in a long time.'

'Escargot swimming in a sumptuous buttery garlic sauce?'

'Yes,' I said laughing, remembering.

'Do you have any Chardonnay up there?'

'I don't think so …'

'That's okay, I'll bring your favorite.'

'Okay, sounds good, just buzz when you get here, and I'll let you up.'

'Oh. I have my keys on me …'

'Oh, okay, that's fine, just buzz the door, will you?'

'Sure! No problem.'

'Okay, see you soon.'

'Bye, princess.'

I hung up the phone. I honestly didn't feel like putting any clothes on, or brushing my hair and putting on my face. And I was slightly annoyed that I knew I would, anyway, because that was just the way I was raised. I thought I'd have at least fifteen minutes to get it together.

I wasn't dressing for a ball; it was just my ex-husband, which felt more than a little weird. But we did have some things to talk about, and I'd like to have his clothes and things out of here, when he could. I didn't want to think about him, and just move on. And we probably had some things to talk about, so …

I was in the bathroom, and had just finished brushing my teeth. I'd barely had time to change when the doorbell buzzed. I was slightly startled, as I hadn't expected him quite so quickly, but when I went out to the foyer and looked through the front door peephole, there was Lewis.

I opened the door.

'Hi,' I said, but then I saw him standing there. His arms were laden with goods: in one arm he carried a huge bouquet of red roses, and a bottle of wine wrapped in paper from the liquor store on the corner; in the other, he was carrying a large brown paper bag, which I assumed was our dinner from the Duck Joint.

'Hey!' he said, kissing me on the cheek as he swept past. I stood out of the way as he strode through the foyer to the dining room table, where he put everything down. Then he came back out and, holding what appeared to be a dozen long-stemmed red roses wrapped in clear cellophane from the upscale corner market, he walked toward me where I was still standing, by the door, and bowed down at the waist in his courtly manner.

'For you, Princess,' he said, flourishing them in front of me.

'Oh,' I said, speechless.

'Aren't you going to take them?' he asked, thrusting them closer, practically into my arms.

I'd been so surprised at his entrance that I was still holding the door open. He closed the door, and the next thing I knew, he pulled me to him, holding the dozen roses behind my back. He buried his face in my hair and said, 'I've missed you so much, Bettye. You have no idea. God, your hair … it smells so good!'

I just started laughing—I couldn't help myself. He pulled back and looked at me, but I kept laughing.

'You're laughing, but there's tears running down your face,' he said, and then he started kissing them.

And that's when I began crying, softly. I moved in closer to him and put my head over his shoulder so he couldn't see me, so that he'd stop kissing me.

'Baby, I hurt you so much. I am so sorry. I had no idea what I was doing,' he whispered.

'Lewis, I can't …'

'Oh, yes, you can,' he said, and then, moving me toward the round table in the foyer, he stepped back and laid the roses down on it. Then he picked me up, swept me off my feet, and carried me into the bedroom in his arms. He didn't turn the light on, but he knew where the bed was, and he put me down on it.

It was dark. I suddenly became cold and started shivering. I didn't know what was going on. He took his leather jacket off and covered me with it, tucking it around my shoulders. Then he sat down next to me. I rolled onto my side and curled up, facing him.

'Here, let me get you under the comforter,' he said, 'you're cold. Why are you so cold all of a sudden?'

I didn't say anything, but he moved me so that he could pull our comforter down under me to cover me with it, then took his coat off and covered me with it, too.

'Stay here a minute, and let me go out into the kitchen and get you a glass of wine. I'll bring the dinner in here, and we can eat by candlelight. How will that be?'

I didn't say anything, but I nodded my head yes.

'I'm going to turn the light on, okay?' he said.

I nodded my head yes, still in the dark.

'Okay, here we go.'

He switched his bedside lamp on. I was laying on his side of the bed, by the door. He sat down on the bed next to me and smoothed my hair away from my face.

'You are so beautiful,' he said.

I covered my face with my hands, because he still embarrassed me when he said those kinds of things.

'Don't cover your face,' he said, gently moving my hands away.

'Lewis, what's going on,' I finally managed to say.

'I miss you, Bettye. I don't think I can live without you.'

'Oh, Lewis …'

'No, stop. Just listen to me a minute. I want us to go out and have dinner in the dining room. You can put the roses in the vase, because I know you've been worrying about them not being in water ever since I brought them in here.'

I smiled, because he was right. I never bite my nails, but for some reason I brought my fingers up to my mouth and started chewing on them.

'Before we eat, I want to tell you something.'

'Yes?' I said, chewing.

'What are you doing?' he asked. 'You don't chew your nails—*stop*.'

He started moving my hand away from my mouth, but I resisted.

'*Let me*,' I said.

He was holding my hand at my wrist between us.

'Okay,' he said, and took his hand away.

I put my ring finger back in my mouth and resumed lightly chewing my nail.

He continued.

'I've been an ass. You're right. I will never shoot drugs as long as we are together, again,' he said.

I didn't say anything, because I just wanted to listen to what he had to say.

'I promise. I give you my word.'

I pushed his coat off me. It was too much.

'Lewis—'

'No, I mean it. I've been so self-destructive. I've brought you down with me, and I'm sorry about that. I'm a fool. You're the best thing that's ever happened to me, and I don't want to lose you.'

'But—'

'I know I already have. But, baby, I want you back. I need you.'

This time, I noticed, he said *wanted* first.

I didn't say anything. I just looked at him.

'I know. How can you believe me?'

'Yes.'

'I can't live without you. I know you can't accept the drugs. So I won't do them. It's not good for me, anyway.'

'Yes …'

'I know…' he said.

'Are you sure?' I asked, blinded once again by my love for him.

'Yes,' he answered.

'*Really?*'

'Yes! I already promised once, but I'll promise again.'

He crossed his heart, then held his hand up in a boy scout salute or something, so I started to giggle.

'You're giggling … *why are you giggling?*' he asked, moving in closer, and putting his face next to mine.

I felt his soft curls on my cheek. His nose under my chin.

'I can't help it,' I said.

'Why?' he asked. And then he started nibbling on my ear, which he knew I loved.

'Baby, take me back,' he whispered.

At the same time as he said this, I said, 'You looked like a kid, crossing your heart.'

'Ah,' he said, chuckling, nibbling my ear. But he heard me.

'I am just a kid,' he said. 'Take me back,' he said again.

'Why would I do that?' I asked. But I was weakening, and he could tell.

'Because I have been a very, very, bad boy, and I need you to make me a good one.'

'Well, you have been a very, very bad boy,' I replied.

'Yes, but I want to be better,' he answered.

'Oh, you do, do you?' I said.

'Yes,' he said, burying his face in my hair and starting to kiss my neck.

'And how are you going to do that?' I asked.

He kept kissing my neck, moving slowly. And lower, with each kiss.

'By doing this,' he said, reaching up, and switching off the light.

last
exit . . . . **CHAPTER FIFTEEN**

We were on the plane flying over to London to record *Berlin*. It was June 1973. Lewis drank several cocktails before falling asleep next to me on the long flight across the Atlantic. For the first time, I was unenthusiastic about being in London while *Berlin* was recorded, and I approached this trip with serious trepidation and a sense of foreboding. I honestly didn't want to go, but I'd promised Dennis and Lou that I would stay by his side through the making of *Berlin*. He believed, and had sufficiently proved to management, that he couldn't work without me.

It was a pain to be needed at this level, but I had already invested several years of my young life with Lewis helping him launch his solo career. Even though we were divorced, a part of me believed it was still my duty to stick by his side through thick and thin, for better or worse. It was an old fashioned concept but one I took seriously.

I don't think anyone likes staying with their partner because they're required to, or are desperately needed. And I probably resented the pressure I got from management to stay. Every time I tried to leave, Dennis would tell me Lewis couldn't make it without me. Extracting a promise from me to stay through *Berlin* was the latest bargain Dennis struck with me. I was sick of making deals and striking bargains with Dennis. I wanted my own life back.

Despite the personal themes included in the album, which were very painful for me, I knew *Berlin* was brilliant. A concept album, it told the story of a couple whose relationship was unraveling. They were reeling out of control with drug and alcohol abuse, marital infidelity, and domestic violence—topics which had never before been explored in rock'n'roll, let alone produced as a concept album in this genre.

Lou and Bob Ezrin, his producer, were calling *Berlin* a rock opera. It was a very dark and sordid story. The drug abuse was detailed, along with the path the woman took in her marital infidelity. Especially disturbing was the protagonist's desire to beat the woman until she was black and blue, then break both of her arms.

You know, fun stuff.

And, of course, in using my parts of my early childhood as the narrative, I felt Lou had betrayed me. Caroline, the lead character in the story, contained elements of me—our looks were similar, she wrote poetry, and we were both having troubles in our relationship due to our partner's alcohol and drug abuse. There were the physical fights, too, however infrequent.

I believe men physically bully women to control them. Until now, I'd never been in a physical confrontation with a person, and I had never hit anybody. The very idea is repugnant to me. But putting my fist through a window was probably my warning to Lou that if he ever tried it again—look out. It was the only way I could tell him I could be driven to physical violence. It wasn't something I thought about—it was a purely instinctive response.

The period during his nearly year-long writer's block was the toughest time in our relationship. As it progressed, his substance abuse got worse. And when he assaulted me on the road and gave me a black eye, as warned, I instinctively fought back.

But we had reconciled, after the twenty-four-hour divorce, and I gave him my promise that I would stay with him through the recording of *Berlin*—and my word means something to me. But I honestly didn't want to relive it, which would certainly happen during the recording of the album. I knew I couldn't go to the studio and hear those lyrics.

Lewis was nervous about recording this album because it was very different from anything that came before it. But he had faith in Bob, who helped Lewis develop the concept behind *Berlin*, and was grateful for his willingness to produce the album. Because the album was so avant-garde, in terms of risk taking—for both of them—it didn't get higher.

Lou assumed RCA would not be pleased with *Berlin*'s subject matter, but this was, in truth, the least of his concerns. By emerging from his writer's block, he had found a way not only to follow *Transformer*—itself a major contribution to his writer's block—but also to forever dispel the notion that he was a glitter-rock pop star. To be taken as such was one of his greatest fears. With *Berlin*, however, Lewis was assured that RCA and the world would have no choice but to consider him a serious artist—his *raison d'être*.

We would be staying, once again, at the Inn On The Park hotel in London, which made me feel more comfortable, as I knew it well. Lewis was happy and content to have me at his side. He was pleased with the details that he'd heard from Bob about the production, which would be much larger than his two previous albums. Ezrin had finished arranging *Berlin* by the end of June, and Lou was ecstatic about the musicians Bob was assembling to record the album: guitarists Steve Hunter and Dick Wagner; Steve Winwood, who I knew and loved from Traffic; Jack Bruce, the bassist and songwriter from Cream; and the drummer Aynsley Dunbar.

So there were positive aspects to this London trip, and I decided to focus on them, hoping for the best. After we had reconciled, Lou had given me his solemn promise that he would avoid hard drugs. It took me about a week to think about getting back with him, and before I did anything I called Uncle Babe. At first he was opposed to the idea, but in the end he told me to follow my heart. He would be there for me if things didn't work out, anyway.

* * *

Lou had been snorting up a storm. I joined him, because I knew it would keep me up and going. I wasn't taking anywhere near half as much as him, but my heart sank as I thought about what we were doing. Lou's cocaine use had escalated to a frightening level.

After checking in to the hotel, we went down to the restaurant and had dinner. Lou chattered away and was looking forward to getting to the studio as soon as possible. Once or twice we had dinner with Bob, but in the main Lou spent his time in the studio.

When we arrived in London, I went to the studio and briefly met everyone. But recording an album is always hard work. *Berlin* was especially difficult, because the subject matter was very dark, and it was incredibly intense. The novelty of watching an album being recorded in a studio had worn off for me long ago. After a while, sitting around and not participating for hours at a time becomes tedious. It's really not a place to be if you're not working on the album. And I wasn't interested in going back anyway, because I knew that listening to those lyrics would upset me.

A private car with a chauffeur was provided for me at the hotel for wherever I wanted to go. In the beginning, I spent my days shopping, catching West End shows or going to museums, especially the Tate Gallery. About a week after we'd arrived in London, I received an invitation from Angie Bowie to visit her at Haddon Hall the next day. I thought it was a bit unusual, but I liked Angie, and it would be nice to see her again.

After the rush-hour traffic in the city died down, we left London for the drive to Beckenham, which took just under an hour. At the appointed time, my driver pulled up to Angie's house—a grand old, rambling residence in an Edwardian mansion that had been converted into apartments. For many years it had been left unattended, but this isn't unusual for old British houses, and comes with its own charm.

I asked my driver to wait outside, as I didn't know how long I'd be, and rang the bell. Angie answered, greeting me graciously, and invited me in. She gave me a glass of wine, then asked if I'd like to go to her bedroom, where she and a friend were reviewing her wardrobe. After offering me some marijuana, I took a couple of drags, then we went to her bedroom, where she introduced me to a man who lived there, whose name I can't remember.

An ironing board was set up, and the man was ironing. Clothes were strewn about the room. Angie was trying on several different outfits.

Assisted by her friend, Angie changed from one outfit into another. Since all the curtains were drawn and the room was lit by only a couple of lamps, it was rather dark. There was nothing else for me to look at but Angie, as she dressed and undressed, changing her clothes. As she walked around the room and modeled them for us, she admired herself in the mirror and asked my opinion about what she wore. I told her everything looked great.

After a short while, meaningful glances were exchanged between Angie and her friend. Then Angie sat down on the bed next to me, as did he. Then they looked at me. Casually, Angie asked if I would like to spend the night. Only then did it dawn on me why I was there.

As Angie talked—she is a very talented conversationalist—it gave me the opportunity to rise from the bed without leaping, although that was my instinct. The moment I got up, more meaningful glances were exchanged.

Soon after I got up, Angie did, too; then, so did he. Suddenly, Angie started talking about how *some people* just don't have the courage to explore all the opportunities presented to them. I casually drifted over to the bedroom door. It suddenly felt stuffy, and I had become uncomfortably warm. They both looked at me disapprovingly. But I had no intention of directly answering Angie's invitation. Angie may have been the wife of an important artist and associate of my husband's, but I wasn't just another groupie. I thought this scene was incredibly inappropriate, although I didn't say anything other than my driver was waiting outside, and I was going to go. I looked around for an uncluttered surface to set down my wine glass, but I couldn't find one.

Angie laughed and said she'd walk me to the front door. Her friend started futzing with all the clothing lying on the bed, ignoring me. I couldn't wait to get out of there.

As Angie walked me to the entrance, she continued chattering away in broad, sweeping gestures. It was clear she was put off, because she was overacting. When we reached the door, I thanked her for the invite and handed her my glass, which she snatched away, closing the door so quickly behind me that I was glad I left with the heels on my feet.

Yeah, okay, I thought, *I'm just a country bumpkin from Pennsylvania, but I'm not interested. You're not going to create a sudden shift in my sexual preferences by maneuvering me into your bedroom to watch you change in and out of your clothes. They were set long before I saw the first light of day on this planet.*

I'm entitled to choose my intimate partners, and I had one—Lewis. The parameters of Angie and David's marriage weren't something they had ever shared with Lou and I, and I was a bit miffed that she made any assumptions. Perhaps that's what she'd been told. Maybe even Lou had told her—he was certainly capable of it.

It was dark outside of Angie's house. She'd turned off the lights and I couldn't see anything. Fortunately, my driver turned on his headlights to illuminate my path. He opened the door for me and I got in. I was damn uncomfortable, and semi-furious.

I hoped Lewis wouldn't be disappointed by the outcome, but he wouldn't have been surprised. In time, I didn't take it personally. Perhaps Angie thought I'd welcome her invitation.

Really? Hadn't everyone already heard I was straight?

Because in Lou's world, being straight was as sensational as being gay everywhere else.

'I am so glad you are here,' I said to the driver. 'Could we please leave?'

He smiled kindly at me in the rear-view mirror and cast a disparaging glance at the house as he turned around in the driveway before driving off. I think I heard him say, 'Humph,' or something that showed his disapproval, which the British are exceptional at doing.

I told Lewis about my aborted social experiment with Angie when he woke up the following day. He threw back his head and cackled. He truly enjoyed hearing about it.

'Poor Angie,' he said, when he'd finished laughing.

I was hoping he wasn't also laughing at me, and the position I'd been put in. Or that he hadn't known about it beforehand. But with Lou, you just never knew.

* * *

After the first two weeks of our stay, I ended up spending most of the time in our hotel room, either reading or watching the tennis at Wimbledon on TV. It was clear that my job had devolved into simply just being there when Lewis came home from the recording sessions, or wherever he was. Since I never knew when that would be, it was just easier to stay in our room. I was probably also depressed, as I hadn't wanted to be there in the first place, and I detested what my job on the road had become.

The *Berlin* recording sessions were very difficult and lasted for long hours, sometimes up to twenty at a stretch. More often than not, Lou returned to our hotel room looking like he'd been beaten up. You never knew what condition he would be in, who would be escorting him, or what hour of the day or night he'd fall through the door.

Naturally, at the time, I was completely unaware of all the heroin floating around the studio.

Most nights, Lou was physically dragged into bed by me or whoever got him up to the room, and this became his routine. He was so exhausted and blown away, all I could do was hold him when he finally made it into bed, and make sure he had his orange juice and coffee to begin the next day's work, whatever time that was.

I heard rumors that everyone involved in the production were depressed because they believed they were recording an album about the breakup of Lou's marriage. They all knew Lou would fall to pieces if we split up forever, and this was a scary thought for them. There might have been some of that, but we were reconciled; and besides, they didn't know the full story behind the album they were working on. Only Lou and I did, and I wasn't talking.

I've always thought that much of what broke him during those recording sessions was his guilt about the content of some of those lyrics. Perhaps I'm giving him too much credit, but I knew he was conflicted about some of the writing in it—especially those snippets about us he'd decided to include for realistic details, and the core story, which rested on very painful parts of my childhood. *Berlin* was written out of sheer desperation to keep his contract with RCA, as he owed them an album in order to retain it. After grappling with his writer's block for nearly a year, it was the only story he could produce.

Usually in the early morning just before dawn, if Lou hadn't arrived home yet, I'd ring my driver and have him take me to the beautiful gardens in St. James' Park. Low-lying mist floating and rising above the beautiful bursts of color flowering in its gardens and groves of trees designed deliberately with a little bit of the wild in mind—the best of British gardening—were highlighted by the moon setting and the sky turning from varying shades of indigo and grey to all the colors orchestrated by the sun as it rose—vermilions, razor-sharp oranges, pinks so rosy I felt I could float away on pillows of clouds. It was incredibly beautiful, and it kept me sane during the recording of *Berlin*.

My favorite place was a swing set near a small pond. Geese, ducks, and swans glided over its glassy surface in perfect tranquility. Birds twittered from the branches in the trees that surrounded the scene. For this Yank, it was a veritable Walt Disney production come to life, each day playing a new reel just before dawn. I could swing like a carefree five-year-old, pumping and pushing higher and higher into the sky slowly lighting above me. Way, way up from this earth, as far as it was possible under one's own might, and into a great beyond.

Then I could almost believe I was flying, far, far away.

* * *

After work on *Berlin* was completed, we returned to New York. The album was set for release in July. Now, Lou needed to rehearse a band to replace The Tots, who had been abruptly retired earlier in April, so that he could tour the new album. A few months earlier, he had quickly put together a replacement band to complete the US *Transformer* tour: Moogy Klingman from Great Neck, New York, a founding member of Todd Rundgren's Utopia, played keyboards; a drummer named 'Chocolate' was the new percussionist; Tom Cosgrove played lead guitar; Ralph Shukett, rhythm; and Bill Gelber on bass. They had done a terrific job, and Lewis was very pleased with them.

The *Berlin* tour was slated to start in Europe in the middle of September. Now that Lou had fulfilled his contractual obligations to RCA with *Berlin*, Dennis was successful in securing sufficient financing for a tour to support its release. Space was arranged for Lewis to rehearse his new band up in the Berkshires, in Massachusetts. I wasn't interested in going with him, so I begged off. I had planned to stay in

New York and fly up to the Berkshires for the first show of the tour, at the indomitable Music Inn in Lenox, on September 1. Thousands of youths were expected to turn out on the Lenox Farm fields to see Lewis perform.

I'd given up monitoring Lou's drinking and drug use, but I agreed to stay with him as long as he wasn't using heroin. I'd fulfilled my promise to Lou and Dennis that I would stay with him through the recording of *Berlin*, but I continued to experience enormous pressure from both Lou and his management to stay on for the sake of the tour. Lou was in critical shape after recording *Berlin*, and everyone was concerned about him. If he had a shot in hell to get back on the road for the *Berlin* tour, apparently, I was the antidote.

After we returned from London, we'd had a month at home to rest and relax before Lou left for the Berkshires. He seemed in much better form when he left at the end of August, and I was looking forward to a week at home alone. Then, the day after Lewis left, I got an urgent call from Dennis. Lou was having difficulty working, and was insisting that I come up to the Berkshires so he could rehearse. He told Dennis he couldn't work without me. There was a very real sense of urgency to get me up to the Berkshires as quickly as possible.

I agreed to go because Lou told Dennis that he needed me, and Dennis was worried that the European tour would collapse. What could I do? I didn't think I had a choice, and there was no time for me to think about it, because they wanted me to leave that day. Within a couple of hours I had packed a bag, and a car was sent to pick me up at home.

The car whisked me down to the heliport at Midtown on the East River, near Fisherman's Warf. Within an hour I was boarding a helicopter to the Berkshires. I felt like a hastily assembled express package being shipped off—everything was happening so quickly. In a little over an hour, we arrived at the Berkshires, where an assistant met me on landing. I was put in a private car and driven to the rehearsal space where Lou was staying with the band, an old barn in a rural setting that had been turned into a rehearsal space. There were rooms provided for the band members to bunk in, but Lou and I had our own private quarters.

It was late summer in the Berkshire Mountains. The leaves were turning gold and burnt orange. There was a mellow, quiet feeling in the peaceful, rustic setting. Lewis came outside to meet me as soon as my car pulled up at the old barn. He looked haggard and pale, and was perspiring heavily. He seemed weak, like the spirit had been knocked out of him. I was alarmed, but I smiled and waved at the sight of him. When he saw me, he was overwhelmingly relieved, which seemed to brighten up everyone a bit, but especially Lou. He drew me to him quickly, and held onto me for a very long time. I was a little taken aback, but then I had been by the entire trip, and was probably in a bit of a daze; however, I held on to him, too. He looked awful, and I wanted to reassure him everything would be okay, but I was also very worried about him and truly concerned with how he looked. What had happened to him since he left New York just two days ago, when he'd looked great and back in good spirits?

After a brief hello with the members of the band and the gentleman who took care of the place, Lou took me to our room. I asked if we could have steak for dinner, because Lou looked like he needed some serious protein, and I was relieved when I saw him wolf it down. Afterward, he poured himself another drink, and confessed how nervous he was to begin the tour.

Because of the lukewarm critical reception to *Berlin*, it was a huge disappointment to RCA, and it wasn't selling. Lou was deeply disappointed and afraid he couldn't go on. I told him I didn't believe him for a minute. The set list they'd put together for the tour included some of his most popular Velvet Underground classics, which would be a hit with audiences, and they were songs he loved performing. Perhaps he was taking a blow with the immediate response to *Berlin*, but he had always known the risk he was taking with its conception and production. Maybe it would take everyone some time to accept it, but now was not the time to give up.

Although his ever-present scotch was always within arm's reach, Lou didn't overindulge that night. He quietly sipped the drink as I gently reassured him. Maybe he just needed to ride this rough patch out for a while. The tour might bolster the sales of *Berlin*, but the fact was that he'd never written the album for commercial reasons. He'd delivered the product RCA required, and it was time to move on. He'd been through this before with the Velvets, and if anyone knew how to handle career ups and downs, it was Lou.

We climbed into bed, and I held him until he fell asleep. I felt terrible for him. As an artist, he'd put everything he had into the making of *Berlin*. He'd nearly destroyed us both, and he had hurt me very badly; the sales of the album had bombed, and what he cared most about—the critical reception to the album—was all over the map. While some heralded the album as highly original and innovative, most had brought down the axe, calling it boring, depressing, self-indulgent. While the *New York Times* called it original, *Rolling Stone* dubbed it 'the most depressing album ever made.' Some of the other reviews were brutal.

But Lou was an artist, and he'd taken a risk. It's what kept him going, but a risk is—well, a risk. He just needed to hang on. Things would work out in the end for him if he just kept going. I believed in him and his work; I always had.

Exhausted from the hurried preparations and the helicopter trip up to Lou, I, too, soon fell asleep.

The following morning we rose early and had bacon, eggs, juice, and coffee for breakfast—Lou's usual fare. Lou got together with the guys in the band, and they began rehearsing. The band was in excellent form, and chomping at the bit to play.

As Lou went over the music they would be playing on tour, his spirits began to improve. I saw him once again become positive and committed. That's what always did it for him—working on his music. If you got him there, he always went back to the work. The rehearsals lasted for several more days, and by the time Lou and the band played the Music Inn, they were primed.

The droves of fans who had come out to hear him reacted positively to the show, although Lewis was exhausted by the time they went on. But as soon as the band struck up its opening chords, he sprang to life and gave a walloping performance. Later, we heard they were so loud the neighbors complained. In retaliation, someone called in a phony bomb threat the following night, and the audience had to be evacuated in the middle of the show.

But the real problem was that no one told me Lewis had been taking heroin before I arrived.

* * *

The next week we flew to Germany via London, for the Scheessel Rock Festival. We checked in to the Blake Hotel, a small boutique property catering to upscale celebrity clientele. After breakfast the following morning, we went off to rehearsals with some new musicians Steve Katz and Bob Ezrin had assembled for the European tour, including dueling Detroit guitarists Steve Hunter and Dick Wagner; Ray Colcord on keyboards; Prakash John on bass; and percussionist Pentri Glan of Bush.

This was the band Lou played with three months later in late December, at the Academy of Music on 14th Street in New York, where his follow-up to *Berlin*, *Rock'n'Roll Animal*, was recorded live. That album, produced by Katz, is still considered among the best live albums in his career.

The boys in the band were amazing, but Lewis was concerned— jealous, really—that Steve Hunter and Dick Wagner were getting so much positive attention in the press. Their opening to 'Sweet Jane,' which would go on for almost fifteen minutes, became legendary. Hunter and Wagner are superb. Steve Katz had correctly assessed Lou's predicament after the reviews came in for *Berlin*, and determined that the best thing Lou could do to offset the disastrous response to the album was return to his roots and do what he does best—good ol' American rock'n'roll.

Many of the VU classics were on the set list, and audiences were ecstatic to hear their old favorites, along with popular selections from Transformer. The band opened on September 15 at the Crystal Palace Bowl Celebration Garden Party, with James Taylor and Beck, Bogert & Appice. Lou had a great time playing, and we enjoyed the party afterward. The show was a great success, and Lewis and the band were wonderful.

But in London, Lou's drinking and cocaine use started reeling out of control again. It got to the point where you took Lou to where he needed to be and set him down like you would a chair. As reliably as a kettle put over a flame, as soon as he snorted some coke, a fire was lit in him—along with apparently whatever else he was taking behind my back. But when I was able to keep his drinking and drug-taking at a manageable level, Lewis performed well.

Everyone thought Lou and I had divorced, which indeed we had. Yet here I was, back in the saddle on tour. I don't think it mattered, really; everyone still called me his wife. But we were no longer in sync anymore. I could see I was in a losing battle, and I became resigned to the conclusion that I had to leave—*again*. We had been together for three months since I'd obtained our twenty-four-hour divorce. Further, even though I'd promised I would stay on for the European tour, it became increasingly apparent to me that my role had degenerated exclusively into being Lou's nursemaid, which I absolutely hated and would never tolerate.

The *Berlin* album was received so negatively in the press and garnered such pathetic sales for RCA that it almost ended Lou's solo career, which we'd spent years working so hard to create. I was as depressed about it as Lou was, but nobody ever considered my role, or the horribly conflicting situation I now found myself in, with the creation and production of the album. I'd worked incredibly long and hard toward Lou's success, but to see it all suddenly come crashing down was a weight that in and of itself was almost too much for me to bear on my own. Yet here I was, helicoptered around and flown across an ocean to bolster and support Lewis, as though my work and I were nothing to be considered. And I wasn't! I don't think one could possibly have felt more minimized than I did during this time. Lewis had recklessly thrown away not only us, but everything we'd worked for—building his career so that everything I believed about in his music could be heard! Everything that I believed in had been annihilated, and I felt like I was a zombie, walking around. I probably was. Other than pain and defeat, there was nothing left for me here—nothing at all.

Ever vigilant about the critical response to his music, it was clear to Lewis that his rock opera—his genius work of art—had tanked. He was devastated by its reception in the press and by the public, and it hurt him deeply. As a result, he was a mess. Suffice it to say, he reacted exactly as he had in the past—an all-points-out alarm for drugs and alcohol to the rescue. *And me.* Although I fought it, I felt so used I could barely go on myself.

After London, Paris was next. The reviews of Lou's shows had been good thus far, so in that sense, the tour was gaining momentum. But I was simply there to keep Lou going. I was his engine. Consequently, I had withdrawn so far into myself to stay on the road that I no longer knew who I was. We were snorting cocaine before rehearsals, after rehearsals, in soundchecks—before and after the show. Lewis was snorting so much his urine turned green, which he thought was hysterical. I laughed along, but I was frightened. I'd made it through three shows at this pace, but I felt like I was walking in slow motion underwater. Nothing was real to me any more.

In Paris, we were booked in to the Bristol, a gorgeous, well-mannered matron of a hotel, and our rooms were lovely. The first night after we flew to the City of Light, Lewis and I had dinner in the restaurant downstairs alone. We were tired and quiet, and I ordered the *poisson du jour* from the menu. But when the waiter set my plate down in front of me, I saw that the entire fish had been broiled with its head, eyes, fins, and skin. Everything on that damn fish was intact. It had been years since I'd spoken French, not since my student travels in 1968, and I didn't remember much.

Looking at the waiter—who, of course, only deigned to speak in French—I sliced my hand vertically through the air over the head of the fish and, grasping for a word to express my concern, said, 'Decapitate? *Please*? Could you—*decapitate*?'

I wasn't used to eating fish with its eye glassily staring at me. The waiter probably got a chuckle back in the kitchen, but he only smiled politely as he took it away, bringing it back a couple of minutes later, *sans* head and eye. It was lovely, tender and delicate, but it also had some small bones, so I picked carefully through the pink flesh as it fell away from my fork.

Lou laughed, but this was the high point of our dinner. He withdrew back into himself; he was preoccupied, it seemed. I was quiet, because being around Lou was like walking on shards of glass. I no longer knew who I was anymore, anyway.

Next, the desert tray was rolled out with a scrumptious array of delicate French pastries. Lewis drank scotch before and during dinner. I had a lovely Chardonnay. Afterward, we sipped on Lou's signature Courvoisiers.

During the soundcheck the next afternoon, at the Olympia, he snorted barrels of cocaine. I was a bit concerned about the green urine thing, and I'd only had a couple of lines to keep me awake. For weeks, I'd been up night and day, back on my 24/7 watch over Lou. The only time I could sleep was when he did. Speeding along as he was didn't leave much time for the old shut-eye. But I had to keep up.

As we ate our dinner quietly back at the hotel after the soundcheck, before it was time to get ready and leave for the theater, we had little to say to each other. I think I had given up, and he probably sensed it, which would only make him nervous and angry, bringing out the most contentious traits in Lou. Now, we were simply co-conspirators.

It was sad, really, I thought. Sitting in these lovely surroundings—this fine restaurant, the grand hotel. The shows were going well, the audiences were happy. Lou was making money and working. But the album was doing very poorly, and the critics had been savage. And Lewis was doing nothing but drinking and snorting. How I felt wasn't considered by anyone. I was at my wit's end.

What the critics wrote about his music had always been of the utmost importance to Lewis. He was convinced that his career was over, and he was only riding out the wake of his accomplishments with the VU and *Transformer*. 'Walk On The Wild Side,' 'Satellite Of Love' (which was taking off), and the VU classics were always a hit with his audiences.

But Lewis was convinced that the world had finally discovered his secret, and his greatest fear: that he was an untalented fake and had been exposed as the loser and phony he'd always been. All his dreams of being recognized as an artist with his rock opera, *Berlin*, had gone up in a plume of white lines and whiskey. *Again.*

And the paranoia that inevitably follows prolonged intake of cocaine sure wasn't helping.

After dinner we went back to our room. I took a long, luxurious bath in the huge, old porcelain bathtub. Finally, something felt divine! I put on the beautiful lapis-blue earrings Lewis had bought me in

London and a long black skirt with a gold silk top. The Olympia was a historic venue; I wanted to, at the very least, dress the part, and wear his beautiful gift to me.

I called room service and chose only healthy things for us to snack on before we left for the theater. We were sitting at the small table the waiter wheeled into our room. I'd ordered fruit, coffee, tea, and a glass of milk—and, of course, a Johnny Walker Red.

Lou was still feeling morose about the reception of *Berlin*, though, and was completely knocked out. He was also stoned. I could feel how angry and disappointed he was, but I no longer had any words to console or encourage him. What could I say? To him, I wasn't even there. He was gone from me.

I looked at him picking at his bowl of fruit and finally asked, slightly irritated, 'What is wrong?'

He looked at me like I was an imbecile.

'What's wrong?' he asked. 'Are you kidding me?'

'No,' I said, looking at him.

'*Everything*!' he yelled. 'We snorted so much cocaine today I don't think there's any left! I don't know how I'm going to do this show!'

'Lewis, what do you want me to say?' I said abruptly. 'You have a show. You have to do it—with or without drugs. I had a couple of lines, that's all, and you know it.' I continued staring straight at him, although I softened my tone for effect. 'So it looks like, in this case—this one time—you're going to have to do this show without the white stuff.'

'I need to be up for this show!' he said, emphatically.

He took another slosh from his scotch glass. That's all he was really putting into his body these days. Scotch and cocaine. I'd ordered something good for us to eat, but all he did was shove it around his plate. I was doing what I could, trying to keep him healthy, yet now he was complaining about *me*? As if I was responsible for his mound of cocaine disappearing?

I can't do anything right anymore, I thought. *Me being here is insane.*

'You know, Lewis, didn't you always want what you've got now?' I asked in exasperation, and with not a little irony. 'You recorded your rock opera. You're doing shows all over Europe. They're going well. We're staying in a beautiful hotel. You're known all over the world. You're a bona fide rock'n'roll star. Now what do you want?'

'I want them to understand!' he cried. 'They hate *Berlin*. Everything we worked so hard to produce in London for that album has been trashed! No one appreciates its beauty and intelligence, or the complexity of the characters in my story. It's all been for naught! Now I have to go and do this show, and there's no coke left! How am I going to perform?'

I really felt like telling him it wasn't just *his* story. But I bit my tongue. What would be the point? Besides, he already knew that.

And he could get more coke as easily as I could get water.

He was already slurring his words, but he took another drink of his ever-present scotch anyway.

He doesn't even know how plastered he is.

I looked away. I couldn't watch him destroy himself anymore. He was destroying me, as well.

I'd become an extension of him, after all, hadn't I?

He continued to whine. 'Maybe if you hadn't had *any*, there'd be some left for me tonight so I could do this show.'

'What did you just say?' I asked quietly, setting down my glass of milk.

'Why did you have to take *any* today?' he cried. 'At least I would have *something* to take before the show. Just to get me on! So I can do this!'

I looked at him, drinking his scotch, pouring it down his throat, and got up from the table.

'So what are you saying?' I asked.

He started trying to push himself up from the small, round table. He was so drunk he could hardly stand. Plates rattled. Some fruit fell onto the floor. My hot teapot filled with steaming liquid fell over. An ugly brown stain spread out onto the crisp, white tablecloth. Finally he managed to get up into a standing position and started yelling.

'*I'm saying that I don't have anything to help me perform tonight, and if you hadn't been such a pig, I would!*'

He took his hand and shoved me on the shoulder. I was knocked off balance and fell back a couple of steps.

'*What?*' I cried, trying to right myself.

'You heard me!' he yelled, staggering toward me.

'Lewis, stop!' I said, so loudly that he did. I moved to my right and reached for the one glass on the table that hadn't been knocked over. It was my glass of milk. I picked it up and threw it in his face.

'Have something healthy to drink for a change,' I said. 'And don't you ever touch me again.' Then I added, without thinking, and purely by instinct, 'No, wait. You're not going to get that chance. Because I'm leaving—this time for good.'

I was finally fleeing. Something had reached up inside and knocked some sense into me. I was a survivor, and I always had been. This was my last exit.

Lou stood like a rock, looking at me. But he didn't advance any farther.

I turned away from the table, took my coat off the hanger, picked up my bag on the bed, and walked toward the door. As I opened it, I turned around.

'I'm walking out of this door, and you're never going to see me again. I'm going to put a note in Dennis's mailbox down stairs that I want a plane ticket tomorrow to fly home. You're going to go and do that show without me. I'm done.'

'Like hell you are!' he cried.

He took a step—or tried to—toward me. But all he could do was hold onto the back of the chair he'd been sitting in.

'You're going to get in that car waiting downstairs for us *with me*,' he said slurring, 'and we're going to the show as planned.'

Instead, I closed the door.

* * *

We never spoke again. The last I saw of Lewis he was standing, holding on to the back of his chair for support. Milk was running down his face, dripping onto his black T-shirt and over the carpet. He was looking at me in utter amazement.

Walking down the hall, I threw on my coat.

And I said, Oh, oh, oh, oh, oh, oh, what a feel-ing.

The end.

epilogue

After leaving a note at the reservation desk requesting a plane ticket home to New York the next day, I stepped out into the Parisian night. It was raining, and I had forgotten my umbrella; but after living in London, I'd learned the necessity of a trench coat, and I always traveled with one. I had mine on now.

The night air was cool. The rain was slightly chilly but felt cleansing. I took off my earrings and thrust them into my coat pocket, and pulled up my collar. I shoved my nose into it, and lowered my head as I stepped out from under the hotel's canopied entrance. For hours I cruised the streets of the 8th Arrondissement, one of the most beautiful districts in Paris. I wandered past the Élysée Palace, and then into the enormous square, the Place de la Concorde—especially beautiful at night—all lit up, even in the rain. Prisms of light distorted by the precipitation created an impressionistic blur I was relieved and awed to brush past, reflecting perfectly the determination I felt to push through all the contradictory emotions I was feeling, however much they continued to roil around inside. After three months I was walking out of my life, once again, and into the unknown. But this time I knew it was good.

I remember feeling incredibly lucky that I was beginning the rest of my life in one of the most beautiful cities in the world, and for that I was grateful. Out on the Champs Élysées, I kept walking until eventually I ended up under the Arc de Triomphe. Although my hair was completely soaked, and I was probably exhausted, the walk had done me good. I leaned on the monolithic structure for a while to rest and enjoy its protection from the rain. But as I raised my head I found myself staring directly into the concerned face of a Parisian policeman. His coat and hat were slick from the rain; the visor of his hat shielded much of his face in the shadow of the great monument, but I could see a look of concern in his eyes.

'Comment allez-vous?' he asked.

'Ca va bien,' I replied. I was fine.

'Pleurez-vous?' he asked, as he indicated tears rolling down his cheeks.

'Quit. Le mari,' I answered, blurting out to this perfect stranger that I'd just left my husband.

'Oh,' he said, with a pained expression, clasping his hands in front of him. Then he asked, 'Hotel?'

'Hotel Le Bristol,' I answered.

Next he asked, 'Viens avec moi?' and gently took my arm, indicating for me to come with him. He took a handkerchief out of his pocket and gave it to me, which I accepted, wiping my face. As we walked out to the Place Charles de Gaulle, he asked, 'Voulez-vous un taxi?'

'Oui.'

As he helped me into the first taxi that pulled over and told the driver to go to the Hotel Bristol, he said something I didn't understand, but I just nodded and thanked him, and then he closed the door.

The cab driver looked in his rear view mirror and said, in English, 'The officer said that you will feel better in the morning once you get some sleep. Are you okay, young lady?'

I smiled and said I was fine, thinking of Blance DuBois in *A Streetcar Named Desire*, when she said she always 'depended upon the kindness of strangers.' Then suddenly I saw Marlon Brando in the movie, as Stanley

Kowalski, standing at the bottom of the front steps of their house, screams like a mortally wounded animal for his mate not to leave and come back to him.

'Stella! Stella! *Stel-la*!' he cries.

But what I said to the cabbie was, 'Let's go back to the hotel.'

Immediately he took off, spiriting me home through the mist and steam rising from the city streets in what had turned into a downpour. The kind Parisian policeman had secured my taxi just in time! And the truth was, there was little to compare me, in Paris, to Blanche DuBois in New Orleans. Nor was Lewis bellowing my name at the bottom of the grand staircase of the Hotel Bristol. The last I saw of him, he could barely walk.

It's about time you see this for what it is, girl! Get it together and learn to think about, and for, yourself first.

It was late when I got back to our room, which was empty, as I expected, but I immediately peeled off my wet clothing and took a steaming hot bath. I poured some lavender-scented salts and bubble bath into the water, and soaked for a while, luxuriating in the warmth and relaxation. Then I crawled into bed and fell asleep almost instantly.

The following morning, I packed my bags, got my ticket, which was left in my box downstairs as requested, said goodbye to a couple of people who met me at the desk, and took a cab out to Orly International Airport for the next plane back to JFK. I was told then that Lou had been hours late for his Paris opening performance, so the audience had become very, very impatient with him, and that he had exhibited some rather bizarre behavior onstage.

* * *

Lewis was my first great love, but we behaved like a couple of teenagers. Well, actually, when I first met him, that's what I was. And Lou never had a steady girl in high school. Our love story was played out on an international stage when I was still just a kid, really, and I was no more prepared for the sudden shot of international fame Lou experienced, and we had both worked so hard for, than he was. But I understood him, and I stood up to him. I told him the truth when no one else would, and that was necessary for Lou, which he had the good sense to understand. First and foremost, a significant component of our love was trust.

Throughout our relationship, he would say to me, 'You're one of the innocents, Princess.' In the beginning, Lewis was paying me a compliment. He thought this quality was beautiful, and something he valued highly. But by the time we parted, I felt like he was really saying I was the host of a disease so strange it eluded diagnosis. Perhaps he was.

The events in this book occurred almost fifty years ago, and however much I tried to be as accurate about facts and the sequence of events, there may be some mistakes that I was not able to catch. I conducted an extraordinary amount of research while writing this book to make up for some of the factual details that I undoubtedly forgot over the years—much of them deliberately—so that I could move on with my life after leaving Lewis.

I am hoping that I have been able to provide a portrait of the man I fell in love with that illuminates the striking complexity of his nature, which resulted in his art. I hadn't see it in any of the books that had been written about him so far, and I wanted the world to know what Lou Reed was really like: his extraordinary ambition, with equal parts humility; his incredible confidence, which contrasted with his equally devastating insecurity and dependency; his tenderness, which was more privately seen only by his partners, and with friends and family, along with his wicked, sometimes cruel tongue and actions. And, yes, I wanted to set the record straight about the part I played in his success and in his life.

But the larger picture, which I also hope emerges in this book, is yet another example of what happens to artists in a country that doesn't value or support the arts. What these already preternaturally sensitive individuals are forced to go through in order to make a living in this field—and what it does to them as people in the process.

Lewis made a decision in his life when he was with me, one that he seriously grappled with for years. In the end, he chose success on a world-class scale, what he thought his art deserved, rather than cultivating and nurturing the personal relationships that might, in fact, have sustained him and his art. Later on in his life, I heard he found that, and I was very happy for him.

Knowing that his last years were spent in a secure and positive relationship helped me when I learned of his passing, which hit me unexpectedly hard. Fortunately, my daughter Samantha called and told me before I heard it on the radio or TV, which was her intention, and for which I will always be thankful.

After leaving Lou, I went back to school the very next week and finished my advanced acting classes. And then I moved to Richmond, Virginia, where my uncle lived, to be with him. And he put me back together again, because I did fall apart for a while.

I was not in the best place emotionally after I left Lewis. He was a larger-than-life personality, and his was not an easy act to follow—for anyone else or for me. He was my first great love, and I adored him. I spent five years working with him and his career during a time when I was very young, and it took a large chunk out of my personal and professional life. He highly influenced how I saw the world, music, art—and writing. He was my first writing teacher, really. And, in broad strokes, he was instrumental in shaping the course of my life.

But I fell in love again, married, and had two wonderful children, who have been the loves of my life, along with my three grandsons. I am extremely grateful for the life I have lived.

I have been very lucky in that I've been able to work and sustain myself in professions that I love—teaching, and freelance writing and editing. I have my own production company, and have produced, directed, and designed theatrical productions, along with teaching theater and speech all over this country, which has brought me great joy.

I also wrote this book because I wanted to bring attention to several things. First, the special challenges of those who are in a relationship with or are related to a person who has an addictive personality, and I hope that I have brought some insight into what it's like living with this person. No matter how brilliant they are, they are deeply affected by this affliction, along with everyone around them—their relationships, their friends, who they love, their family.

Lewis should have been provided with professional help, rather than relying on me, someone who was incredibly unprepared to deal with the issues surrounding this problem. But during the time that I was with him, addiction was not dealt with on a large scale as it is now. I am hoping that I have been able to illustrate that you can change your role in the addict's life, even if he is personally very close to you.

Having your own escape clause, one that is meaningful to you and that you will adhere to no matter what happens, is extremely helpful in getting you out of the relationship if that becomes necessary, and it often is with addicts. Boundaries must be set—what you will tolerate from the addict and what you will accept into your life. You don't need to accept minimization of yourself, which can happen when you are in a relationship with an addictive personality. And you don't need to blame yourself—that somehow you are attracting this kind of person into your life.

Know that there is a kind of predatory nature to addictive personalities. They look for people who they think will enable or tolerate the demands they will make upon your life. They actually put people through tests—some very small and not easily noticeable in the beginning—to see if you are the kind of person who will. Someone who is kind and thoughtful or sensitive is often mistaken for someone who is weak or who can be easily bullied. You don't need to stay in these relationships. Try to look out for the signs, be careful and take care of yourself. *You can walk away, if need be.* I know, because I did it.

Often, this kind of predatory behavior also goes along with people who are the perpetrators of domestic violence. I wanted to highlight the special challenges of children who grow up in abusive homes, and especially—as in my case—the families of veterans of war. Professional services must be provided to our veterans in this country, as well as to their families. In my years of studying domestic violence, as well as working with children as a teacher who are coming from homes afflicted with domestic violence and my volunteer work in the field, I have learned that veterans who suffer from PTSD must, of course, be counseled and cared for. But so must their families, who end up contracting PTSD just by living with veterans, as they struggle with theirs.

Be aware and try to remember that people will treat you the way you treat yourself. This is a major reason why we must learn to be kind to ourselves, and try to treat ourselves with a responsible and reasonable amount of self-respect, even when we don't always feel like it. We all disappoint ourselves and travel through self-doubt during periods in our lives: in our childhood, our adolescence, as young adults out in the world on our own. Sometimes, things just happen in life. *Life happens*, and it affects us all, but most of the time we come out on the other side stronger and richer for the experience, which is also extremely valuable.

At the end of the day, good can come from bad, so don't despair.

It's a good thing to remember that everyone is watching how you treat yourself, especially predatory types. Nowadays, with social media, with everyone sharing their thoughts openly on the internet—the whole world is watching us. The world is full of good people, and I don't think it's terribly helpful to think otherwise, but it's also good to be careful. And to take care of yourself.

I probably have another fifteen, twenty productive years, and am at a place where I can reflect back upon my years with some perspective. My years with Lou Reed were tumultuous, sometimes frightening, incredibly creative, quite an education, and rarely boring. But it is in the rest of my life, *post Lou Reed*, for which I am incredibly grateful. Where I found mutually respectful love in my relationships; my incredible family to whom I owe so much for the values with which I was raised and sustained me throughout my life; my children, and now my young grandsons, who are the stars in my life that I am so very grateful for.

For all the practical considerations most of us face nowadays in our challenging economy, and the political unrest that has once again befallen our country and throughout the world—just like in 1968—despite all of it, what sustains me most is my ability to work in professions that I love, for which I feel very, very lucky, and the family I raised who have given me more life and love. I am truly blessed!

BETTYE KRONSTAD SUMMER 2016

acknowledgments

To Valerie Swenson, for your encouragement, kindness, and support. It would have been hell on wheels without you! Peter Wilson, for your technical support, kindness, and generosity. Samantha Terrio—you are my heart; Krista Koerperich—the keeper of the flame. Lauri Warren, thank you for your incredible support in a new land. Cindy Privette, a superb Spiritual Architect. Gives great support to alien newbies! Barbara Wilkinson—thanks for your generosity and snapshots! Christopher Garvey, for your moral support and advice. Fred Weinhagen and Dianne Maughan, for your moral and moving support (Have Drive Travels). Julie Compton, technical support. To Charlotte Cripps, my editor— thank you, thank you, thank you! To Cole and to Lola—welcome to the world! And finally, to my agent, Carrie Kania, at Conville & Walsh, for your encouragement and inspiration; to Tom Seabrook at Jawbone Press, for your subtlety, sensitivity, grace under pressure, and British grammar rules; and to Nigel Osborne, Jawbone Press, my enabler—thank you!

ALSO AVAILABLE IN PRINT AND EBOOK EDITIONS FROM JAWBONE PRESS